MARTIN LUTHER
Learning for Life

CONCORDIA SCHOLARSHIP

SCHOLARSHIP

Today

MARTIN LUTHER

Learning for Life

Marilyn J. Harran

CPH
SAINT LOUIS

Copyright © 1997 Concordia Publishing House
3558 S. Jefferson Avenue, St. Louis, MO 63118-3968
Manufactured in the United States of America

Library of Congress Cataloging-in-Publication Data.

Harran, Marilyn J., 1948–
    Martin Luther: learning for life / Marilyn J. Harran.
       p.   cm.   —(Concordia scholarship today)
    Includes bibliographical references and indes.
    ISNBN 0-570-05315-3
    1. Luther, Martin, 1483–1546—Knowledge and learning. I. Title. II. Series.
    BR327.H365   1997
    284.1'092—dc21   97-33547

1 2 3 4 5 6 7 8 9 10   06 05 04 03 02 01 00 99 98 97

In memory of my parents
Eugene Daniel Harran
Barbara Biegelow Harran

Contents

Abbreviations

LW *Luther's Works*. 55 vols. General Editors: Jaroslav Pelikan, vols. 1–30; Helmut T. Lehmann, vols. 31–55. St. Louis: Concordia Publishing House; Philadelphia: Fortress Press, 1955–1976.

WA *D. Martin Luthers Werke: Kritische Gesamtausgabe.* 58 vols. Weimar: Hermann Böhlau and Hermann Böhlaus Nachfolger, 1883–

WA Br *D. Martin Luthers Werke: Kritische Gesamtausgabe. Briefwechsel.* 15 vols. Weimar: Hermann Böhlaus Nachfolger, 1930–1978.

WA TR *D. Martin Luthers Werke: Kritische Gesamtausgabe. Tischreden.* 6 vols. Weimar: Hermann Böhlaus Nachfolger, 1912–1921.

Foreword

If today's analysts and critics are correct, education is in deep crisis, morally, academically, and financially, sorely in need of basic reform. What better way, then, but to tackle the problem by reviewing what education reformers of an earlier day advised? The author of *Martin Luther—Learning for Life* provides insights to sixteenth-century education that are of more than passing interest and seem strangely applicable at the moment.

Professor Harran presents a clear, succinct, and sprightly overview of (1) Luther's own education, (2) Luther's educational ideas and program, and (3) the impact (and limitations) of Luther and the magisterial reformers' work on the educational enterprise and institutions in Luther's day down to the present.

This volume is the result of research in a number of archival sources and especially of a respectable number of printed sources. It represents a "zusammenfassende Darstellung" of much scholarly literature on the subject, including heavy German tomes not available in many American libraries or to most American and English-speaking readers. It is based on a prodigious volume of Reformation scholarship and reflects wide reading and sound judgment. Though not aggressively apologetic, as some writers, the author's approach is in line with an orthodox Lutheran understanding of the theology and church history of the period and thus makes a very positive contribution to the understanding of the Reformation's importance for education, its relation to Renaissance humanism, and its role as the fulcrum leading to the modern from the medieval age.

Obviously, Martin Luther was not encumbered by the "no establishment" clause that the Founding Fathers wrote into the Constitution, which some later altered to mean "separation of church and state" and more recently have virtually interpreted as "freedom from religion." But Luther did emphasize a distinction of "the two kingdoms." On the one hand, God deals with those who are in the "kingdom of grace," who recognize that they are sinners but redeemed sinners and freely subject to God's will and ways. On the other hand, some are not in the kingdom of grace; and even those who are still succumb, more than they wish, to the sin that afflicts us all. Therefore, rulers must carry out their responsibility as heads of the kingdom of power, compelling obedience. That includes making sure that all functions of life, including education, are cared for and properly monitored.

Professor Harran alludes to the two kingdoms frequently, but limitations of space require her to assume the reader's understanding of this, as well as other tenets of Lutheran theology. For example, Luther, and probably most Christians of his day, assumed that everyone sensed a natural knowledge of God and felt bound by its moral requirements. But Christians today who seek to effect a return to that basic, biblical view face an almost insurmountable challenge.

Likewise, it will be necessary to refer to some of the sources the author has cited to enjoy more supporting detail for her generalizations and Luther's very comprehensive and far-reaching views. Examples: he urged that before a youth is ordained into the ministry, he should practice music in the school and voiced numerous other views in support of music education. History, Luther said, always offers and teaches more than laws and statutes. Society needs the learned professions. Education is a good investment. A little knowledge is a dangerous thing because it leaves the impression that one knows everything.

This volume, then, is a valuable study of a highly productive period in history from which the "general reader" as well as Reformation scholars can glean much that can be applied to current concerns—learning for this life and that to come.

The Publisher

Preface

No stranger to the difficulties of writing, Luther once proclaimed: "Some think that the office of writer is simple and easy, that real work is to ride in armor and suffer heat, cold, dust, thirst and other discomforts. ... True, it would be hard for me to ride in armor; but on the other hand I would like to see the horseman who could sit still with me all day and look into a book—even if he had nothing else to care for, write, think about, or read" (*LW* 46, 249). Anyone who has written a book, and especially anyone who has attempted to do so in the midst of teaching and administrative obligations, knows precisely what Luther means. To realize how much Luther wrote in the midst of his myriad duties as preacher, teacher, theologian, husband, father, dean, resolver of conflicts, and reformer, is to have one's admiration for him increase all the more. In comparison with his accomplishments, any writer, including this one, must stand in awe.

A considerable number of works have been produced on the topic of Luther and education, to say nothing of the vast number of biographies that have examined his upbringing and education. Many are in German; many go into far more exhaustive detail than this work, which is intended to be an introduction to those interested in knowing about Luther the learner and Luther the teacher. This book draws upon the work of many scholars, from writers of earlier times like Heinrich Boehmer and Otto Scheel to contemporary scholars such as Lewis W. Spitz, Martin Brecht, Leif Grane, Heiko Oberman and Eric Gritsch. The three-volume biography of Luther by Martin Brecht has been an especially important source for this book, and the interested reader who wants to learn more about the many facets of Luther's life and career should turn to it.

As with any book, the author owes much to many people. My move from New York and Barnard College meant I no longer had the superb resources of the Columbia University Libraries and the Union Theological Seminary Library right at hand. I could never have completed this book had it not been for the extraordinary helpfulness of Gina Wilkinson, head of interlibrary loan at the Thurmond Clarke Memorial Library of Chapman University. I am grateful for her patience and intrepid pursuit of even the most difficult to locate nineteenth-century German sources. I also owe a debt of thanks to Betty Bolden, head of interlibrary loan and reader privileges at the Burke Library of Union Theological Seminary, for allowing me to use that excellent collection on my visits to New York.

This book has taken far longer than I had ever anticipated and so my debt of gratitude has become ever larger and now encompasses two coasts. At Chapman University, special thanks are due to the Griset family for their support of my scholarly activity during the time when I held the two-year appointment as the Griset Chair in Religion. I owe thanks as well to the administration of Chapman University, particularly President James L. Doti, for his encouragement of faculty to be active teacher-scholars.

My initial studies on the topic of Luther and education were facilitated by the Graves Award administered by Pomona College and the American Council of Learned Societies. Further research in libraries and archives in Leipzig, Dresden, and Weimar was supported by a travel-to-collections grant from the National Endowment for the Humanities, and by the International Research and Exchanges Board. The grant from IREX yielded the unanticipated benefit of experiencing at first hand the dramatic changes and peaceful revolution that unfolded in the autumn of 1989. To join a congregation of hundreds singing *Ein feste Burg* on October 31 of that year in Wittenberg was an incomparable experience of Evangelical hope and faith. For support, consultation, and friendship during my months in Leipzig I owe special thanks to Prof. Dr. Helmar Junghans and Prof. Dr. Dr. Günther Wartenberg and their families, and to Ms. Renate Rochler. The many pages of visitation records which the Staatsarchiv Dresden permitted me to microfilm are the foundation for a continuing project researching the progress of education in Germany over the sixteenth century in the areas of Grimma and Chemnitz.

Without the support and encouragement of several wonderful friends this project would never have been completed. My special thanks go to Alberta Graham, Nancy Hill, Barbara Gooden Mulch, and Mary Sellen on the west coast, and to David Sperling on the east. Dr. Lewis W. Spitz, William R.

Kenan Professor emeritus at Stanford University, continues to be my mentor. I am deeply grateful for his willingness to review the completed manuscript and to suggest improvements. My editor at Concordia Publishing House, Dr. Wilbert Rosin, never flagged in his conviction that this work would be completed nor failed to give excellent advice and thoughtful criticism. I am grateful to Concordia Publishing House, St. Louis, and to Augsburg Fortress Press, Minneapolis, for their kind permission to quote from *Luther's Works*.

Finally, this book is dedicated to the memory of my parents. As Luther's parents did for him, they supported me through school and university, making extraordinary sacrifices and never failing in their support of me and my dreams. It is thanks to them that I was the first in my family to go to college and eventually to become a university professor. My debt to them can never be repaid, but will never be forgotten.

Marilyn J. Harran
Chapman University
Orange, California
June 1997

Hans Luder, Luther's father

Margarethe Ziegler Luder
Luther's mother

Katherine von Bora, Luther's wife

Introduction

Luther and Education in the Age of the Internet

In his recent book *The Road Ahead*, Bill Gates, the chairman of Microsoft, paints a fascinating portrait of the twenty-first century.[1] His intriguing vision of a world linked by the information highway would have sounded fantastic to Martin Luther, a professor at a small university on the fringes of civilization at the beginning of the sixteenth century. Yet, in some ways, different as these two men and their visions are, separated by almost five hundred years, they both beckon us toward new ages and new ways of thinking. Luther stood on the threshold of a new European age shaped by the invention of the printing press, by the discovery of the "new world," and by the energy and optimism of humanism. Gates beckons us toward a new era where technology overcomes distances and offers us extraordinary possibilities for building new communities. For both Luther and Gates, education is central to their visions.

If Gates is correct, the new century will look very different from even the latter years of this one. The information highway will yield dramatic shifts in the ways we live, do our work, and educate our children. The Information Age offers us exciting opportunities, while at the same time shaking our individual and social foundations. Luther and his generation too experienced the social upheaval generated by the power of the printing press and the sudden swirl of new ideas, available to all who were literate. Like the twentieth century, the sixteenth century was an age of dramatic transitions—in commerce, in

---

[1] Bill Gates, *The Road Ahead*, 2nd ed. (New York: Penguin Books, 1996).

education, in the ways that people lived their lives and viewed their world. The decline of feudalism brought an end to the Middle Ages; the Renaissance and Reformation provided more freedom and opportunity for discovery and invention on the one hand, and more insecurity and confusion on the other.

In Luther's time, few could read, and many must have wondered what the printing press and the growing stress on literacy would mean for them, just as many of us now wonder where the information highway will lead. Luther recognized that the success of the Reformation rested with the young, and, as we will see, he was committed to furthering education and increasing literacy. Yet, at the same time, he realized that he could not concentrate on the new generation at the expense of their elders. The lessons of the schools would be wasted if they were not reinforced in church and home by pastors and parents—and thus they too must be taught. "Adult education" became an urgent goal even as Luther and his colleagues struggled to develop and institutionalize new curricula and pedagogies in schools and universities. The emerging Information Age similarly challenges us to teach the young while not leaving behind those who are even a few years older. As Bill Gates insists: "The younger you are, the more important it is that you adapt. ... If you're twenty-five today and not comfortable with computers, you risk being ineffective in almost any kind of work you pursue."[2]

There are, of course, dramatic differences between the Reformation Age and the Information Age, and in many instances Luther's responses cannot be ours. However, the questions we face call us to look afresh at Luther and the challenges he faced as theologian, reformer, and educator. Luther, who perceived so clearly the value of education to individual, church, and society, compels us to ponder what goals and values education, with all its new technological dimensions and possibilities, should serve in our time.

In the winter of 1542-43, just three years before his death, Luther told the listeners gathered around him, "When schools flourish, things go well and the church is secure. Let us make more doctors and masters. ... When we are dead, where are others [to take our place] if there are no schools? God has

---

[2] Gates, *The Road Ahead*, 294.

preserved the church through schools."[3] This remark alerts us to the interrelationship Martin Luther saw between religion and education, between church and school, and between one generation and its successor. It also introduces us to a host of issues, some more controversial than others, that comprise the topic of Martin Luther and education, and that are central to this work. To begin with some apparently straightforward questions: What type of education, what curriculum, did Luther see as necessary for furthering the well-being of society and of the church, the community of faith? Which pedagogy did he find most effective and appropriate? What value did he ascribe to education apart from its role in preparing knowledgeable parishioners and pastors? How did new problems and possibilities lead Luther to alter his vision of education and its purpose? To move from the sixteenth century to our own time, can we affirm any of Luther's educational goals and pedagogies as relevant to our diverse and secular age? Does Luther's goal of Christian education connect at all to public education today?

Like all young people, both the reformer and his educational ideals were shaped in large part by his schooling. As we will see, not all of those experiences were positive as Luther noted in his 1524 writing *To the Councilmen of All Cities in Germany That They Establish and Maintain Christian Schools*: "Today, schools are not what they once were, a hell and purgatory in which we were tormented with *casualibus* and *temporalibus*, and yet learned less than nothing despite all the flogging, trembling, anguish, and misery."[4] When it came time for Luther to construct a curricular plan, he envisioned something quite different, although the break with the past was not so dramatic as we might imagine.

So too did Luther's experiences at both the University of Erfurt and the new University of Wittenberg shape his understanding of higher education, first in the liberal arts and then in theology. Indeed, Luther's career as a reformer began with the university rather than with the church. In early

---

[3] *WA TR* 5, 239, 30–34; *Luther's Works*, vol. 54: *Table Talk*, ed. Theodore G. Tappert (Philadelphia: Fortress Press, 1967), 452.

[4] *WA* 15, 46, 6–9; Luther's Works, vol. 45: The Christian in Society II, ed. Walther I. Brandt (Philadelphia: Muhlenberg Press, 1962), 369.

September 1517, some eight weeks before the *95 Theses* were posted, he prepared ninety-seven theses for debate. In the *Disputation Against Scholastic Theology*, Luther questioned the role of Aristotle in the theology curriculum. As a professor, one who had been called against his will to become a doctor of theology and to assume the daunting responsibility of teaching others, Luther saw it as his duty to press for a renewed emphasis on the Bible, as well as on those languages essential for biblical exegesis, Greek and Hebrew. As Robert Rosin notes, "if the universities had not changed (and hence the theologians produced had not changed), the Reformation would not have happened, at least not as we know it."[5]

One of the principal qualities of the reformation that Luther launched was its stress on education. Luther argued eloquently for more funding for schools and libraries, for support for needy students, for adequate pay for hard working teachers. Not all proponents of ecclesiastical reform in the sixteenth century were equally committed to education, indeed, some saw education as a threat. Particularly those who believed that the day of judgment was imminent tended to devalue learning, or at least to limit learning simply to religious education strictly interpreted, principally the study of the Bible. Modern Amish, for example, continue to refuse to send their children to public schools and to limit their education to the eighth grade with a very restricted curriculum, arguing that education in other subjects is at best unnecessary and at worst threatening to their faith and way of life.

Why then did Luther and some of his Wittenberg colleagues—although not all—argue for a more encompassing view of education? The answer lies in Luther's own conversion or evangelical breakthrough. The hard won understanding of Romans 1:17 and Romans 3: 21–24 that Luther achieved came after long hours of study and meditation. As has been often noted, it rested upon a point of grammar, that the righteousness of God is what God gives to the believer who trusts in him. Luther's firm conviction that God speaks through the word as it is preached or read, along with his belief that faith is an individual matter of trust and personal relationship with God,

---

[5] Robert Rosin, "The Reformation, Humanism, and Education: The Wittenberg Model for Reform," *Concordia Journal*, vol. 16, no. 4 (October 1990), 306.

means that each Christian must learn to read and understand the Bible for himself or herself. The moment of revelatory insight that Luther experienced is available to every Christian who has the tool of literacy. Justification by faith means that the biblical door is open and the Christian is able to return again and again to the text to gain new insights and a greater depth of faith as he or she encounters the trials and challenges of Christian life. Justification by faith initiates a life of learning and a life of service of which education is the foundation.

Anchored to conversion, education is joined as well to vocation, a sense of calling that means much more than narrow careerism. Justified by faith, the Christian is able to act freely in the world as both lord and servant, the famous dualism that Luther described in his treatise on *The Freedom of a Christian*. Through one's calling, one serves God and contributes to the kingdom of God. Education provides both the context in which one comes to know one's vocation and the tools for becoming proficient in it. Viewed more broadly, education connects to ethics, to service in the world. Luther was convinced that human effort furthers the cause of either good or evil. As he warned parents in his *Sermon on Keeping Children in School*, God "has not given you your children and the means to support them simply so that you may do with them as you please, or train them just to get ahead in the world. You have been earnestly commanded to raise them for God's service."[6]

Luther and education is a complex and multifaceted topic. It might also seem to be territory that has been well trod and need not be investigated again. One need think only of such older works as F. V. N. Painter, *Luther on Education: A Historical Introduction* (1889); Gustav Marius Bruce, *Luther as an Educator* (1928); Erwin Mülhaupt, *Reformatoren als Erzieher: Luther—Melanchthon—Calvin* (1956), as well as more recent interpretative studies such as the one by Gerald Strauss, to question whether there is need for another book on this topic. However, these studies give either little or no attention to Luther's own education and upbringing and their role in shaping his pedagogical goals.

---

[6] *WA* 30 II, 531, 1–4; *Luther's Works*, vol. 46: *The Christian in Society III*, ed. Robert C. Schultz (Philadelphia: Fortress Press, 1967), 222.

In his study published in 1978, *Luther's House of Learning: Indoctrination of the Young in the German Reformation*, Gerald Strauss evaluated the impact of Luther's ideas on his own time. He argued that the Evangelical Reformation scored at the very most limited success in educating the young and that "if it was its central purpose to make people—all people—think, feel, and act as Christians, to imbue them with a Christian mindset, motivational drive, and way of life, it failed."[7] Strauss ascribed to education a transformational role with regard to both individual and society, a role which Luther affirmed only up to a point. Luther did in fact believe that education effects change, but he also anchored education to both conversion and vocation.[8] While education remains valuable in and of itself—Luther had a healthy respect for the liberal arts, for example—its power to transform is linked to God's purpose for individuals and their societies.

This study is intended for general readers, those who have an interest in the Reformation and education and want to learn more about Luther's role. It is divided among three major topics: Luther's education and the ways in which his experiences in school, university, and cloister shaped his educational vision; his impact on the education of the time and his place in the history of education; and the relationship between religious and curricular reform. Grounded in the principles of Luther's theology, the Evangelical Reformation offered both the possibility of a new relationship of trust in God and the opportunity for a new educational adventure that was grounded in *vocatio* or calling, learning put to service in love of God and neighbor. Luther challenges us to ponder if that

---

[7] Gerald Strauss, *Luther's House of Learning: Indoctrination of the Young in the German Reformation* (Baltimore and London: The Johns Hopkins University Press, 1978), 307.

[8] Heiko Oberman argues that a distinction must be made between "reformation and visitation, between 'gathering' and 'amendment' (in the sense of improvement, which Luther did not share), between a battle in the name of a faith stripped of all illusions and a rational attempt to improve the world." *The Reformation: Roots and Ramifications*, trans. Andrew Colin Gow (Grand Rapids, MI: William B. Eerdmans Publishing Company, 1994), 52; 23–24.

adventure may not also be ours, one as meaningful to the twenty-first century as it was to the sixteenth.[9]

---

[9] In a fascinating and provocative article, Gertrude Himmelfarb considers the implications of the electronic revolution, especially with regard to libraries. While applauding the "democratization of access to knowledge" (p.199), she argues it should not be confused with the democratization of knowledge itself" (p.200). She stresses: "It takes a discriminating mind, a mind that is already stocked with knowledge and trained in critical discernment, to distinguish ... between the trivial and the important, the ephemeral and the enduring, the true and the false. It is just this sense of discrimination that the humanists have traditionally cultivated and that they must now cultivate even more strenuously if the electronic revolution is to do more good than bad." "Revolution in the Library," *The American Scholar* 66, no. 2 (Spring 1997), 200; 197–204.

Christmas in Luther's Home

1

"Planting" and "Raising": Educating the Young Martin Luther

"A pastor and schoolteacher plant and raise young trees and saplings in the garden. Oh, they have a precious office and work and are the finest jewels of the church, they preserve the church."[1] As former schoolboy and student, Luther affirmed the crucial role of teachers in shaping the lives of young people, and as theologian and teacher, he underscored their importance in preparing the next generation for these vocations. Pastors and teachers are the bridges from past to present to future.

Like any person who has undergone long years of schooling, replete with both positive and negative experiences, Luther's encounters were vital to the shaping of his educational goals, to his deciding what he would keep and what he would change, what was good and what was bad. Indeed, years before he became a father, he wrote: "For my part, if I had children and could manage it, I would have them study not only languages and history, but also singing and music together with the whole of mathematics. ... How I regret now that I did not read more poets and historians, and that no one taught me them."[2] In these words we sense the wistfulness of a man who realized what he might have learned from these studies, and who was intent that such mistakes not be repeated in the schooling of a new generation.

---

[1] WA 50, 617, 18-21; Ewald Plass, ed., *What Luther Says: An Anthology*, vol. III (Saint Louis: Concordia Publishing House, 1959), 1337.

[2] WA 15, 46, 13–19; L W 45, 369–70.

Given the importance of childhood and youth in shaping the adult, we might wish for more complete records about Luther's early life and education.[3] As a remarkably self-conscious adult, Luther had a deep understanding of the role that parents and teachers play in shaping the lives of young people, and he addressed this concern programmatically in his writings. Within these same writings he also offered some of his most piercing comments about his own schooling. As we encounter these remarks, we need to keep in mind the context in which they occur, often as dramatic illustrations to particular pedagogical points.

The author who has generated the most debate about Luther's early years, his testimony about them, and their effect on his subsequent life and work, is Erik Erikson. In his daring book, *Young Man Luther: A Study in Psychoanalysis and History*, published in 1958, Erikson utilized his psychoanalytical skills to place Luther on the couch and examine him as a patient. While Erikson's approach raised many questions and his work was troubled by historical inaccuracies, he nonetheless did much to focus attention on the importance of Luther's early years. Erikson argued that a series of crises revolving around Luther's adolescent identity and his relationship to authority led him first to the safety of the monastery and then eventually to a rebellion against hierarchical authority, both father and pope. Erikson states his thesis as follows:

> We will therefore concentrate on this process: how young Martin, at the end of a somber and harsh childhood, was precipitated into a severe identity crisis, for which he sought delay and cure in the silence of the monastery; how being silent, he became "possessed"; how being possessed, he gradually learned to speak a new language, *his* language; how being able to speak, he not only talked himself out of the monastery, and much of his country out of the Roman Church, but also formulated for himself and for all of mankind a new kind of ethical and

---

[3] On childhood and education during the Middle Ages, see Philippe Ariès, *Centuries of Childhood: A Social History of Family Life*, trans. by Robert Baldick (New York: Alfred A. Knopf, 1962) and Shulamith Shahar, *Childhood in the Middle Ages*, trans. by Chaya Galai (London and New York: Routledge, 1990).

psychological awareness: and how, at the end, this awareness, too, was marred by a return of the demons, whoever they may have been.[4]

The problems with Erikson's psychoanalytic method and use of sources have been addressed by several scholars, principally those contributing to the volume, *Psychohistory and Religion: The Case of Young Man Luther.*[5] Although Erikson's work has rightly been critiqued, it can also be credited for bringing to center stage a topic within many, especially older, biographies of Luther, namely, "his somber and harsh childhood." Let us then begin our consideration of Luther's early years, the education he received at home and at school, with this question in mind: how harsh and somber was Luther's childhood and what was its effect on him?

Answering this question would be much easier if we had more information. Indeed, given Luther's fame, it is surprising how many facts remain either unknown or under debate. For example, we do not know for certain how old Luther was when he began school nor do we have records of the names of the schools he attended and the circumstances of his living arrangements. We have only an occasional comment about the training he received from his parents at home and school, about what he learned and what he found most and least rewarding in his studies. We do not even know precisely whose idea it was that Martin be sent to school. The usual assumption is that the idea originated with Hans Luder, Martin's ambitious father. In his monograph *Luther and His Mother*, Ian Siggins states that it was Margarethe, not Hans, who came from a family where academic life was valued and where it was usual for boys to

---

[4] Erik H. Erikson, *Young Man Luther: A Study in Psychoanalysis and History* (New York: W.W. Norton & Company, 1962 [1958]), 47–48.

[5] Roger A. Johnson, ed., *Psychohistory and Religion: The Case of Young Man Luther* (Philadelphia: Fortress Press, 1977). See also the essays by George Lindbeck, Robert Bellah, and Lewis Spitz in Donald Capps, Walter H. Capps, and M. Gerald Bradford, eds., *Encounter with Erikson: Historical Interpretation and Religious Biography* (Missoula, MT: Scholars Press, 1977).

progress through school and on to the university.[6] We also do not know why Martin was taken out of school in Mansfeld, where his family lived, and sent first to Magdeburg and then to Eisenach.

Born in 1483, Martin moved with his parents in his earliest days of infancy, perhaps around six months, from Eisleben to Mansfeld. Biographers agree that the reason for the move was Hans Luther's desire to improve himself financially. Since he was not the youngest son, Hans did not stand to inherit the family farm and, although he perhaps could have remained on the land and worked for his brother, Hans had larger ambitions. He chose to engage in the profitable copper mining industry, moving first from Möhra to Eisleben. When he found his possibilities to rise from worker to owner limited in Eisleben, he and his wife moved to Mansfeld where he found the opportunities for which he was searching and where he prospered. Ian Siggins locates the reasons for Hans' success in "his native energy and the established status of his wife's relations" while Heiko Oberman concludes that Hans' ability to progress from worker to owner may have been partly due to the financial guarantees of his wife Margarethe's family on his behalf.[7] Certainly Margarethe came from more prosperous circumstances than her husband. Born a Lindemann, Margarethe came from a well-established family in Eisleben.[8]

---

[6] Ian Siggins observes: "Hans Luder's ambitions for his oldest son— that he should make an 'honorable and wealthy marriage' and enter the law—also appear in a new light when seen in the context of the Lindemann family, where ... the normal expectation of sons in Martin's generation was that they should enter one of the learned professions and become men of influence." *Luther and His Mother* (Philadelphia: Fortress Press, 1981), 47. Siggins also suggests that of Martin's two parents, his mother may have been the better educated and the "more literate." 48. In general, however, during the Middle Ages girls received significantly less education than boys.

[7] Siggins, *Luther and His Mother,* 47; Heiko A. Oberman, *Luther: Man Between God and the Devil,* trans. by Eileen Walliser-Schwarzbart (New Haven and London: Yale University Press, 1989), 91.

[8] Siggins discusses Luther's two first cousins, "Johann (II) Lindemann of Eisleben (1475–1519), doctor of civil and canon law at the

Unlike his mother's relatives who were men to be emulated, his father's side of the family included at least one black sheep, "Klein Hans" or "Little Hans" who followed his brother from the familial home in Möhra to Mansfeld, but who unlike his brother came to public attention not through his hard work and ambition but through his participation in brawls and his enjoyment of one too many brews at the local tavern.[9] Hans moved his family to Mansfeld in early summer 1484 and may have become a leaseholder of a foundry as early as 1502.[10] Records of contracts show that by 1508 he was part owner of eight copper shafts and three smelting works.[11] Hans earned not only financial success but the esteem and trust of his peers as a solid citizen and a man of honor. Town records indicate that by 1491 he was one of four men elected to represent the town before the magistracy, a sure sign of the esteem in which he was held by his community, with or without a black sheep for a brother. When Martin entered the University of Erfurt in 1501 he was listed in the registration records as one whose economic situation was such that he could pay full fees. And

University of Leipzig in 1514, and councillor of ducal Saxony. Johann's brother was Caspar Lindemann (1485–1536), who studied at Leipzig, Frankfurt an der Oder, and Bologna, and graduated as both master of arts and doctor of medicine. He became professor of medicine at Leipzig and also personal physician to both Frederick the Wise and John of Saxony. ... Luther's maternal cousins and their children included two pastors, two lawyers, a physician, two schoolmasters, a university docent, and three public officials; among their qualifications, three attained the degree of doctor, three the degree of magister, two were ducal councillors, and three were mayors of their respective cities. The Lindemanns were a highly distinguished family." *Luther and His Mother*, 46.

[9] See further Otto Scheel, *Martin Luther: Vom Katholizismus zur Reformation*. Vol. I: *Auf der Schule und Universität*, 3rd ed. (Tübingen: J.C.B. Mohr [Paul Siebeck], 1921), 6.

[10] Scheel, *Martin Luther*, vol. I, 7.

[11] Heinrich Boehmer, *Der junge Luther*, 6th rev. ed. (Stuttgart: K.F. Koehler Verlag, 1971 [1939]), 17.

when Hans died in 1534 he left behind an inheritance of 1250 *Gulden,* a not inconsiderable sum.

We do not know how much schooling Luther's parents had or how their experiences in school might have shaped their hopes for their children. It is very unlikely that either of them had the opportunity to gain more than a rudimentary education. Eisleben, where Margarethe was born, would have offered a parish school and Margarethe's brothers were well-educated. However, as a girl, she would have received significantly less schooling than her male siblings.

As the son of a farmer, Hans probably was needed to help with the work on the farm, and thus whatever schooling he received would have been in those months when there was no planting or harvesting to be done. There was no school in Möhra.[12] However, that does not mean that Hans may not have learned the basics of reading from a priest or gained the skill later in life. As a businessman, he would have found it useful to know how to read and write in German. Regardless of his educational limitations, Hans was an ambitious man. As he reflected on his son and his future, it is not surprising that he wished for him even greater opportunities, the sort of opportunities which a good education could provide. As Martin proved to be a gifted pupil, it is also not surprising that his parents', and most especially his father's, hopes for him continued to rise. Little did Hans know that in time his ambitions for his son would dramatically diverge from those of the young man himself. Eric Gritsch notes that education provided the "bridge from slavery to freedom in the medieval world for those not born into nobility."[13] Martin would one day come to define "slavery" and "freedom" in quite different terms.

We do not know precisely how old Martin was or in what year he first attended school in Mansfeld. Luther's biographers offer a variety of proposals, ranging from Boehmer's assertion that he entered school as early as possible, probably in the year 1488, an assertion with which Gritsch, Schwiebert and Kittelson agree, to the contention that he entered the Mansfeld school at

---

[12] Siggins, *Luther and His Mother,* 48; Oberman, *Luther,* 85.

[13] Eric Gritsch, *Martin—God's Court Jester: Luther in Retrospect* (Philadelphia: Fortress Press, 1983), 3.

the usual age of six or seven, a view held by Brecht and Oberman, among others.[14] The usual time would have been six or seven, the age at which Aristotle held that a person knew the difference between right and wrong. We would have no reason to think that Martin entered school any earlier than the normal age if it were not for Melanchthon's report that Luther had once said he had been carried to school by an older friend, Nicholas Oemler.[15] Since the distance to school was not great and a boy of six or seven would have been well able to walk the distance, this comment suggests that Hans may have sent his son to school at an earlier age than usual.

Whether Martin began school in 1488 or in 1491, the Mansfeld school provided his first and perhaps most formative educational experience. Based largely on the reformer's assertions about all that was wrong with his school years, the Mansfeld school has often been judged negatively by Luther's biographers as offering precisely the type of education against which Luther would later consciously rebel.[16] As we will see, there is some truth to this assessment, but it is at least equally interesting to note that many parts of the schooling he experienced, both content and method, Luther retained in his

---

[14] Boehmer, *Der junge Luther*, 17; Gritsch, *Martin—God's Court Jester*, 3; E. G. Schwiebert, *Luther and His Times: The Reformation from a New Perspective* (St. Louis: Concordia Publishing House, 1950), 111; James Kittelson, *Luther the Reformer* (Minneapolis: Augsburg Publishing House, 1986), 36. In Magdeburg Martin most likely attended the cathedral school and in Eisenach the school attached to the parish church of St. George. See Martin Brecht, *Martin Luther: His Road to Reformation, 1483–1521*, trans. James L. Schaaf (Philadelphia: Fortress Press, 1985), 12. Brecht notes the most likely time for Luther's entering school is March 1491, St. Gregory's Day, the traditional start of the school year. See also Oberman, *Luther*, 94.

[15] Philipp Melanchthon, *Prefatio Melanthonis in tomum secundum omnium Reverendi Doctori Martini Lutheri*, in *Philippi Melanchthons Opera quae supersunt omnia*, ed. Carolus Gottlieb Bretschneider (Halle: C. A. Schwetschenke et filium, 1838), vol. 6, no. 3478, col. 156–157.

[16] For example, see Oberman, *Luther*, 96.

school plan. Although at least one scholar has suggested that Martin may have attended a so-called "Winkelschule" or German school before attending the Latin school at Mansfeld, there is no evidence to suggest that such a school existed.[17] With Hans' apparently high ambitions for his son, it is very unlikely that he would have sent his son to a school that would not have offered preparation for subsequent study, possibly even for the university, where his wife's brothers had gone. Given his aspirations for Martin, and his willingness to send him later to schools in Magdeburg and Eisenach, it is improbable that Hans would have kept his son at the school in Mansfeld for several years, from the ages of either five or seven to thirteen or fourteen, if the school were as deficient as many scholars suggest. Indeed, Otto Scheel offers a helpful corrective to the usual negative assessment when he cites the names of several students *"ex Mansfelde,"* from Mansfeld, in the matriculation register of the University of Wittenberg.[18] While the term "from Mansfeld" indicates the region and does not prove that they attended school in the town of Mansfeld, it is unlikely that many students followed the path taken by Martin to several different schools. In addition, Martin's later success in the schools at Magdeburg and Eisenach suggests that his early years of schooling did not leave him seriously deficient.

What may we assume that Martin learned during these first years? The Latin school or "trivial school" was devoted to teaching the *trivium*, the three subjects of Latin grammar, rhetoric, and logic. There is no doubt that of those three subjects the stress fell unrelentingly upon learning Latin grammar which was, in a variety of ways, drummed into the students. Since declining and conjugating belonged to the early years of

---

[17] Dietrich Emme, *Martin Luther: Seine Jugend und Studentenzeit, 1483 –1505. Eine dokumentische Darstellung mit 10 Abbildungen und 1 Karte* (Verlagshaus Wienand, 1982), 89. Emme suggests that Luther may have attended Latin school in Eisleben before Magdeburg, and that his later proficiency in German is testimony to the fact that his first schooling may have occurred not in a Latin school, where the speaking of Latin was strictly enforced, but in a German school where he became fluent in the vernacular. I can find no evidence to support these suggestions.

[18] Scheel, *Martin Luther,* vol. I, 52–53.

schooling, the following critique contained in the *Table Talk* of 1543 probably refers to Martin's years in Mansfeld and his experience of what it was like to have knowledge pounded into his head, perhaps by a new or "substitute" teacher who had no idea that the material on which he was quizzing the boy was as yet unassigned: "Some teachers are as cruel as hangmen. I was once beaten fifteen times before noon, without any fault of mine, because I was expected to decline and conjugate although I had not yet been taught this."[19] While technically the school taught the trivium as defined above, Boehmer's description may more accurately reflect the reality of what was taught: "reading, writing, singing, and Latin, with Latin as the most important discipline."[20] Developing skills in reading, writing, and singing were also intended to increase proficiency in Latin. The speaking of German was strongly prohibited, although some teaching for the youngest pupils may have occurred in the vernacular.

In school, the pupils were divided into various levels or groups (*Haufen*) to facilitate their learning (and in the case of larger schools, to help the teacher keep his pupils straight). Schwiebert succinctly describes what was expected at each level:

> First there were the *Tabulisten*, or beginners, who learned the ABC's of Latin, which was largely a memorization of elementary forms and the contents of the *Fibel*, or Latin primer. [Thus these beginning students were also often referred to as *Fibulists*.] These little youngsters also learned *the Benedicite*, *the* prayer before meals, and the *Gratias*, the giving of thanks after eating. In addition they learned the *Confiteor* or the Confession of sins, the Creed, the Lord's Prayer, the Decalog, and the Hail Mary. ... The second group, often called the *Donatisten*, was so named after the *Donat*, a medieval Latin textbook. ... The study of the Latin language in this division became much more formal. Frequently the assignment was an entire Psalm or a section from the Latin Vulgate. ... The upper division group was known as the *Alexandristen*, named after a

---

[19] *WA TR* 5, 254, 8–10; *L W* 54, 457.

[20] Boehmer, *Der junge Luther*, 18.

textbook by Alexander de Ville Dieu, in which the
students were given more advanced Latin grammar and
syntax.[21]

There was a strict and clear progression from *Fibulist* or
Tabulist to *Donatist* to *Alexandrist* with pupils moving to ever
higher levels of accomplishment, principally in Latin. This
progression moved from the first stages of the "ABCs" to a
systematic study of the elements of grammar as a *Donatist* to
the study of meter and syntax as an *Alexandrist*. Along with
these studies, pupils at the second level read from Cato the
Elder while those at the third read Aesop's *Fables*, a writing that
Luther always cherished, preparing a German edition of it and
asserting that it was the best book there was next to the Bible.[22]
In addition, pupils memorized the *Cisio Janus*, a "mnemonic
poem about how important saints' days fell in the various
months, which served both as an introduction to the church
year and as an aid to learning the calendar."[23] In spite of some
negative comments from Luther in *To the Councilmen of All Cities
in Germany That They Establish and Maintain Christian Schools*
about the ineptitude of his teachers and the stupidity of the
books they used, the reality is that much of what Luther learned
during that time, from Latin grammar to the church calendar to
the liturgy, stayed with him and provided the foundation for
his subsequent study and vocation. The text by Donatus
continued to be used even in schools of the Reformation, and
Melanchthon himself formulated a new version of the *Cisio
Janus*.[24]

Among the studies of most lasting importance to Martin
was his introduction to singing and music. The school day
began with prayer and song, usually "Come, Thou, Holy Spirit,
Come" and closed in the same way, often with the hymn,

---

[21] Schwiebert, *Luther and His Times*, 111–12.

[22] Boehmer, *Der junge Luther*, 20; Brecht, *Martin Luther: His Road to
Reformation*, 14.

[23] Brecht, *Martin Luther: His Road to Reformation*, 14–15.

[24] Schwiebert, *Luther and His Times*, 112. On Luther's critique of
what he learned, see *W A* 15, 51, 8–16; *LW* 45, 375.

"Come, Holy Ghost, Our Souls Inspire."[25] When Luther the reformer turned to the task of educating the young, he stressed music and gave it a significant place in the curriculum. In Luther's day, pupils and their teachers were expected to participate in church services. Thus, young Martin had ample opportunity for "practical" application of what he learned in school. Long before formally studying the quadrivium at the University of Erfurt, Luther had learned by heart not only the liturgy and many hymns, but had probably gained at least some basic theoretical knowledge in music.[26] Given Luther's accomplishments and his lifelong love of music, one or more of his teachers may have been gifted in this area. Luther is quoted as saying in the *Table Talk*: "Music I have always loved. He who knows music has a good nature. Necessity demands that music be kept in the schools. A schoolmaster must know how to sing; otherwise I do not look at him. And before a youth is ordained into the ministry, he should practice music in school."[27] Erikson suggests that Martin's love of music may predate his school years and be traced to his mother's influence on him.[28]

From a modern perspective, the schooling that Martin received in Mansfeld could be categorized as anything but balanced. Boehmer, for example, asserts that Martin probably gained very little skill in arithmetic, and Luther himself complains about the absence of history and literature.[29] However, before we wax too critical of what appears to us to be a very limited curriculum, we should remember that the majority of those who attended such schools and progressed through the three classes would become members of the

---

[25] Brecht, *Martin Luther: His Road to Reformation*, 15.

[26] Brecht, *Martin Luther: His Road to Reformation*, 15.

[27] *WA TR* 5, 557, 18–21; translated in Plass, *What Luther Says*, vol. II, 980.

[28] Erikson, *Young Man Luther*, 72. Although there are no sources indicating that Luther's mother sang to him, it certainly would have been expected that a mother would sing her baby to sleep with lullabies and hymns.

[29] Boehmer, *Der junge Luther*, 19.

spiritual order, and for their needs precisely the most important subjects were Latin and the liturgy, along with such information as that provided by the *Cisio Janus*. Those intending to pursue secular occupations would usually attend a "German school" where they would learn reading and writing in the vernacular, along with some rudimentary arithmetic, and would then apprentice themselves to someone who could train them in their occupation. The idea that all children need a firm grounding in history, literature, mathematics, and other subjects in order to be well-balanced and informed people would have been regarded as an unheard of luxury in an age when a bad harvest could still threaten survival and when outbreaks of the plague threatened to end life painfully and quickly. Life was short, and when parents sent their children to school, it was with the intention that they learned what they needed as quickly as possible in order to put it to use. It is perhaps ironic that we as college and university educators sometimes face the same attitude today, although in a very different context.

This pervading sense of the shortness of life yielded an impatience that may explain why both parents and teachers made such fervent use of the rod to correct mistakes and teach lessons. We have already noted that Martin complains he had once been struck fifteen times in a single morning for failing to learn a lesson that he had not yet been assigned. Likewise he recounts that he experienced beatings at home. Luther tells only two such stories, one about his father and one about his mother, and it would be a mistake—one that some biographers have made—to regard them as thematic for Martin's childhood. With regard to the beating he received from his father, Luther reports: "My father once whipped me so that I ran away and felt ugly at him until he was at pains to win me back."[30] Of his mother, Luther recounts: "My mother caned me for stealing a nut, until the blood came. Such strict discipline drove me to the monastery, although she meant it well."[31] What should we make of such comments?

If Erikson were writing today in the current climate of concern about child abuse, he might well suggest that Luther

---

[30] Cited in Roland Bainton, *Here I Stand: A Life of Martin Luther* (New York and Nashville: Abingdon Press), 23; *WA TR* 2, 134, 5–7.

[31] *WA TR* 3, 415, 29–416, 2, cited in Bainton, *Here I Stand*, 23.

had been the victim of such abuse, or at the very least of excessive physical discipline. Instead, Erikson argues that Martin was a victim of his father's frustrations disguised as righteous anger: "Martin, however, seems to have sensed on more than one occasion that the father, behind his disciplined public identity, was possessed by an angry, and often alcoholic, impulsiveness which he loosed against his family ... under the pretense of being a hard taskmaster and righteous judge."[32] Erikson proposes that the punishment delivered by his father permanently disfigured Luther's understanding of authority, as would later be demonstrated in his challenges to the papacy and by his becoming—in reaction to his father's unwillingness to tolerate any back-talk—"one of the biggest and most effective back-talkers in history."[33] The conclusions that Erikson draws from this single report have been successfully challenged and refuted by numerous scholars, including Roland Bainton and Lewis Spitz. There is absolutely no historical evidence to suggest that Hans was an alcoholic or that he had a murderous temperament. Indeed his economic success and standing in the community would argue strongly at least against the former. It *may* be the case that he beat his children and perhaps even his wife, but we have no evidence to suggest that this was the case. Indeed, as Bainton discusses, the quotation that Erikson cites suggests that Hans took considerable pains to win back the trust and confidence of his young son.[34] Bainton rightly underscores the fact that Luther says "once", certainly not suggesting that he was the victim of regular beatings.

The same interpretation can be offered to the beating that Martin received at the hands of his mother. There is one single reference to such a beating. It came about as a result of a theft, which trivial as it may seem, was nonetheless taken very seriously as the beginning of a behavior which was morally

---

[32] Erikson, *Young Man Luther*, 66. See further the well formulated response by Roland Bainton in Johnson, ed., *Psychohistory and History*, 19–56, especially 34–35.

[33] Erikson, *Young Man Luther*, 66.

[34] Bainton, "Psychiatry and History: An Examination of Erikson's Young Man Luther," in Johnson, ed., *Psychohistory and History*, 34–36.

wrong. In both *Table Talk* accounts, Luther's objective was to stress that excessive corporal punishment is to be avoided since it intimidates children and makes them question the love of their parents for them, even when, as Luther said of his mother, they mean well. It is difficult to know precisely what the mature Luther meant when he comments that the strict discipline he received from his mother drove him into the monastery. Perhaps he was suggesting that she succeeded all too well in imbuing in him a sense of guilt and repentance and that he felt he could never do enough to atone for the sins he had committed. Such a conclusion fits well with what we know from Luther about his struggles to please a righteous God and the sort of self-inflicted punishment, including both fastings and whippings, which he inflicted upon himself in the monastery.

There is every reason to think that Martin sincerely loved his parents as is evidenced by the comments he made at their passing. There are no signs that he harbored any animosity toward them, only that as he reflected later in life on the most appropriate way to discipline children he recalled these two instances as occasions when discipline went too far. There is also no evidence to suggest that Martin was regularly beaten at school. The pedagogy of the time emphasized memorization, and errors could be corrected either by word or by rod or both. The education that Martin received was medieval in both content and method, and there was a continued emphasis on the dictum "spare the rod and spoil the child."

There is no reason, however, to believe that Martin's teachers were unfeeling tyrants. First, most teachers were on short-term contracts and could readily be fired if there were accusations of excessiveness in the enforcement of discipline or if the teachers proved themselves inadequate. Second, although virtually all parents would have seen pedagogical discipline as warranted, they also loved their children and would not have tolerated discipline that exceeded normal bounds. There were other practices that plagued schoolboys, including young Martin, but Luther and Melanchthon also continued several of these. There was the practice of the *lupus*, the pupil who was appointed to spy on his fellows and to report to the teacher any occurrences of speaking in German rather than Latin. Since these instances were recorded secretly, the culprit never knew what his punishment would be until it was delivered on Friday. The other practice that was followed was the *asinus*, the donkey mask, which the poorest student had to wear until he was replaced by another. While Luther complains of these practices, it is worth noting that they remain part of Reformation schools as demonstrated by records from 1580.[35]

Biographers differ markedly in their assessment of the effect of these early years of schooling on Luther. Representing those who judge these years negatively is Heiko Oberman who writes: "Luther thought he had learned deplorably little during those long years. His experiences in Mansfeld provided a negative model that impelled him toward radical educational reform."[36] Martin Brecht offers a more positive interpretation of these years: "A few unpleasant memories of an excessively severe and inadequate education remained with Luther from his school days. But here also one should not one-sidedly emphasize the negative experiences. He did have good teachers as well. ... The ability to think in the Latin language, to use it and to express himself in it, he owed primarily to the school."[37] For his part, Roland Bainton concludes: "But, despite all the severities, the boys did learn Latin and loved it. Luther, far from being alienated, was devoted to his studies and became highly proficient."[38] Although we have no way of knowing precisely how much Martin learned at Mansfeld in comparison with the subsequent year in Magdeburg and the years in Eisenach, he evidently learned enough to allow him to proceed to those schools and to perform well there.

Given Luther's loquacity we may assume that if the punishment had been consistently harsh and Luther a consistent victim, he would have commented on it far more often. Luther's academic success and the paucity of his comments about his negative school experiences encourage us to conclude as Brecht and Bainton do that in spite of the discipline and an often boring pedagogy, Luther came to love learning, or at least to demonstrate sufficient proficiency to encourage his ambitious father to keep him in school, certainly not an automatic decision. At the same time, Oberman correctly

---

[35] Scheel, *Martin Luther*, vol. I, 35.

[36] Oberman, *Luther*, 96.

[37] Brecht, *Martin Luther: His Road to Reformation*, 15.

[38] Bainton, *Here I Stand*, 25.

notes that his school years led Luther to become a staunch critic of the pedagogy he had experienced, as he writes in his 1524 treatise *To the Councilmen of All Cities in Germany That They Establish and Maintain Christian Schools*: "Now since the young must always be hopping and skipping, or at least doing something that they enjoy, and since one cannot very well forbid this—nor would it be wise to forbid them everything—why then should we not set up such schools for them and introduce them to such studies? By the grace of God it is now possible for children to study with pleasure and in play languages, or other arts, or history."[39] In short, probably in reaction to his own experiences, Luther later affirmed that the most effective pedagogy mixes study with play, something he probably experienced all too seldom during his own school years.

We do not know how much Martin had learned at the time that his father made the decision to take him out of the Mansfeld school and send him to Magdeburg. Whether he began school in 1488 or later, after seven or more years of schooling, we can surmise he had developed proficiency in Latin, including reading, writing and grammar. He had also gained a firm knowledge of the liturgy, numerous hymns, and perhaps the rudiments of musical theory. By this time as well he had encountered Cato the Elder and perhaps even Aesop, as well as excerpts from Virgil and others in the *Donat* text.[40]

We also do not know what motivated Hans to send Martin to Magdeburg. We know that the son of a business associate of Hans, Peter Reinecke, decided to send his son, Johannes, to school in Magdeburg, and that the two boys went to school together. We also know that a former resident of Mansfeld, Paul Mosshauer, was at that time a well-placed official with the archbishop and a member of the cathedral chapter.[41] There is a paucity of information regarding Martin's year in Magdeburg, and historians propose various interpretations of his time there. Although we do not know for certain which

---

[39] *W A* 15, 46, 1–6; *L W* 45, 369.

[40] Schwiebert, *Luther and His Times,* 113.

[41] Scheel, *Martin Luther,* vol. I, 67; Brecht, *Martin Luther: His Road to Reformation,* 15.

school Martin attended, it was most likely the cathedral school. Scheel states that at the time Martin was in Magdeburg, although there were several other schools in the city, the cathedral school was the best known, widely recognized throughout northwest Germany.[42] Given Mosshauer's association with the cathedral, and the possibility that he was the one who recommended to the parents that their sons attend the school there, we have every reason to believe that the boys were at the cathedral school.[43] There is only one reference by Luther to his time in Magdeburg, in a letter written to the mayor, Claus Storm, on June 15, 1522 in which he recounted his memory of meeting Storm in the home of Dr. Paul Mosshauer, where he was often a guest during the time when he and Hans Reinecke went to school "zu den Nullbrüdern," to the Brethren of the Common Life.[44]

This comment has elicited a great deal of discussion and debate. Did Luther in fact attend a school run by the Brethren of the Common Life? If so, what was their influence upon him? Did he live in a hostel run by the Brethren and attend their school or did he live with them and attend school elsewhere, most likely the cathedral school? Did the Brethren in fact teach in the cathedral school so that Martin and Hans would have come into far more sustained and regular contact with them? Or did the two boys come into contact with the Brethren only through extra lessons, largely focusing on the inculcation of piety, which they offered to schoolboys? It is impossible to achieve definite answers to most of these questions, and biographers of Luther have addressed these issues quite differently. For example, Atkinson and Boehmer maintain that Luther attended a school run by the Brethren, with Boehmer arguing that Mosshauer took Luther into his house, although he needed to earn his keep as did other boys, singing as part of a boys' choir in churches and in the streets for food, an accepted practice.[45] Kittelson notes that Luther "lived and studied at a

---

[42] Scheel, *Martin Luther*, vol. I, 67.

[43] Brecht, *Martin Luther: His Road to Reformation*, 15.

[44] *WA Br* 2, 563, 3–7.

[45] James Atkinson, *Martin Luther and the Birth of Protestantism* (Atlanta: John Knox Press, 1968), 23; Boehmer, *Der junge Luther*, 26.

foundation operated by the Brethren of the Common Life."[46] Brecht, Gritsch, and Scheel all maintain that Luther attended the cathedral school.[47] Scheel, Schwiebert, and Todd argue that some of the Brethren taught at the school, while Brecht is more cautious in suggesting that, although Luther undoubtedly resided with the Brethren, it is not clear what role they might have had as teachers in the cathedral.[48]

Luther's 1522 letter would seem to argue for more than a merely casual association with the Brethren, and it is certainly possible that Luther lived in a hostel supported by them. However, sources do not allow us to conclude this fact with certainty. The one report that may refer to Luther's living with the Brethren comes from the biography of Matthäus Ratzeberger, not regarded as a highly trustworthy source. Ratzeberger recounts a time in Magdeburg when Luther was quite ill with a high fever and was left alone, forbidden to consume any liquids.[49] Ratzeberger reports that Luther awoke to find himself alone and in spite of the prohibition he had received, he arose and went to the kitchen to drink some water, after which he began to feel much better. In favor of the validity of the report, Brecht argues that the "recollection ... fits completely into this context."[50] Scheel, however, contends that if Luther had been living with the Brethren, they never would have left him completely alone in the house, since the Brethren were highly regarded for their care of the ill and had rules concerning attendance upon them. This fact suggests to Scheel

---

[46] Kittelson, *Luther the Reformer*, 37.

[47] Brecht, *Martin Luther: His Road to Reformation*, 16; Gritsch, *Martin—God's Court Jester*, 4; Scheel, *Martin Luther*, vol. I, 77.

[48] Scheel, *Martin Luther*, vol. I, 70–74; Schwiebert, *Luther and His Times*, 7; John Todd, *Luther: A Life* (New York: Crossroad, 1981), 7; Brecht, *Martin Luther: His Road to Reformation*, 16.

[49] D. Chr. Gotth. Neudecker, ed., *Die handschriftliche Geschichte Ratzebergers über Luther und seine Zeit* (Jena: Druck und Verlag von Friedrich Mauke, 1850), 41–42.

[50] Brecht, *Martin Luther: His Road to Reformation*, 16.

that Luther was in fact living not with the Brethren, but in a private house. Since the cathedral school was well-established with good teachers before the Brethren were permitted to establish a house in Magdeburg in 1482, and there is no record of the Brethren playing a leading role as teachers in the school, it is unlikely that Luther would say he went "to the *Nullbrüder*" to school, if he meant that they had been among his teachers at the cathedral school. Nor, as was noted earlier, is it likely he would have made this comment if he had simply voluntarily attended their sermons and lessons. At the same time, the research of R. R. Post has demonstrated that the Brethren, who encountered considerable opposition from both citizens and monastic orders in Magdeburg, did not open a school of their own there.[51] Post further maintains that "Luther's assertion that during this period the Brothers taught in the cathedral school is completely unacceptable. ... It is difficult to imagine that the *fratres* from Hildesheim were competent to teach successfully."[52] The most likely explanation for Luther's association with the Brethren of the Common Life would seem to be that he boarded with them, at least for a time, while he attended the cathedral school.

The question of the nature and degree of Luther's contact with the Brethren is important because of the type of education that the Brethren espoused. Through their teaching and manner

---

[51] R. R. Post, *Modern Devotion: Confrontation with Reformation and Humanism*, in *Studies in Medieval and Reformation Thought*, vol. III (Leiden: E. J. Brill, 1968), 440. Albert Hyma's assertion that the Brethren opened a school at Magdeburg is not supported by the evidence. *The Brethren of the Common Life* (Grand Rapids, MI: William B. Eerdmans Publishing Company, 1950), 117.

[52] Post agrees with Scheel that the Brethren would not have neglected a sick boy in their care, but he does not find the Ratzeberger account a persuasive argument against the fact that Luther lived with the Brethren: "I agree that one can not imagine them as failing in their duty towards the boys entrusted to their care. However, they may not have been convinced of the seriousness of the illness in question and thus left the boy alone without scruples." He concludes: "The only remaining solution is that young Martin boarded with the Brothers and went to school elsewhere." *Modern Devotion*, 629 and 630.

of living they articulated a specific attitude toward learning that has been characterized as "learning in the service of piety."[53] Undoubtedly, regardless of where it occurred, Martin's schooling in Mansfeld incorporated religious training since the boys participated in both regular and special church services. However, the Brethren took the connection between learning and religion several steps further and fostered a particular attitude of devotion, of learning in service to God, among those boys with whom they came in contact. Scheel describes the Brethren as more concerned with education than with instruction, in other words, more committed to encouraging the boys to follow a certain model of life than simply to teaching them facts.[54]

Founded by Gerhard Groote of Deventer, Holland, the Brethren of the Common Life was a lay religious organization whose members combined their funds and lived a common life under a rule formulated by Groote around 1387. Over the course of the fifteenth century the Brethren spread from Holland into several areas, including northwestern and southwestern Germany. The Brethren dedicated themselves to a life of poverty, but unlike the mendicants, they did not beg for their livelihood. Instead, they lived partly from their combined funds, from donations, and from their work as book copiers and illuminators. Groote himself was greatly interested both in learning and in furthering pious education among the young. Over time the Brethren began to admit schoolboys as boarders into their houses and to open hostels for poor boys from rural areas and villages who sought to achieve an education in towns such as Deventer that had good schools. With the advent of printing, some of the Brethren moved from copying to printing books, while increasingly as a group they devoted themselves to educating the young, boarding and helping schoolboys with their lessons in the hostels they ran, as well as opening their own schools in those towns where the city council would give them permission or where they were allowed to teach in established schools. The school in Deventer, attended by Erasmus of Rotterdam, and the one in Zwolle became the most famous.

---

[53] Oberman, *Luther*, 96.

[54] Scheel, *Martin Luther*, vol. I, 82.

Scholars have long looked upon the Brethren as precursors of, and contributors to, northern humanism. Although the Brethren used some classics in their teaching and prepared some textbooks, scholars now agree that the Brethren did not decisively contribute to fostering humanist learning.[55] However, as Oberman suggests, their contribution to fostering education through enabling boys from outlying areas to attend good schools should not be underestimated.[56] Luther was probably a beneficiary of this commitment to education on the part of the Brethren.

Assuming then that Martin lived with the Brethren for a time, he experienced daily a devotional milieu anchored by sermons and prayers. The Magdeburg house was founded by Brethren from Hildesheim in 1482. The two brothers who first came to the city experienced considerable opposition from the city council and from monastics and mendicants. The city had little desire for another tax exempt group in their midst; the monastics and mendicants did not desire any additional competition for donations and alms.[57] Only intercession from the archbishop and the cathedral chapter allowed the Brethren to succeed in their goals and eventually, in the year in which Martin most likely came to Magdeburg, 1497, to be able to increase their membership to twenty.[58] It would be interesting

---

[55] Based on extensive research in primary sources from the various houses of the Brethren of the Common Life, Post concludes: "It has been established that despite their merits in training and supplementing the education of small groups of students with a particular aim within their hostels, the Brothers were essentially pastors and not teachers in the late medieval and first Humanist schools. Their main task was the pastoral care of schoolboys and nuns. Only in exceptional cases and in a few cities did they introduce their charges to the humanistic culture, and here too they only developed after the new concepts had already gained a hold in the schools. In any case they were not trained to be pioneers in this domain." *Modern Devotion,* 630.

[56] Oberman, *Luther*, 96.

[57] Scheel, *Martin Luther*, vol. I, 78.

[58] Brecht, *Martin Luther: His Road to Reformation*, 16; Scheel, *Martin Luther*, vol. I, 82.

to know what role Paul Mosshauer may have played in the Brethren's triumph and whether or not his interaction with them may have impressed Mosshauer to the point of suggesting to Reinecke and Luther that they send their sons to live with the group.

Under the guidance of the Brethren, Martin would have encountered an environment analogous to a monastic one, with regular periods for study and prayer, as well as lessons and prayers delivered by members of the community. Their goal was to foster a sense of inner devotion and spirituality, as epitomized in Thomas á Kempis' book *The Imitation of Christ*. We simply do not know how much influence this devotion had upon Martin and what role it may have played in his decision to choose the monastic life. The Brethren themselves were frequent critics of the monastic life and its failure to live up to its apostolic ideals. In his *Lectures on Romans*, as a young professor of Bible, Luther approvingly cites Gerhard Groote (although he means Gerard Zerbolt, as Oberman notes) on the topic of original sin, stating that Groote speaks "not as an arrogant philosopher but as a sound theologian."[59] Although Luther later became an outspoken critic of the monastic life, he spoke harshly only once of the Brethren of the Common Life, and that was in the year 1529 in regard to a Bible translation prepared by his enemy Jerome Emser and printed by the community in Rostock.[60] Indeed, the contrast that Luther draws between "arrogant philosopher" and "sound theologian," an opposition that was very much on Luther's mind in 1515–17 as he was developing his critique of Aristotle's inappropriate influence on theology, suggests high praise for Zerbolt, aligning him, and by implication the Brethren, with the sound theology of the Bible and such church fathers as Augustine. Given Luther's outpourings against monastic life, his few positive references to the Brethren should be taken seriously. The fact that the Brethren remained a lay organization, freely choosing to live in common and to donate

---

[59] *WA* 56, 313, 13–17. *Luther's Works*, vol. 25: *Lectures on Romans*, ed. Hilton C. Oswald (Saint Louis: Concordia Publishing House, 1972), 300; Oberman, *Luther*, 97.

[60] Post, *Modern Devotion*, 628.

their resources, would certainly be compatible with Luther's concept of the freedom of the Christian. Their voluntary adherence to a semi-monastic life may well have proven attractive to an impressionable boy away from home for the first time.

Some of Luther's biographers suggest that the way of life followed by the Brethren may have proven too attractive to Martin, and for that reason his father chose to remove him from school in Magdeburg and send him to Eisenach, where relatives could more closely supervise him.[61] Once again the absence of sources leaves us in the realm of speculation. And the few sources we have leave many questions about Luther's years in Eisenach unanswered. What we know from Luther's account is that these were happy years and that for the rest of his life he looked back fondly upon the town and upon the friends he made there.

The best known remark from Luther concerning this time in his life occurs in his 1530 writing *On Keeping Children in School*, where he proclaims: "I too was such a crumb collector [beggar] once, begging from door to door, especially in my beloved city of Eisenach—though afterward my dear father lovingly and faithfully kept me at the University of Erfurt, by his sweat and labor helping me to get where I am."[62] Much has been made of this remark suggesting that Martin was destitute during his Eisenach years and supported himself by begging for bread from door to door. Current biographers of Luther reject this portrait of the poor and lonely boy begging for his daily bread for several reasons. First, we know that such "singing for bread" was a well-accepted practice in which many schoolboys, rich and poor, participated. Second, Luther's fond memories of Eisenach offer no hint that this was a time of poverty and struggle. Third, several of his letters that refer to the Eisenach time suggest that he become acquainted with people there who took an interest in his welfare, as well as teachers who made learning a positive experience. Fourth, we know that Martin had relatives in Eisenach, who although they may have been unable to house him, nonetheless would not have allowed him to wander hungry upon the streets. Had that

---

[61] Erikson, *Young Man Luther*, 81.

[62] *W A* 30 II, 576, 11–15; *LW* 46, 250–51.

been the case, his father, given his concern for Martin's welfare and future success, would have brought him home or sent him elsewhere where he could have received more adequate care.

Luther indicates that he spent four years in Eisenach, and, since the matriculation records of the University of Erfurt specify that he was accepted into the student rolls in spring of 1501, we can assume that Martin moved to Eisenach in 1497 or 1498, with most scholars agreeing that 1498 is the more likely date.[63] Most biographers agree that Hans transferred Martin to Eisenach because of relatives who could look after him, although this may not have turned out precisely as Hans had wished. The Eisenach school did not enjoy any special reputation; so other reasons must have been behind Hans' decision.[64]

In Eisenach Martin had an abundance of relatives, perhaps on both sides of the family. Although there is some dispute on the precise relationship, Brecht argues that Conrad Hutter, the sacristan at the St. Nikolai Church, was "the husband of ... [Luther's] paternal grandmother's sister."[65] Playing a more prominent role were Martin's maternal relatives. Heinrich Lindemann, probably Luther's uncle, "was a city councellor from 1484 to 1507 (together with Heinrich Schalbe) and mayor

---

[63] WA TR 5, 76, 25–26: "1497 Magdeburgam in scholam missus; ibi annum fui. 1501 ab Isanach Erphurdiam; 4 annos fui Isanach." If Luther went to Magdeburg in 1498, he would have spent three rather than four years in Eisenach. While agreeing with most other biographers that Luther arrived in Eisenach in 1498, Kittelson errs in suggesting that Luther spent six years there. *Luther the Reformer,* 39.

[64] Scheel, *Martin Luther,* vol. I, 116.

[65] Brecht, *Martin Luther: His Road to Reformation,* 17. Scheel holds that Hutter was married to the sister of Martin's grandmother on his *mother's* side of the family. *Martin Luther,* vol. I, 103. Clemen in a note in *WA Br* 1 also indicates that Hutter was married to a sister of Luther's grandmother on his mother's side of the family (12–13). Gottfried Krodel in his note 5 on the letter to Braun in *Luther's Works,* vol. 48: *Letters I* (Philadelphia: Fortress Press, 1963) concurs with the editor of *WA* (4).

in 1497."[66] We do not know precisely where Martin stayed during this period or if he roomed in two or three different locations during those four years. Boehmer suggests that at least for a time Martin may have lived in a hostel or at the school itself.[67] Scheel believes that Martin lived for a time in the family of Heinrich Schalbe and then moved later to that of Kunz Cotta whose wife Ursula was born a Schalbe. She may be the distinguished lady (*Matrone*) of whom Mathesius reports, so impressed by Luther's singing and praying that she took him into her house.[68] Scheel argues that it is more likely that Martin lived with the Cottas since they were closer to the school he attended, St. George's. Brecht offers a possible resolution to the problem, noting that Ursula was the daughter of Heinrich Schalbe, and that the young Cotta couple "lived in the same house as the Schalbes."[69] Siggins describes the "Lindemanns, Schalbes, and Cottas ... [as] all part of the same patrician circle of Eisenach burghers and [they] were closely related. ... It was here, among his mother's people and their values, that Martin Luther lived throughout the years of his early adolescence."[70]

Sources, including Luther's early letter to the priest Johannes Braun inviting him to his first mass, establish that Luther had links to both families, particularly to the Schalbes, whose young son Caspar he took to school.[71] Both families were very distinguished, with members serving on the city council. Heinrich Schalbe served as mayor of Eisenach for two terms, during 1495 and 1499.[72] He and his family founded a circle, the "Collegium Schalbe", which was deeply interested in both religion and culture. The reference to the "Collegium Schalbe",

---

[66] Siggins, *Luther and His Mother*, 45.

[67] Boehmer, *Der junge Luther*, 27.

[68] Scheel, *Martin Luther*, vol. I, 106–107.

[69] Brecht, *Martin Luther: His Road to Reformation*, 19.

[70] Siggins, *Luther and His Mother*, 50.

[71] *WA TR* 5, 95, 4–6.

[72] Brecht, *Martin Luther: His Road to Reformation*, 18.

however, is not entirely clear. It may refer to the group that Schalbe formed around the small Franciscan monastery to which the Schalbe family was particularly devoted, or it may refer, as Oberman suggests, to "a regular house-soirée."[73] Probably within their circle Martin met Father Braun, who seems also to have been at the center of a social group, to have opened his home to schoolboys, and to have had a strong interest in music.[74] With Braun, the Schalbes and the Cottas, Martin encountered an environment that encouraged both his religious and his musical gifts and interests. As Brecht concludes, these years are especially important ones because they introduce Martin to a new and more refined social milieu and constitute a significant change in his background, now more "middle class and urban" than peasant and rural.[75]

We know little about Martin's studies during those four years, although we can surmise that in large part these years were dedicated to increasing his proficiency in Latin, and that during this time he had the opportunity to read at least a few classical authors, such as Terence and Aesop. According to Melanchthon, Luther encountered in Eisenach a teacher who taught grammar better than anyone else.[76] Ratzeberger recounts that the rector of the school, Trebonius, doffed his beret when he came into class in honor of so many future distinguished citizens, doctors, lawyers, and theologians. Scholars have questioned whether or not Ratzeberger invented Trebonius and the anecdote to serve as a prophetic statement of Luther's subsequent fame.[77] Following the editor of the *Weimar Ausgabe*,

---

[73] Oberman, *Luther*, 100.

[74] Brecht, *Martin Luther: His Road to Reformation*, 20.

[75] Brecht, *Martin Luther: His Road to Reformation*, 21. Siggins stresses the values that Luther learned during this period. *Luther and His Mother*, 74–75.

[76] *CR* 6, col. 157.

[77] Brecht, *Martin Luther: His Road to Reformation*, 19–20. The only evidence about Trebonius stems from Ratzeberger. We do not know what association Trebonius may have had with Luther, and therefore it is difficult to know how much of an effect he may have had upon Luther. Kittelson suggests that Trebonius had a great

Brecht suggests that Ratzeberger may have confused Trebonius with the humanist Trebelius in Eisenach, whom, however, Luther did not know.[78] Nonetheless, Luther did regard highly another teacher, Wigand Güldenapf, who later became a pastor and whom Luther recommended to the elector in 1526 as deserving of a pension.[79]

Few as the references are to the Eisenach years, they convey an unmistakable impression of joyous and productive years, the memories of which stayed with Luther throughout his life. Although the St. George's school did not possess any special repute, its teachers, Güldenapf certainly, and perhaps others, appear to have been men of genuine knowledge who were concerned for their pupils' welfare. Although the *asinus* and the *lupus* would have been a part of this school as well, there are no references in the *Table Talk* or in Luther's writings, to the infliction of punishment and humiliation during these years. Indeed, the very fact that Luther referred to Eisenach with such warmth as his "beloved Eisenach" suggests that these were years he remembered happily and believed were well-spent. What seems to have been especially the case during these years and probably was a new experience for him was the fusion of academic and social life. We can sense that in Eisenach Martin came to achieve a clearer sense of his independence, identity, and social standing. The fact that Martin was made welcome in these two circles, particularly in that of the Schalbes, is an indication that his hosts found him enjoyable and engaging company. His responsibility for escorting young Caspar Schalbe to school, and perhaps helping him with his lessons, are indications that the elder Schalbes viewed him as responsible and trustworthy. Although one cannot draw too many conclusions from the limited evidence about this period, its

impact upon Luther: "He found a teacher who could awaken his imagination while sharpening his mind. In this case the teacher was the headmaster of the school, one John Trebonius, whom Luther later praised as a gifted man." *Luther the Reformer*, 39. Luther may well be referring to Wigand Güldenapf, a teacher whom he highly respected and with whom he maintained a correspondence.

[78] Brecht, *Martin Luther: His Road to Reformation*, 19–20.

[79] Brecht, *Martin Luther: His Road to Reformation*, 20.

positive qualities decry any assertion that Luther's youth was somber and oppressive.

By the time Luther had completed his years in Eisenach he had successively progressed from the *Fibulisten* to the *Donatisten* to the *Alexandristen*, although some of the works Martin had encountered in the trivial school, such as the advanced grammar of Alexander de Ville Dieu, he would meet again as he studied for his bachelor's degree. While we can justifiably assume that by the end of his schooling, Luther had become proficient in Latin, it is more difficult to determine how far he had progressed in the other two components of the *trivium*, rhetoric and logic. Increasingly rhetoric had come to be displaced both by the study of grammar in the schools and then subsequently at the university level by logic, about which Luther would have a good deal to say. We have no reason to think that Luther was anything other than well-prepared to enter the university since he was able to attain his bachelor of arts degree in the minimum time.

The associations that he established in Eisenach became pivotal transitions to the University of Erfurt. It is unlikely that it was only on the recommendation of his Eisenach teachers that Martin and his father entertained the idea of his attending the university.[80] Given Hans' strong ambitions and the fact that he had already committed his son to schools in three locations over a considerable period of time, there is every reason to believe that it had long been his intention to send his son to the university. Of the two possible choices, Leipzig and Erfurt, Erfurt, the older of the two universities, had by far the more prestigious reputation, particularly in law. There were other reasons why Martin would have been far more inclined to Erfurt, not least among them the fact that his close friend, Father Braun, had attended that university. Braun must have been acquainted with the rector of the university, Jodocus Trutfetter, one of the two professors who would come to have the most influence on Luther, since Trutfetter had served as a

---

[80] Kittelson to the contrary suggests: "It was undoubtedly they [his Eisenach teachers] who recommended that the young man, then 17 years old, continue his studies at a university. ... It was unusual for a man in his position to send his son to the university." *Luther the Reformer*, 39.

cleric in Eisenach during 1493. Several of Luther's mother's relatives had also attended Erfurt.[81]

Although no one would deny that the upbringing of children during the Middle Ages was strict and sometimes harsh, there are no indications that Martin's was unusually so or that he experienced a particularly, "somber and harsh childhood," in the words of Erikson. Certainly Martin must have had some difficult and lonely days when he was away from home, especially in Magdeburg, where unlike Eisenach, there is no evidence that he was part of a close circle of friends and mentors. However, there is no reason to believe that his early upbringing and schooling left him bitter and afraid, ready after a few more years of education, to seek—in Erikson's words—a moratorium. At home and at school he experienced—as did every other schoolboy of the Middle Ages—discipline in the form of corporal punishment. He emerged from these experiences of punishment able to distinguish when it was rightly applied and when not. The older Luther, as he formulated his pedagogical program, spoke critically of the beatings he experienced and of some of the subjects he studied. Partly in reaction to those studies, Luther became an advocate of history and literature and of a pedagogy that includes play to reinforce learning and to make it enjoyable. While biographers often opine that Luther argued this way because he had experienced no such joy in his own schooling, it may in fact be the case that the Eisenach years and the teachers he admired there gave him some inkling of how enjoyable learning could be. His positive feelings about his years at Eisenach, where discipline too was an essential part of the pedagogy, suggest that by the end of his school years, discipline had not proven to be an impediment to his enjoyment of learning. It may have been these years of schooling that eventually led Luther to see God as a teacher whose discipline and justice serve the larger purpose of bestowing grace, just as Luther's favorite teachers in Eisenach used discipline to serve the purpose of learning.

It is difficult to be too critical of Luther's schooling when we witness what strengths it allowed him to bring to his subsequent education, first as a student of the arts and then of theology, as well as to his vocations as theologian and educator. By the time Luther went to the University of Erfurt, he was highly proficient

---

[81] Siggins, *Luther and His Mother*, 45.

in Latin and had come into enough contact with classical writers to desire to read more. He had become thoroughly familiar with the liturgy and had some opportunity to develop his love of music, which he would one day make an integral part of his educational program for young and old.

The education Luther received in those early years shaped his character. Required to adjust and to succeed in new schools and new living situations, Luther developed at a young age psychological stamina, independence, and the ability to accomplish the task that was set before him. The rest of Luther's life, from his days as a student of arts to his decision to enter the Augustinian Order, known for its scholarship, to his many years as a professor, suggest that his school years imbued Luther with a true love of learning. This is not to deny his critical comments about both the content and method of the education he received, but for all his complaints, Luther was never deterred from continuing to study and learn.

While we would not say that Luther emerged from his school years with a well-rounded education, he had achieved what was expected from him. Indeed, given the fact that his father was willing to pay the costs to send him to the university, he had far exceeded the norm. He was now ready to make the leap from school to university.

2

Martinus ludher ex mansfelt: Student of the Liberal Arts

As Americans of the late twentieth century, we prize our independence. We often define ourselves as individuals first and only second as members of communities. That is not to say, of course, that identification with a community is not important to us, but unlike western Europeans of the sixteenth century, it tends not to be our starting point, perhaps because we change our residences, our jobs, and our communities so often. We also have a plethora of communities among which to choose—one need only think of the multitude of Christian denominations. In contrast, at the beginning of the sixteenth century, there were far fewer types of communities that one could join. One's choices were largely determined by one's social class and gender, although Martin is a good example of what a boy of humble origins could accomplish with brains and parental support. At the age of seventeen he now joined a new community, the university, which would do much to shape and transform his identity and which would become the vocational anchor for his life. From the day he entered the university until the day he died, Martin Luther was a university man. Thus, understanding the university and its social context is vital to understanding Luther the educator. What were the intellectual currents in Germany at the beginning of the sixteenth century? Which ideas and ways of thinking influenced Luther? Which of them would he incorporate into his theology and pedagogy?

At the beginning of the summer semester 1501, Martin Luther matriculated as a student at the University of Erfurt. Unlike our tendency to define universities in terms of *place*, physical location and plant—the university campus—throughout the Middle Ages and even at the beginning of the sixteenth century, universities were defined in terms of *people*.

Universities were composed of two communities, the teaching association and the learning association, professors and masters on the one hand, and students on the other. The boundary between the two associations was in some respects quite fixed—masters and professors had rights and privileges which students did not—but in other respects it was fluid. For example, after receiving his master's degree in philosophy, the terminal degree in the liberal arts at the time, Martin was obliged to become an instructor for two years—thus joining the association of teaching masters—while at the same time maintaining his status as a student in the higher faculty of law.

Governance of the university was determined by its members. In the south, at such universities as Padua and Bologna, students largely controlled governance, and the rector, or in American educational terms, the president, was chosen from among the students. In the north, at a university such as Erfurt, the teaching association wielded more power and chose the rector from its ranks. Above the rector stood the chancellor who represented the authority of the church, since no university at that time was founded without papal approval. In the case of Erfurt, the chancellor was the Archbishop of Mainz, who appointed a vice-chancellor resident in Erfurt to represent and protect the church's interests.

To become a university student meant accepting certain obligations and a prescribed way of life while there, as well as affirming a lifelong oath of loyalty to the institution. The ambitious seventeen-year old who matriculated as Martinus ludher ex mansfelt probably perceived his university study as the means to an end, a law degree and a well paid position as councillor to city or prince. At least that was what his father intended for him. Although that goal may have been Martin's as he entered the university in 1501, Erfurt would change him and his ambitions in ways that neither father nor son could anticipate. Martin brought to his university studies a brilliant and searching mind, and he would find much in Erfurt to engage him, ideas of long standing, as well as new ones.

By matriculating at the university, Luther joined a special and privileged minority. Each stage of education that he completed placed him within an increasingly elite and distinguished group, with expanding possibilities for social and financial success. It seems likely that such thoughts were very much on Hans Luther's mind as he sent his son to the university to receive a level of education far higher than his own. It is unlikely he would have been willing to accept the burden of costs associated with that education if he had not anticipated long term financial rewards and increased honor and recognition for the family. When Luther was matriculated he was listed as in *habendo*, as financially capable of paying the entire matriculation fee of twenty groschen.[1]

Hans Luther undoubtedly gave much thought to choosing a university for his promising son. The University of Leipzig, founded 1409, was close to Luther's hometown of Mansfeld.[2] However, much spoke in favor of the University of Erfurt. It had a distinguished history, and there were strong connections between Erfurt and Eisenach where Martin had established such warm relationships. Erfurt was much closer to Eisenach than was Leipzig. The rector at the time Luther matriculated was Jodocus Trutfetter from Eisenach, known as "Doctor Eisenach", who was acquainted with Luther's mentor and friend, the Eisenach priest, Johannes Braun.

Erfurt was among the oldest of Germany's universities, and its roots within the cathedral schools of St. Maria and St. Severi went back even further. Erfurt's reputation as a lively center of learning was already established in the thirteenth century. While the institution was well regarded even then, it lacked the permission granted Paris and other universities to award academic degrees.[3] One could study the same subjects as at Paris, but would be unable to claim the degree and therefore unable to enjoy the privileges associated with formal status as a bachelor or master.[4] Although Erfurt preceded even Prague as a center of advanced study, it did not gain its university status

---

[1] Brecht, *Martin Luther: His Road to Reformation*, 29; Scheel, *Martin Luther*, vol. I, 148.

[2] Boehmer, *Der junge Luther*, 29.

[3] Sönke Lorenz, "Das Erfurter 'Studium generale artium'— Deutschlands älteste Hochschule" in Ulman Weiss, ed., *Erfurt 742–1992: Stadtgeschichte Universitätsgeschichte* (Weimar: Verlag Hermann Böhlaus Nachfolger, 1992), 129.

[4] One could become a master in Erfurt prior to 1392, but could not receive the *"licentia ubique docendi."* Lorenz, "Das Erfurter 'Studium generale artium'," 130.

until 1392, long after not only Prague but such institutions as Vienna and Heidelberg. Recognizing the educational and financial challenge posed by Prague, the city appealed to the papacy for the privilege of granting degrees, but papal politics, including the split within the church, prevented the granting of permission until 1389, with the university officially opening only in 1392.[5] For that same reason, Erfurt lost out to Cologne the distinction of being the first university founded by a city.[6] Reflecting the political complexity of the time, although the university was founded by the city, it was the Archbishop of Mainz—within whose domain Erfurt fell—who held the position of chancellor, authority he generally delegated to a vice-chancellor resident there. The university also fell victim to the tug of war over the city of Erfurt that was played out between the Archbishops of Mainz and the Electors of Saxony, both of whom claimed it as part of their territory.

Its unusual status as a university founded by a city rather than by a prince or king worked in Erfurt's favor for many years in spite of tensions between the city and the Archbishop of Mainz. There were, as might be expected, conflicts between town and gown, disagreements over judicial authority, tax exemption, and the like. As long as Erfurt continued to thrive economically and the university did well, bringing in new endowments and enjoying high matriculation rates, the tensions could usually be resolved amicably. However, when Erfurt began to experience serious economic problems, stemming partly from Erfurt's loss to Leipzig of its premier position as a trading center, partly from a shift in power from city to territory, partly from economic tensions between the various social classes, and partly from downturns caused by severe outbreaks of the plague, the city council found itself unable to support its university and foster its growth as it had in the past.[7] The city might have been able to weather these problems

---

[5] Lorenz, "Das Erfurter 'Studium generale artium'," 133. The reasons for the delay between the granting of papal permission and the official opening of the university are unclear.

[6] Lorenz, "Das Erfurter 'Studium generale artium'," 133.

[7] Erich Kleineidam, *Universitas Studii Erffordensis: Überblick über die Geschichte der Universität Erfurt. Teil II: Spätscholastik,*

had it not suffered enormous penalties from its involvement in the dispute between Dietrich von Isenberg and Adolf von Nassau over the position of Archbishop of Mainz.[8] As it turned out, the city council backed the losing candidate and was obliged to pay a heavy price by the winner, resulting in virtual financial ruin.[9] No longer the recipient of the city's generosity, the university had to furnish loans to the city, money which the university's leaders were well aware would never be repaid.

Erfurt also faced competition from new institutions, founded with strong princely financial support, such as Tübingen and Mainz, and later Wittenberg. Students who had traveled long distances to study in Erfurt now enjoyed excellent educational opportunities closer to home, at institutions whose sponsors were able to attract the leading intellectual lights and guarantee a more peaceful climate. Meanwhile in Erfurt, town and gown tensions and animosities between the well-to-do and the impoverished boiled over into violence in the bankrupt city when the lower classes rebelled in 1509 against the high taxation and misrule of the elite.[10] Violence was the order of

---

Humanismus und Reformation 1461–1521, 2nd expanded ed., vol. 22: Erfurter Theologische Studien (Leipzig: Benno Verlag, 1992), 75.

[8] Brecht, *Luther: His Road to Reformation*, 23–24.

[9] Brecht offers an excellent summary of the complex relationship among Erfurt, Mainz, and the territory of Saxony. *Martin Luther: His Road to Reformation*, 24. Kleineidam puts the debt of the city even higher than does Brecht, at about 600,000 gulden. *Universitas Studii Erffordensis II*, 184. He reports that in 1483 the city incurred a debt of about 200,000 gulden as a result of the two treaties with Mainz and Saxony, 74. As a result of ill-fated efforts to keep the serious financial situation as secret as possible and failed policies by the elite who ran the city council, the situation was utterly out of control by 1509–10 when the city declared bankruptcy in response to its huge debt.

[10] Brecht outlines how the city's economic tensions generated political ones with the lower classes siding with Mainz and the upper ones with Saxony. The university was caught in the middle: "As a result of a revolt between students and mercenaries in 1510 the Great College was laid waste." *Martin Luther: His Road to Reformation*, 25. Kleineidam places part of the blame for the events

the day culminating in the execution of the mayor by a mob. In 1510 the fighting resulted in the plundering of university buildings and the destruction of the university library. Not surprisingly, immediately thereafter Erfurt experienced a decrease in enrollments, further damaging the economic situation of both town and university. Kleineidam reports that in the winter semester of 1509–1510, 128 students matriculated, a substantial decline from previous years, and by winter semester of the next year the number had dropped to 61.[11] This decline is all the more remarkable when compared with the numbers over the period 1451–1460 when the university was at its height. In those nine years some 4,032 students matriculated, averaging out to roughly 200 each semester.[12]

In fairness to Erfurt, however, as Kleineidam notes, other cities and universities also had their problems during this time of increased social tension and turmoil. Outbreaks of violence occurred in other cities and universities, although the extraordinarily serious debt of the city and its resulting bankruptcy made violence in Erfurt far more widespread and serious. However, even in Wittenberg, still a mere village, in Electoral Saxony, at the newly established and well supported University of Wittenberg, there was a serious act of violence— the murder of the rector by a student.[13]

When the tumult occurred in Erfurt in 1510, Luther was in the final stages of his education, having joined the Augustinian Order and recently returned to Erfurt from a teaching stint at the University of Wittenberg. The violence and destruction against his *alma mater* deeply disturbed him, particularly the damage that was done to the library of the Great College, and heightened his awareness that universities could no longer be seen as islands of tranquillity in the heavy seas of social unrest.

---

of 1509 and 1510 on the arrogance and ostentatious display of wealth by the upper classes, which further infuriated those who had nothing. *Universitas Studii Erffordensis II, 74.*

[11] Kleineidam, *Universitas Studii Erffordensis II, 187.*

[12] Kleineidam, *Universitas Studii Erffordensis II, 20.*

[13] Kleineidam, *Universitas Studii Erffordensis II, 192.*

Already at that time he may have begun to ponder the relationship between university and society.

In spite of the problems it faced, when Luther entered the university in 1501 it was still a strong institution, although its glory days at the top of the list of German universities in terms of enrollments were past. From 1471–1501 it occupied third place, after Cologne and Leipzig, and then beginning in 1501 it dropped to fifth.[14] Nonetheless, at the time Luther entered the arts faculty, Erfurt was still regarded as an outstanding institution, whose degrees meant something. Its graduates, such as the distinguished theologian Gabriel Biel, had gained positions of honor within other universities and garnered widespread fame for themselves and their *alma mater*. Among Erfurt's graduates and former students were not only many professors, but also high ranking churchmen, including many bishops and archbishops. Of the three higher faculties of medicine, theology, and law, the law faculty continued to be regarded as particularly distinguished.[15] If law was indeed Luther's goal from the day he entered the university, all indications would be that he had made the right choice in Erfurt.

Matriculation at the university bore little resemblance to the procedure now. It was far more than a bureaucratic or financial formality. It was in fact a ceremony of considerable solemnity. It signified joining the corporation or body of the university, an association that included both rights and responsibilities. Young

---

[14] Kleineidam, *Universitas Studii Erffordensis II*, 75.

[15] Oberman notes that at the beginning of the sixteenth century "the higher faculties were not Erfurt's particular strength," while the arts curriculum was. *Luther,* 116. Kleineidam, however, argues that during the time when Luther was at Erfurt the law faculty was still notable, particularly through the presence of Henning Göde, known as "prince of the jurists." He suggests that the reputation of the law faculty was established through the success of its graduates, such as Johannes Muth aus Homberg, the brother of Mutianus Rufus, who became the chancellor to the Landgrafen of Hessen. Another graduate, Siegfried Uttesberg, became rector of the new University of Frankfurt/Oder. *Universitas Studii Erffordensis II,* 90. It seems likely that it was the reputation of the law faculty that encouraged Hans Luther to send his son to Erfurt.

Martin had to swear an oath to the rector, at that time Jodocus Trutfetter, to uphold the statutes of the university and to live according to its rules. Only after swearing this oath was he permitted to register in a bursa—what we might define as a very well-supervised fraternity—where his daily life would be closely monitored. Later Luther would speak of the bursa in less than positive terms, commenting that it provided the environment of a "whorehouse and a beerhouse."[16] However, in spite of these criticisms, both the bursa and the university were probably quite strict and Luther certainly made good use of his time. Given the fact that he applied to take his bachelor's examination in the minimum time allowed under the statutes of the university, Martin appears to have been among the most determined and industrious of students.

What was his life like? Students were required to arise early; to attend morning prayers; to go to the required lectures, either in the bursa or in another building; to participate in the mandatory practices, repetitions and discussion of the lectures; and lastly, to participate each year in a set number of disputations, culminating in the *quodlibet* disputation that all members of the university attended. Students slept in large dormitory rooms and were expected to spend their time in the common study room when they were not sleeping, eating, or attending lectures and practices. There was little opportunity to be alone or to be elsewhere than one was expected to be. To study late in preparation for a disputation or examination a student had to secure special permission. He had to do the same if he had reason to be out late in the evening. Such expeditions required a lantern, an essential given the fact that there were no street lamps in Erfurt, and acquiring one meant securing special permission from the dean of the bursa.

Life in a bursa should certainly not be equated with modern university dormitory life. Students had little independence or free time. At the same time, bursa life was not entirely monastic in character, even though that was certainly its spirit. Women were entirely excluded from the bursa, but students did enjoy social time together and did have fun during their school years. Luther, if we are to believe his contemporary at the university, Crotus Rubeanus, was no exception. He played the lute and

---

16 *WA* 42, 504, 18ff., cited in Brecht, *Martin Luther: His Road to Reformation*, 32.

was generally regarded as "one of the boys," although he also had the nickname *philosophus* which may suggest either his interest in humanist concerns or his skills during disputation, perhaps both. At any rate, when Luther made the apparently sudden decision to enter the monastery, his friends were dismayed and tried to persuade him to reject his vow as made under duress. Their clear pain at his departure suggests that he was well liked and that his presence as part of a lively social group of students would be missed. All of this is to say that if bursa life was highly regulated and monastic in character, it was also not without its lighter side. Indeed, the very stringency of the rules that kept young men in a highly supervised environment day in and day out led to close and lifelong friendships, such as that between Luther and Crotus Rubeanus (although Crotus later turned against Evangelical ideas) or between Luther and Johann Lang, who like Luther later joined the Augustinian Hermits.

While the university records tell us in which semester Luther matriculated at Erfurt and the fact that he had to pay full fees for his studies, they do not tell us to which bursa he was assigned. There is conflicting evidence for two different bursae, St. George's and the Amplonian College, known as Heaven's Gate or *porta coeli*.[17] The case for the *porta coeli* is the stronger of the two. There are indications that Crotus Rubeanus, who recounts that he lived in the same bursa as Luther, resided in the *porta coeli*, as perhaps did Johann Lang.[18] The *porta coeli*

---

[17] Scholars remain divided on this question. Heinrich Boehmer, *Der junge Luther* (p. 30); Todd, *Luther:* (p. 15); and Hans M. Tümmler, *Luther und Erfurt* (Erfurt: Gebr. Richters Verlagsanstalt, 1943), (p. 7) state that Luther lived in the St. George's bursa while Schwiebert, *Luther and His Times* (p. 132) leans in that direction. Brecht, on the other hand, after a review of the evidence on both sides states that "an entire series of proofs, independent from one another, points to the Heaven's Gate as Luther's bursa." *Martin Luther: His Road to Reformation*, 31. Heiko Oberman, *Luther*, suggests the Amplonian College "may have been Luther's residence hall for several years" (p. 116). Several biographers remain silent on the issue, including Gritsch, *Martin—God's Court Jester* and Kittelson, *Luther the Reformer*.

[18] Brecht, *Martin Luther: His Road to Reformation*, 51; Martin Burgdorf, *Der Einfluss der Erfurter Humanisten auf Luthers*

was also regarded as the leading bursa at the university, and, given Hans Luther's ambitions for his son, it seems likely that he would have sought admission for him there. Debate continues as to whether or not a letter of September 9, 1501, sent from the *porta coeli*, was written by Luther. Possibly intended for Luther's Eisenach friend and mentor, Johannes Braun, it is signed Martinus Viropolitanus, a Latinized (with a bit of Greek thrown in) version that may refer to "Martin from Mansfeld"— although Martin from Manstedt would be more accurate, as the introduction to the letter in the *Weimar Ausgabe* notes. Scholars question whether or not Luther would have referred to himself in this humanist style at this very early stage of his studies.[19] Martin Brecht argues for the authenticity of the letter, suggesting that Luther's cousin Dietrich Lindemann may have been mistaken in his much later letter in which he noted that he had briefly stayed with Luther in St. George's bursa.[20] The question is not of great importance for our knowledge of Luther's student years since both houses would have followed the same rules and both appear to have been open to humanist ideas. This was perhaps more the case in the *porta coeli*, where Johannes Knaes aus Bercka, who was promoted to doctor of law in October 1498, was dean from 1481 until his death in 1505.[21] Knaes studied at Erfurt with the Italian humanist Jakob Publicius during his brief stay from 1466–67 and recorded his lectures *"De arte distinguendi und rhetorica seu ars dictandi."*[22]

If matriculation into the university was a serious and formal matter, initiation into the bursa had quite a different character. Brecht describes this event as follows: "When one entered the bursa, a 'deposition' took place. This involved discarding the uneducated animalistic person, represented by an animal mask with the donkey's ears and swine's teeth, initially placed on the

---

Entwicklung bis 1510 (Leipzig: Kommissionsverlag von Dörfling & Franke, n.d.), 56.

[19] See the detailed discussion in *WA Br* 1, 1–7.

[20] Brecht, *Martin Luther: His Road to Reformation*, 30.

[21] Kleineidam, *Universitas Studii Erffordensis II*, 326–27.

[22] Kleineidam, *Universitas Studii Erffordensis II*, 53 and 327.

newcomer, and the acceptance of the new academically educated person. The newcomer was absolved of his old state and cleansed by a dousing, which corresponded to baptism, and by other levity of this sort."[23] Embarrassed as he may have been at the time, Luther maintained the tradition of depositions at the University of Wittenberg. In 1539 he refers to his deposing of three students at the University of Wittenberg and comments on the act in this way: " 'This ceremony is intended to make you humble, so that you may not be haughty and arrogant and given to wickedness. Such vices are horns and other monstrous parts that are not becoming to a student. Therefore humble yourselves. Learn to be patient. You'll be subjected to hazing all your life. ... When this happens, don't go to pieces. Bear your cross with equanimity and your troubles without murmuring. Remember that you have been initiated into annoyances at Wittenberg. Say that you first began to be hazed in Wittenberg when you were a young man, that now that you have become a weightier person you have heavier vexations to bear. So this deposition of yours is only a symbol of human life in its misfortunes and castigations.' And so when the wine had been poured on their heads he absolved them from their fledgling status."[24] In spite of the theological interpretation, Luther may also have thought the deposition was fun, since part of the process involved the new boys buying beer for the bursa.

This induction into academic life, both matriculation and deposition, made a considerable impression on Luther. In addition to matriculation before the rector and induction into the bursa, Luther had to appear before the dean of the arts faculty and swear an oath of loyalty. The academic year began with a university-wide church service in which those who had died over the past months were remembered and in which all dedicated themselves to the university's statutes and to pious and worthy behavior. Now the new academic year could begin.

At least initially Luther may have found his university studies quite familiar. The main difference was what was emphasized within the *trivium*. In school, it had been grammar,

---

[23] Brecht, *Martin Luther: His Road to Reformation*, 31.

[24] *WA TR* 4, 443, 17–444, 3; *L W* 54, 362–63, cited in Brecht, *Martin Luther: His Road to Reformation*, 31.

but now the curriculum unrelentingly stressed dialectics, and within dialectics, Aristotle. Rhetoric, the third part of the *trivium*, was often conjoined with lectures on grammar and received substantially less attention. We do not know precisely what Luther studied and just when he did so, but we can map out generally the lectures he attended. Given the fact that he was able to take the examinations for his degree in the minimum time allowed, we may infer that he attended two or three lectures each weekday. Scheel suggests that Luther attended at least eleven series of lectures during the three semester period from summer 1501 through summer 1502.[25] The university stipulated that a candidate for the bachelor's degree must have resided within the bursa for at least a year. Otherwise, however, there was no "residence" requirement. Unlike American universities of today, the length of a course—a series of lectures on a particular book—was not determined by semesters, but by the number of months that it took for the professor or master to complete his exposition of them. In some cases, that might be as little as a month, but in most cases it was considerably longer, perhaps as much as eight months.[26] To gain his degree, Luther would have had to have completed the prescribed lectures on the following works in the *trivium*: in grammar, the lesser Priscian and the second part of the grammar of Alexander de Ville Dieu; in rhetoric, the *Laborinthus* of Eberhard of Bethune; and in dialectic or logic, the tractate of Petrus Hispanus and the so-called *ars vetus* which was the "commentary on Aristotle by the Neoplatonist Porphyry."[27] In the area of logic, there were more lectures than in the other two areas. In addition to Hispanus and the *ars vetus*, there were lectures on the *Prior* and *Posterior Analytics* and the *Elencorum*, which dealt with fallacies. Luther also attended lectures in natural philosophy, including the *Physicorum* and *De anima*, and in astronomy.

Besides lectures, Luther was required to participate in certain exercises in the areas of logic and philosophy, including

---

[25] Scheel, *Martin Luther*, vol. I, 158.

[26] Scheel, *Martin Luther*, vol. I, 154.

[27] Brecht, *Martin Luther: His Road to Reformation*, 33. Scheel gives a similar listing of lecture courses, *Martin Luther*, vol. I, 158.

physics and psychology. In the bursa he participated in repetition sessions designed to assure that he was remembering what he was hearing in the lectures. He also attended the required disputations, including defending theses three times in both *"ordentlicher"* (regularly scheduled) and *"ausserordentlicher"* (special) disputations.[28] What seems to have distinguished the Erfurt curriculum from those of its competitors was a stress on the text of Aristotle himself rather than on commentaries. Luther's two main professors in the arts, Jodocus Trutfetter and Bartholomäus Arnoldi von Usingen, both prided themselves on their ability to deal directly with the sources. To better understand the education that Luther received, it is helpful to know something about these two teachers.

Jodocus Trutfetter matriculated as a student at the University of Erfurt in 1476, gained his bachelor's degree two years later and his master's degree in 1484.[29] As was required, he began his teaching career that same year as a master in the arts faculty while also pursuing advanced studies in theology.[30] He became a *baccalaureus biblicus* (the initial degree in theology) in 1484 and received his licentiate in theology in 1493. However, it was only in 1504 that he was able to afford the cost of the promotion to doctor of theology.[31] During his long career at Erfurt, he occupied many positions of responsibility within the university, from bursa rector, to representative of the *magistri de communi* in the faculty council, to dean of the arts faculty, and eventually, in 1501, to rector of the university. As was the norm, his main source of support came through the church positions that he held, including eventually that of canon at the St. Severi Church.[32] For a time, beginning in 1507, Trutfetter was lured away from Erfurt to Wittenberg by Elector Frederick the Wise, who pursued a vigorous policy of attracting the best and the brightest to his new university. However, as the

---

[28] Scheel, *Martin Luther*, vol. I, 167.

[29] Kleineidam, *Universitas Studii Erffordensis II*, 153.

[30] Kleineidam, *Universitas Studii Erffordensis II*, 141.

[31] Kleineidam, *Universitas Studii Erffordensis II*, 153.

[32] Kleineidam, *Universitas Studii Erffordensis II*, 153.

sole representative of the *via moderna* at Wittenberg, Trutfetter apparently longed for the more congenial environment of Erfurt, and he returned there in 1510—much to the delight of his colleagues.[33]

Along with Bartholomäus Arnoldi von Usingen, Trutfetter recognized the educational possibilities that the printing press provided, and he became an active publisher. His first work appeared in 1500 and his major work, the textbook in logic, *Summule totius logice,* was published in 1501, the year Luther entered the university.[34] Trutfetter's works were highly regarded at the time, and not only by his fellow scholastics. Leading humanists wrote prefaces to his works, including most frequently Maternus Pistoris and Nicholas Marschalk, but also Eoban Hessus, Jodocus Windsheim and others.[35] These literary associations testify to peaceful coexistence on the part of humanists and scholastics during Luther's student years, although some may already have sensed the potential for conflict.[36] As Brecht describes, a student like Luther did not yet have to choose sides, but could be interested in both dialectics and the classical languages.[37] Indeed, such laudatory prefaces and poems as Trutfetter received would have encouraged a student such as Luther to search for ways in which the new learning might augment the old. This ecumenical attitude would change only as the humanist challenge became more evident,

---

[33] Maria Grossmann, *Humanism in Wittenberg 1485–1517* (Nieuwkoop: B. de Graaf, 1975), 69.

[34] Kleineidam, *Universitas Studii Erffordensis II,* 154.

[35] Kleineidam, *Universitas Studii Erffordensis II,* 154.

[36] Brecht notes the less than enthusiastic endorsement of Trutfetter's work by Pistoris when "he admonishes the reader not to be vexed by the study of the book." *Martin Luther: His Road to Reformation,* 40.

[37] Brecht, *Martin Luther: His Road to Reformation,* 40. Kleineidam too describes a "coexistence" between scholasticism and humanism in the period around 1500, prior to the formation of the group around the Gotha canon Mutianus Rufus, but he notes that it was humanism that was the way of the future. *Universitas Studii Erffordensis II,* 159.

particularly with regard to the authority of ancient texts over medieval commentaries. In theology, the Bible and church fathers would be placed against Aristotle and his commentators. However, when Luther was studying the liberal arts at Erfurt, these challenges were not yet explicit.

Although it was Trutfetter who was known as *"sapientissimus doctor,"* most wise or learned doctor, his colleague, Bartholomäus Arnoldi von Usingen, did not stand far behind Trutfetter in the respect he was accorded from colleagues and students.[38] Arnoldi matriculated at the university in 1484 and received his master's degree in 1491 at the age of thirty, suggesting that he was considerably older than most students when he began his arts education. Like his colleague Trutfetter, Arnoldi was active in university governance and in publishing, even surpassing his colleague in producing clear and thorough textbooks on a variety of topics, including grammar and logic.[39] His handbook on natural philosophy was used in Erfurt for some fifty years, even after the reform of the university curriculum.[40] Well respected by his colleagues, Arnoldi was elected to a number of important posts, from rector of the Great College to dean of the arts faculty in 1504, to serving as one of two faculty members, along with the dean, to represent the university in negotiations with the city of Erfurt regarding university privileges.[41] Arnoldi too enjoyed a positive association with his humanist colleagues. His work on natural philosophy, *Compendium philosophiae naturalis*, was prefaced with rhapsodic verse from the young Eoban Hessus who proclaimed that this work encompassed all of nature in a way that had hitherto never been achieved.[42] Like Trutfetter, Arnoldi earned his doctorate in theology, achieving this distinction only in 1514, at the age of 53, two years after his

---

[38] Kleineidam, *Universitas Studii Erffordensis II*, 154.

[39] Kleineidam, *Universitas Studii Erffordensis II*, 154; Brecht, *Martin Luther: His Road to Reformation*, 36.

[40] Kleineidam, *Universitas Studii Erffordensis II*, 154.

[41] Kleineidam, *Universitas Studii Erffordensis II*, 155.

[42] Kleineidam, *Universitas Studii Erffordensis II*, 156.

entrance into the Augustinian Order.[43] In 1519 he became prior of the Erfurt monastery and in 1521 dean of the theological faculty.[44]

Along with the humanistically inclined Maternus Pistoris, Trutfetter and Arnoldi constituted the leading lights of the arts faculty during Luther's student years. It was they who set the tone for studies within the liberal arts. As scholastics, Trutfetter and Arnoldi represented the philosophical school known as nominalism, which affirmed the teachings of the Englishman William of Occam in distinction to the school known as realism, taught at such universities as Leipzig and Cologne, which followed the teachings of Thomas Aquinas. It would be a mistake to think of these "schools" in a monolithic sense or to suggest that their adherents were in absolute agreement on all issues at all times. Scholasticism itself—which was composed of nominalists, realists, and Scotists, those who affirmed the teachings of John Duns Scotus—is often compared to a giant edifice such as a medieval cathedral, with reason, like a spire, soaring toward heaven; but neither nominalism nor realism comprised such a singular structure. It is true that Erfurt, and even some of the bursae, such as the *porta coeli* where Luther most likely resided, were dedicated to the *via moderna*, the modern way or nominalism, in distinction to the *via antiqua*, the old way or realism; but there was nothing in the university's statutes that committed it to this school.[45] Although nominalism reigned, Kleineidam argues that there is no evidence that this commitment led to a lack of freedom of thought or to an unwillingness to disagree, even with William of Occam himself.[46] This tolerance and intellectual freedom helped to

---

[43] Kleineidam, *Universitas Studii Erffordensis II*, 298.

[44] Kleineidam, *Universitas Studii Erffordensis II*, 299.

[45] Oberman observes: "The Amplonian College (also called, impressively, 'Heaven's Gate'), which may have been Luther's residence hall for several years, was expressly instructed to teach according to the modern way, 'secundum modernos.'" *Luther*, 116.

[46] Kleineidam, *Universitas Studii Erffordensis II*, 140. Kleineidam explains that Trutfetter began his teaching career in the arts faculty and completed several of his commentaries before he knew Biel's

shape the academic outlook and expectations of the young liberal arts student Luther. Not only did Trutfetter and Arnoldi provide Luther a foundation of philosophical knowledge, they also trained him in the tools of sophisticated analysis and argumentation that would one day enable him to challenge teachings he had received from them. In a 1497 disputation, Trutfetter and Usingen sought to clarify their intellectual position and develop nominalist "principles into a cohesive program."[47] They affirmed that, while Aristotle was the foremost guide with regard to matters of reason, he was not to be given the same authority in theology.[48] Luther asserted it was his teacher Trutfetter who taught him that one was to believe, to accept as absolute authority, only the Bible, and all other sources were to be viewed critically; in other words, one should apply to them the tools of reason and logical analysis.[49]

The differences between the two schools of realism and nominalism centered on their way of perceiving, on their differing epistemologies.[50] For the realists, the individual receives its identity and existence through its participation in the universal. For example, individual humans exist as such because they are preceded by and represent the universal, "humankind." The nominalists went about matters in just the opposite fashion, affirming that such a concept as "humankind" is constructed as a category to comprehend the individual characteristics of various humans. The word "humankind" is a *nomen* or name that we assign to a group or

---

work. Thus, Trutfetter does not simply follow Biel in more narrowly restricting his authority to Ockham, 141.

[47] Oberman, *Luther*, 118.

[48] Heiko Augustinus Oberman, *Masters of the Reformation: The Emergence of a New Intellectual Climate in Europe*, trans. by Dennis Martin (Cambridge University Press, 1981), 250.

[49] *WA Br* 1,171, 72ff.; cited in Brecht, *Martin Luther: His Road to Reformation*, 35.

[50] In summarizing the differences between realists and nominalists, I found especially helpful the works of Oberman, and especially, his discussion, in *Luther*, 116–17.

category based on our perception of the unity or sameness of their individual qualities and characteristics. Thus, much depends on proper perception and analysis, and on following the appropriate steps to assign the name or category. Not only human perception but the conveying of those perceptions in language depended on precisely following the rules. Misperception or the drawing of inaccurate conclusions from empirical evidence would lead to false terminology or concepts and thus to the breakdown of humans' ability to communicate with one another. Knowing the rules and following them without error were crucial. In other words, as Martin Brecht summarizes the situation, "through general concepts such as nature, appearance, distinctions, characteristics, and additions, it was possible for dialectics, which dealt principally with logic, on its part to distinguish again the definition of nature and persons. By means of distinctions the unequivocal significance of a concept could be determined. The proof then had to lead to the conclusion in accordance with fixed rules."[51] To gain these tools of perception, analysis and definition, one utilized the teaching of Aristotle in various fields of knowledge, including natural philosophy, and above all logic. Since the assignment to a category was based upon experience, there was an obvious break between the worlds of experience and revelation. Nominalists affirmed that humans must trust in revelation to present that which is infinite or transcendent to human reason.

Even as a beginning student of the liberal arts, Luther would have learned the fundamental epistemological assumptions of nominalism with its stress on careful observation, analysis, and logical deduction. A forceful argument has been made by many scholars that nominalism's emphasis on experience, on the careful testing and analysis of reality, provided the cradle for modern science. In a nicely put phrase, "once experience became experiments, modern science was born."[52]

For a gifted student such as Luther, learning the rules and applying them was not a problem, and there is every reason to think that he excelled in dialectics and debate, as his nickname *philosophus* may suggest. At the same time, he also came to realize that much of the argument was about matters of very

---

[51] Brecht, *Martin Luther: His Road to Reformation*, 37.

[52] Oberman, *Luther*, 119.

little substance indeed, and that at least at times the conceptual arguments could degenerate into meaningless intellectual tournaments, leading into an abstractness far distant from experience and reality. While there is no denying that Luther gained many important tools from his study of logic and dialectics, as a mature scholar he would choose quite deliberately the situations in which he might appropriately apply dialectics over against those where other forms of discourse were more appropriate.[53] Dialectics, as Luther had learned it, would prove unable to move the heart or even to offer the most stirring image to help the intellect to grasp an idea and appreciate its significance. It was for that reason that Luther came to emphasize rhetoric over dialectics.[54] He also complained that his studies in logic had prevented him from reading the poets and studying history.

Already during Luther's student years, some faculty began to voice their frustration and dissatisfaction with the status quo. Evidence from the records of the University of Erfurt cited by Erich Kleineidam indicates that already in the years before Luther became a student there, there was resistance among the faculty to the annual *quodlibet* disputation.[55] Rather than take on the responsibility of supervising the disputation at which all members of the university were expected to be in attendance, faculty members who were elected to the position chose instead to pay a fine. The faculty records are replete with annual struggles to persuade one or another faculty member to assume

---

[53] Brecht develops this argument very cogently, particularly with regard to Luther's preaching where he realized the inappropriateness of dialectic. At the same time, it is undeniable that Luther made use throughout his life of the tools he gained at Erfurt, so that he could carefully analyze meaning and work his way methodically toward a conclusion. As Brecht notes, "Luther owed the precision and methodological training of his intellectual power to his study in Erfurt. A portion of his later weapons came from this old arsenal." *Martin Luther: His Road to Reformation,* 38.

[54] See the discussion by Lewis W. Spitz, "Luther, Humanism, and the Word," *Lutheran Theological Seminary Bulletin,* vol. 65, no. 1 (winter 1985), 3–24, especially 11–12.

[55] Kleineidam, *Universitas Studii Erffordensis II,* 76.

the task. What the records do not tell us is precisely why the faculty members were so resistant to assuming responsibility for the debate. One possible explanation is that the disputation was regarded as a "make work" activity in which serious open debate degenerated into mere word play and argument over irrelevant or absurd propositions. The fact that the regular debates scheduled throughout the academic year continued to be well attended lends substance to the suggestion that the problem with the *quodlibet* was its implicit encouragement of debate for the sake of debate, leading to intellectual showmanship at the expense of genuine learning. These debates were intended to demonstrate the universality of all truth and the compatibility of truth from one area of knowledge with truth from another. Dialectics had the honorable task of resolving seemingly inconsistent positions and thereby achieving a clear and consistent statement of the truth. The unfortunate reality was that at least in the case of the Erfurt *quodlibet* disputations this noble goal no longer drove the enterprise. When Luther became a professor at the University of Wittenberg he would for a time join with his colleagues in suspending the granting of doctoral degrees in theology, because of their belief that the scholastics had corrupted the doctoral disputation.[56] Yet Luther was also an enthusiastic proponent of debate and encouraged its legitimate use within the university curriculum, and he was delighted when the doctoral degree—and the disputation—were reinstated in Wittenberg.

The beginnings of humanism in Erfurt long predate Luther's student days. Humanism was influential from the opening of the university in the fourteenth century, since it was from the University of Prague that Erfurt drew its first professors. Prague was the origin of humanism in the Empire under the auspices of the emperor's chancellor, Johann von Neumarkt, who was a friend of the first theologian appointed to the university, Angelus von Döbeln, a member of the Augustinian

---

[56] Marilyn J. Harran, ed., *Luther and Learning: The Wittenberg University Luther Symposium* (Selinsgrove: Susquehanna University Press, 1985), 32. See also Gustav Adolf Benrath, "Die Universität der Reformationszeit," *Archiv für Reformationsgeschichte*, 57 (1966), 41. On the resumption of the disputations for the doctorate, see Paul Drews, ed., *Disputationen Dr. Martin Luthers in d.J. 1535–1545 an der Universität Wittenberg gehalten* (Göttingen: 1895).

Hermits.[57] The earliest days of the University demonstrated not only a close connection with Prague, but an unusual openness and receptivity to humanism, the study of the classical languages and texts, along with rhetoric. Erfurt was also visited by wandering humanists, such as Peter Luder, who arrived at Erfurt from Heidelberg in 1460.[58] The first humanists to lecture at the university found an open and congenial environment, a situation created in part by the fact that the university enjoyed an unusual degree of autonomy over its own affairs.[59] The "German arch-humanist" and poet laureate of the Empire, Conrad Celtis, spent time in Erfurt during 1485 and 1486, although he did not matriculate at the university.[60]

What seems to have gone unrecognized for several decades was the implicit contradiction we have already mentioned between the scholastic and humanist ways of thinking. As Kleineidam describes it, while the scholastics thought logically and dialectically, the humanists thought anthropologically and linguistically.[61] Coexistence was possible as long as humanism minded its place and served as an aid and embellishment to the scholastic enterprise—very much like the prefaces and poetic introductions that Marschalk and Pistoris gave to the textbooks of Trutfetter and Arnoldi. Initially the two existed side by side, with occasional forays from the one into another. On the whole, however, the scholastics continued their main pursuit of dialectics and the humanists theirs of grammar,

---

[57] Kleineidam, *Universitas Studii Erffordensis II*, 39–40.

[58] Kleineidam, *Universitas Studii Erffordensis II*, 52. On Luther's contact with humanism in school and university, see Helmar Junghans, "Der Einfluss der Humanismus auf Luthers Entwicklung bis 1518." *Lutherjahrbuch* 37 (1970), 37–101.

[59] Kleineidam, *Universitas Studii Erffordensis II*, 55. Kleineidam notes that many of the leading German humanists of the mid- to late fifteenth century studied at Erfurt, including Rudolf Agricola.

[60] Kleineidam, *Universitas Studii Erffordensis II*, 54. See also Lewis W. Spitz, *Conrad Celtis—the German Arch-Humanist* (Cambridge, Massachusetts: Harvard University Press, 1957).

[61] Kleineidam, *Universitas Studii Erffordensis II*, 39.

rhetoric, and history. The battle was joined, however, when those who furthered the study of classical languages and texts made the claim of offering more than logic and dialectic could, including a larger appreciation of the world, and, even challenging the scholastic approach in perceiving and describing reality.

During Luther's time in the Erfurt cloister and his first years in Wittenberg, a more aggressive humanist circle formed around Mutianus Rufus in Gotha, a *sodalitas* that would have little patience with the alleged irrelevance and obscurity of the scholastics. A letter from Frederick the Wise's chaplain and Luther's friend, Georg Spalatin, to Mutian recommending Luther to him offers proof that the two did not meet during Luther's Erfurt days. Nonetheless, Luther had ample opportunity to hear the more critical views of Mutian not only from Spalatin, but from his close friend and fellow Augustinian, Johann Lang, who joined the monastery in Erfurt about a year after Luther.

Educated, like Erasmus, by the Brethren of the Common Life in Deventer, Mutian enjoyed the benefits of coming from a well-to-do family in Homburg, Hessia, where he was born in 1471.[62] Like many who would comprise the first generation of German humanists, Mutian studied at Erfurt "where he received his B.A. degree in 1488 and his M.A. in 1492."[63] For two years he taught at the university before journeying to Italy where he had the good fortune to meet some of the leading humanists of the day, including the well known poet Baptista Mantuanus, who was known as the "modern Vergil" and who was the first of the poets Luther was to read.[64] Mutian was especially influenced by the thought of the Florentine Platonists, whose religious universalism proved particularly congenial to him. Lewis Spitz describes him as combining universalism with an "ethical Paulinism," not unlike that of Erasmus, with a strong focus on piety, on following Christ as one's model, an attitude

---

[62] Lewis W. Spitz, *The Religious Renaissance of the German Humanists* (Cambridge: Harvard University Press, 1963), 131.

[63] Spitz, *The Religious Renaissance of the German Humanists*, 132.

[64] Spitz, *The Religious Renaissance of the German Humanists*, 135; 240.

that also stressed human freedom and responsibility.[65] In 1503, after a short stay in Hessia, Mutian returned to the neighborhood of Erfurt, becoming canon in Gotha, a position he was to retain until his death. Although Luther most likely did not meet Mutian until 1516, a consideration of his thought and career is integral to a discussion of Luther's arts education for several reasons. It was Mutian and the circle around him, including such close friends and associates of Luther as Georg Spalatin and Johann Lang, that constituted the more confrontational and antischolastic humanism of the next decades. This was a humanism quite self-conscious of its own identity and its own educational agenda. For example, in a sarcastic letter of 1513, Mutian wrote: "It would be enough in a great university, if there were one sophist, two mathematicians, three theologians, four jurists, five doctors, six orators, seven Hebraists, eight Graecists, nine grammarians, and ten right-minded philosophers as presidents and chiefs of the whole literary undertaking."[66] By philosopher Mutian meant a humanist not a practitioner of scholasticism. In fact this was a title he sought for himself, preferring it to being regarded as a "rhetorician or *literatus* in the purely humanist sense of the word."[67] Mutian understood the title philosopher along the lines of the Florentine Platonists. Those who were suspicious of his ideas also ascribed the term to him, meaning, however, something quite different. For them, the title "*philosophus*" was linked to a highly critical attitude toward those who pursued Greek and the study of poetry. In the words of one contemporary critic, "Urban, Spalatin, and Mutian are poets, speak Greek and think godlessly about divine matters."[68] Mutian responded to this insult by proclaiming that those who criticized him simply labeled as Greek everything they did not

---

[65] Spitz, *The Religious Renaissance of the German Humanists*, 149; 140ff.

[66] Cited in Spitz, *The Religious Renaissance of the German Humanists*, 137.

[67] Spitz, *The Religious Renaissance of the German Humanists*, 137.

[68] Burgdorf, *Der Einfluss der Erfurter Humanisten*, 27.

understand.[69] Here we see a preview of the battle that was yet to unfold, between the scholastics, who perceived themselves as the defenders of truth and godliness, and the humanists, who understood themselves as the true philosophers able through their study of the original sources to proceed beyond obscurant dialectics to true knowledge, what Erasmus termed the "*philosophia Christi*." It is quite possible that Luther's nickname "the philosopher" reflects this humanist understanding of the term.

In addition to the set curriculum of the *trivium* and subsequently the *quadrivium*, it had long been possible for students, with the permission of their bursa rector, to enroll in the *Allotria*, ancillary lectures—in our terms, electives. Although we know that Luther attended such lectures, we do not know when he did so or how many lectures he heard. There are a few intriguing references to Luther's humanist interests as a student. His later opponent, Jerome Emser, offered a course during the summer semester 1504 on Johann Reuchlin's play *Sergius*, and in a letter to Luther written years later he referred to the fact that Luther had attended the course and that Emser had met him then. We also know that after his sudden decision to enter the Augustinian cloister, Luther sold or gave away all of his books, with the exception of Vergil and Plautus. As Helmar Junghans notes, Luther frequently quoted Vergil throughout his career, although he referred only rarely to Plautus.[70] It would seem that, compared with Vergil, Plautus had much less meaning for him. Why then did he take the book with him into the monastery? The most likely suggestion would be that Luther had just purchased the copy of Plautus and had not yet had the opportunity to read it. Such a suggestion implies that Luther was actively engaged in reading the classical authors whenever his studies permitted, offering proof again of his humanist interests. Another testimony to Luther's humanist leanings is offered by his close friend Lang who comments in a letter of 1515 that during his Erfurt days Luther had been no small help

---

[69] Burgdorf, *Der Einfluss der Erfurter Humanisten*, 27.

[70] Helmar Junghans, *Der junge Luther und die Humanisten* (Göttingen: Vandenhoeck & Ruprecht, 1985), 88.

to him in the "good arts."[71] This reference to the "good arts" may simply refer to humanist studies generally, since we know that Luther did not emerge from his Erfurt arts education with any knowledge of Greek, and that he began to study Hebrew only when he was in Wittenberg.

Perhaps more important than determining the extent of Luther's linguistic skills and knowledge of the ancient poets and historians is simply recognizing that during his time in Erfurt Luther gained an interest in these areas. Indeed, such a development was to be expected. The flourishing of the presses, especially in the printing of Greek sources; the laudatory words of humanists prefacing the works by Trutfetter and Arnoldi that Luther would have encountered in his studies; the adulation that even then was accorded Erasmus and Conrad Celtis, who himself had studied at Erfurt, all suggest an atmosphere filled with humanist ideas. There was also strong interest in the latest humanist critique of abuses in the church and of scholasticism, even though Luther's teachers would hardly have been enthusiastic about this side of humanism. Undoubtedly, such an attitude on the part of their teachers led students to delve even more enthusiastically into the new ideas.

After all, it was Erfurt where Johann Rucherat von Wesel had been an admired theologian and rector of the university. The university remained firm in its commitment to Wesel even after he was charged with heresy by the Inquisition and sentenced to a life of cloistered imprisonment. Although his books were banned and scholars were ordered not to teach from them, we know that Wesel's books remained in the university library. While the university's instructors were willing to accept the church's condemnation of Wesel with regard to specific aspects of his thought, such as his condemnation of indulgences, and his belief that the laity should receive communion in both kinds, they were not willing to reject his entire theological contribution.[72] In this respect too, the

---

[71] Brecht, *Martin Luther: His Road to Reformation*, 41; Junghans, *Der junge Luther und die Humanisten*, 78.

[72] Oberman notes that Wesel's association with Erfurt, even though he was not a member of its faculty when he was condemned, served to "cast a dark shadow on the theological faculty of Erfurt—the shadow of Hussite heresy." *Luther*, 116. Assuming that this negative association with condemned heresy was perceived as such at the

university showed a genuine independence of judgment that could not have but influenced Luther. Heiko Oberman characterizes this independence as integral to the nominalist principles taught by Trutfetter and Arnoldi, who cited experience and Scripture as the twin poles against which the authority of all statements in philosophy and theology must be measured.[73] The willingness to take an independent attitude toward the authorities of one's own school went beyond Luther's generation of professors to Wesel himself, who, although firmly in the nominalist camp, frequently quoted the realist Thomas Aquinas.[74] At the same time, Luther's professors drew limits on the extent to which authority could be questioned. Arnoldi, for example, made clear that Scriptural interpretation must be based on the authority of the church, i.e., Scripture must be interpreted according to the church's teachings.[75] Otherwise the Bible could become the instrument or occasion for sedition—an attitude of distance and fear toward the literary source of Christianity which stands in stark contrast to the humanist call for a return to the sources, *ad fontes*.[76]

---

time, it is even more interesting that the Erfurt theologians took such a moderate attitude toward Wesel's works and continued to quote him.

[73] Oberman, *Luther,* 118–19.

[74] Kleineidam, *Universitas Studii Erffordensis II,* 23–24.

[75] Burgdorf, *Der Einfluss der Erfurter Humanisten,* 17; Oberman, *Luther,* 118–19. Brecht formulates Arnoldi's position a bit differently: "He made use of the writings of Johann von Wesel, although not uncritically. To a greater extent than did Trutfetter, he followed Occam and was certainly also more interested in theology than he. On this basis he could also criticize Aristotle. Yet later he remained faithful to traditional scholasticism. Undoubtedly he gave the student Luther the restrictive advice to read the Bible exclusively according to the exegesis of the church fathers." Brecht, *Martin Luther: His Road to Reformation,* 36, citing WA TR 2, 5, 38–6, 5; L W 54, 127–28.

[76] WA TR 2, 6, 3; L W 54, 128.

Another matter of debate during the time when Luther was studying at the university and which carried on into his days in the Erfurt cloister concerned the arguments of the humanist and preacher Jakob Wimpfeling. Lewis Spitz characterizes Wimpfeling as "the most conservative of the leading humanists … a dedicated institutionalist."[77] Yet this conservative humanist set off a firestorm of debate with his arguments in *De Integritate*, a work that was primarily designed to defend celibacy and attack concubinage. Within this same work, however, Wimpfeling asserted that Augustine had not been a monk and "that wisdom did not dwell in cowls."[78] In subsequent writings he continued his arguments undermining the special privileges of the monks, arguing both that Augustine was not the author of the *Sermones ad Eremitas*—thus neither advocate of monasticism nor himself a monk—and that the monks were tainted with "ignorance, greed, and leading the people from parish churches to monastery chapels."[79] Needless to say, the Augustinians vociferously challenged Wimpfeling's assertion that Augustine was neither a monk nor the author of the treatise praising the monastic life. While sympathetic to Wimpfeling's statements that a person did not need to become a monk to gain wisdom, Luther nonetheless denied Wimpfeling's statements regarding Augustine. In at least this situation, Luther was unwilling to challenge the position of his own order.

It is difficult to know to what degree Luther was influenced by the humanism he encountered. While he did not neglect his required studies, he appears to have sought the opportunity to attend humanist lectures, such as those by Emser, and to read the classics such as Vergil, as well as those authors whose goal was to recreate classical literature for their own time, such as Baptista Mantuanus. Luther's subsequent comments and references to classical authors, as well as his colleague Philipp Melanchthon's observations, indicate that in spite of his lament that he had little time to absorb the classics, Luther read such authors as Quintilian, Livius, Cicero, and Terence. In so doing,

---

[77] Spitz, *The Religious Renaissance of the German Humanists*, 41.

[78] Spitz, *The Religious Renaissance of the German Humanists*, 54.

[79] Spitz, *The Religious Renaissance of the German Humanists*, 54.

he developed his own criteria by which to assess the writings of the scholastic philosophers and theologians, and those of the ancients as well. As Helmar Junghans observes, although Luther could praise Cicero and refer positively to him as he did to the church fathers, it is Scripture that conveys the full truth and against which all other sources must be judged.[80]

Although Luther did not have contact with the more "radical" humanism of Mutian until after his Erfurt years were behind him, he gained from his teachers Trutfetter and Arnoldi an appreciation for the classical authors, a desire to read more of their works, and to become proficient in their languages. He could not but be intrigued by the critical stance of a Wesel or a Wimpfeling, even though he might disagree with them on specific points. In the long run, the critical stance he encountered in nominalism itself and the critical attitude of the humanists toward scholasticism and the church would lead Luther to a new concept of authority, sola Scriptura, that would challenge the very foundations of both scholasticism and humanism.

Whatever he may have thought of the education he had received in the trivium, Luther was sufficiently prepared to gain the support—by oath—of the rector of the bursa to allow him to stand for the bachelor's exam at the earliest date possible. Much has been made of the fact that Luther did not particularly distinguish himself in this exam, coming in as thirtieth among fifty-seven candidates. Oberman, for example, suggests that however good the education he received in Eisenach was, it could not compensate for the deficits of his Mansfeld years.[81] While it is true that Luther did not distinguish himself in this exam, it is worth noting that Luther was still quite young (although not in comparison with Philipp Melanchthon who gained his bachelor of arts degree at fifteen!), and—even more importantly—that he had taken the exam in the minimum time permitted by the statutes of the university. His place in the order of the examination may also have been influenced by whether or not any nobles or clergy had stood for the baccalaureate examination at the same time, since regardless of the level of competence they had demonstrated, they would

---

[80] Junghans, Der junge Luther und die Humanisten, 198.

[81] Oberman, Luther, 113.

have been moved ahead of any commoner or member of the laity in the rankings.

Having completed his B.A., Luther turned to climbing the next rung on the academic ladder, gaining his Master of Arts degree. While his first studies had focused on the *trivium*, those that concerned him now were the *quadrivium*, including geometry, arithmetic and music, and astronomy. In geometry the source was Euclid; in arithmetic and music Johann de Muris; but, as in his previous studies, above all the emphasis fell upon Aristotle.[82] To complete his education in logic, he attended lectures on Aristotle's *Topics*. In addition, he also went to those on the *Nichomachean Ethics*, the *Politics, Economics,* and *Metaphysics*.[83] The length of time for the lectures varied from one month for the *Economics* to eight months for the *Nichomachean Ethics*.[84]

In his pursuit of the M.A. Luther was once again on the fast track, ready to take his examinations in the minimum time permitted. Permission to take the examinations meant not only that the candidate had completed the required series of lectures, practices, and disputations—attending some thirty and participating in fifteen—but that his behavior had conformed to the statutes of the university, and his masters had found no fault with either his character or his work habits. A far fewer number were permitted to apply for the master's examination than were allowed to do so for the bachelor's degree. As the terminal degree in the liberal arts, the M.A. was jealously guarded by the university's masters. The candidate had to swear that he had attained the minimum age of twenty-two, as required by the university statutes. Assuming that Luther was born in 1483, he had not attained the required age when he applied to take his examinations in January 1505. As Brecht suggests, perhaps the statute was not vigorously enforced at that time or Luther "did not know his exact birth date and gave an earlier date."[85] It was also possible for

---

[82] Boehmer, *Der junge Luther*, 31; Brecht, *Martin Luther: His Road to Reformation*, 33.

[83] Brecht, *Martin Luther: His Road to Reformation*, 33.

[84] Brecht, *Martin Luther: His Road to Reformation*, 33.

[85] Brecht, *Martin Luther: His Road to Reformation*, 34.

exceptions to be made and for students to be allowed to take the examination at an earlier age. Luther's colleagues in Wittenberg, Justus Jonas and Philipp Melanchthon, were in fact much younger than he when they gained their degrees. Although the arts professors valued the master's degree for its own sake, for many if not most of those who applied to take the examinations, the gaining of the degree was simply an intermediate hurdle to be conquered before turning to the ultimate goal of a degree in one of the higher faculties. Such was the case for Luther. At the same time, for some—and only very few could afford the cost of "graduate study"—the master's degree was their ultimate achievement. As a master, one could become the rector of a bursa or a schoolteacher or seek an office within the administration of city or prince.

The university's records tell us that Luther excelled during his master's examination, emerging as second among seventeen candidates, a considerable accomplishment. Luther tells us nothing of the examination itself, and we do not know what impression this challenge made upon him. However, he did comment at several points about the ceremony surrounding the awarding of the degree, which clearly constituted the high point in his life to that time. He later spoke of the master's ceremony as symbolizing the height of earthly joy and accomplishment while the deposition into bachelor of art's study had been a useful experience in humility. In his *Table Talk* from 1532, he recalled: "How majestic was the promotion of the masters, and the torches, which were given to them. No earthly joy can compare to it."[86] Luther's father validated his sense of accomplishment by no longer addressing him with the familiar "*Du*" but with the more formal "*Ihr*," offering clear evidence of precisely how much education had changed his social standing and relation to family and friends.

Each successful achievement on the academic ladder was marked by a change in outward status. For example, after receiving the bachelor's degree, a graduate could carry a dagger. In the Master of Arts degree ceremony, Luther received the master's beret and ring. As part of the requirement for the degree, he was obliged to deliver an address and to pay the costs of a festive meal. More importantly, he also had to swear

---

[86] *WA TR* 2, 660, 16–18.

to teach two years at the university, during which time he could simultaneously pursue advanced studies in a higher faculty. For Luther, that faculty was law, and his father once again signaled his approval of his diligent and ambitious son by presenting him with a copy of the major law text he would study, the *Corpus Juris Civilis*. Law students had the option of beginning their studies either with canon or civil law, both of which they had to study to attain their degree, but the fact that Luther's father presented him with the text in civil law suggests that Martin began his studies in this area. The summer semester for law students began on May 19, "the day of their patron Saint Ivo."[87] Thus, there was a break between Luther's gaining of his master of arts degree, which was probably awarded some time in February, and the official beginning of his law studies. However, he may have already begun his teaching obligations, perhaps chairing some disputations, if not lecturing in the arts faculty.

Much has been written about the reasons that Luther suddenly chose to break from the academic path that he had been following with so much success. The events of the story are well known. Returning from a visit to Mansfeld, Luther suddenly found himself in the midst of a frightening thunderstorm. Fearing for his life, he vowed to St. Anne, the patron saint of miners, that if she saved him he would become a monk. Having made the vow, Luther found himself with no choice but to obey it—lest by breaking his word to a saint, and implicitly to God, he condemn his soul—and thus on July 17, 1505 he entered the cloister of the Augustinian Hermits in Erfurt.

Scholars have made extraordinary efforts to decipher the causes behind Luther's decision. From Erik Erikson's affirmation that a mentally and emotionally exhausted Luther sought a moratorium from his father and from the pressure to succeed in the only place he could, the monastery, to the more recent suggestions of Martin Brecht and others that a number of recent deaths of both fellow students and professors may have led Luther on a path of reflection focusing more on his immortal soul and less on his mortal successes, various efforts have been made to probe beyond Luther's action to the motives behind them. Several factors may have contributed to his action, from a

---

[87] Brecht, *Martin Luther: His Road to Reformation*, 44.

new concern with mortality as he witnessed the deaths of
fellow academics, to a desire to choose a life more dedicated to
God than to worldly success. And it is equally plausible to
suggest that Luther was as surprised by his vow as were his
friends and family. However, regardless of whether or not we
think Luther's dramatic action was preceded by a period of
reflection about the direction in which his life was headed, there
is no doubt that his decision regarding which religious order to
join shows genuine reflection and careful consideration. He had
various options before him in Erfurt, from the Benedictines to
the Franciscans, but he chose the Augustinian Hermits. Recent
works have challenged the assertion that the Augustinians were
head and shoulders above the other orders in piety and
academic reputation, but the significance to Luther and his
contemporaries of the positive association between the
monastery and the university, where the Augustinians were
responsible for a chair in theology, and between at least some
members of the cloister and the Erfurt humanists, still is an
important factor to consider in evaluating his choice. Georg
Eberbach, himself a humanist, whose two sons were later part
of the circle around Mutian, thought so positively of the
Augustinians that he asked to be buried within their cloister.[88]
Some scholars suggest that if Luther's humanist friends could
not dissuade him from joining a religious order, they at least
were able to influence him to join one which demonstrated a
spirit of openness and toleration toward humanist ideas—and
where he would almost certainly be allowed to pursue the life of
the mind.

The education that Luther now received was in large part
practical in nature as he progressed through the novitiate into
full standing in the order. His intellectual gifts were quickly
recognized and he was required to prepare himself for the
priesthood. He soon came to the attention of Johann von
Staupitz, the vicar general of the Order in Germany, who
recognized Luther's talents and placed him once again on the
road toward achieving academic degrees, first at Erfurt and
then at the recently founded University of Wittenberg. Although
in many respects this education in theology would proceed
along the same lines as Luther's previous studies, especially

---

[88] Brecht, *Martin Luther*, 40–41; Burgdorf, *Der Einfluss der Erfurter
Humanisten*, 88.

with regard to nominalism and to the stress on the authority of Aristotle, there would also be new influences—the writings of mystics, such as Johannes Tauler; of church fathers, above all, Augustine; and of the Bible itself.

Especially the Bible would cause Luther to reflect in new and radical ways upon the theological principles he had been taught by his nominalist professors. In so doing, Luther would come not only to challenge the theology and ecclesiastical practices of his time, but much of the education he had received as well. Above all, he would question the role that Aristotle played in theology and the assumption, articulated by his nominalist professors, that without knowledge of Aristotle one could not become a theologian. Although we will need to examine more closely Luther's path to his theological breakthrough and to his critique of the education he had received, his liberal arts training provided the foundation for those future accomplishments.

Through his arts studies, Luther had learned of the separation of the realms of reason and revelation, and of the spheres in which experience and authority operate. He had also learned from the humanists that the sources could speak directly to him. Even in the course of his arts studies, he may have begun to question the assertion that one's reading of the Bible must be guided by the teachings of the church. It is unclear precisely when Luther encountered his first complete Bible, but its very magnitude was a revelation to him, and he was overwhelmed by the desire to dive as fully as possible into its mysteries. Luther never shared the concerns of many humanists, the love of eloquence for its own sake, the study of the languages as a pursuit in and of itself, but he had learned enough from the impassioned and dedicated humanists of his own generation, such as Crotus Rubeanus, to realize that humanism offered tools to allow him to bridge the two worlds that his nominalist teachers told him were unbridgeable—the driving concerns of his own experience and the resulting questions that filled his reason and his heart, and the world of revelation. As Luther so clearly outlines in his Preface of 1545, in searching for the answers to the questions that occupied his every waking hour and in preparing honestly for his role as teacher, Luther used the tools of grammar and textual analysis provided to him through his study in the liberal arts, to find the answers that would transform his life, the church, and the very content and role of education.

3

Frater Martinus Lutherus: Augustinianus

On July 17, 1505, an earnest twenty-one year old knocked upon the heavy outer door at the cloister of the Augustinian Hermits in Erfurt. Close as the cloister was to the university and at least one of its bursa, Martin Luther must have passed by its entrance many times without a second thought. This time, however, was quite different, for on this day Luther sought admittance to the cloister, his entrance marking the transition from secular to religious life. His request for admittance was at the same time an affirmation that he would obey the authority of this community and follow its rules without question. For a young person today, the transition from college to cloister would be a dramatic one, but for Martin the change in communities was much less startling.

As we have seen, life in a university bursa was itself monastic in character with set hours for prayer, study, classes, and meals. There was close supervision; only rare opportunities for an evening excursion; and little, if any, possibility of enjoying the company of women who were never allowed within the bursa itself. Certainly on those occasions when Martin traveled home, he enjoyed more freedom, but such vacations were infrequent. Since the day when Luther had matriculated at the university, he had spent most of his time within its confines and following its rules. With close supervision of days and evenings and a required dress code within a single-sex environment, university life was itself monastic and cloistered, and the change must in some respects not have seemed very great to Luther. The best example from today might be the transition from one of the service academies (although the change would be more noticeable since the academies now admit women) to a monastery. However, while the outward routine that governed the day and even the expectation of obedience to authority must have seemed familiar to Luther, there were other aspects of life that were very different indeed.

To this point the young man had sought success, in part no doubt to fulfill his own ambitions, and in part to satisfy those of his family. Now he was challenged to direct his ambition in a new way, one that required him to distinguish himself in obedience to his superiors and to God. Fulfilling this goal required that Luther in fact *not* seek to distinguish himself from his fellows but above all to seek, *humilitas*, humility. On the one hand, the training the Augustinians gave their novices was directed toward achieving that goal through earnest prayer, reflection upon one's past life, and confession. On the other hand, Luther soon found himself on the "fast track" as his talents were recognized, and he rapidly received new responsibilities. For Luther, as he recounts in his 1545 *Preface to the Complete Latin Writings*, the real challenge lay in fulfilling the demands of a righteous God, as he then understood Him. The young monk found this much harder than meeting the expectations of his superiors.[1] At times it must have seemed to him that meeting those increasingly numerous demands deflected him from his efforts to concentrate inwardly upon his soul and upon meeting the expectations that he believed God had of him.

For the Augustinians the intense young man who sought membership in their community posed a dilemma. The Order valued the life of the mind, and they must have been delighted to have welcomed into their midst a young man who had already attained the highest degree in the liberal arts. At the same time, at least some of them were taken aback by his single-minded intensity. Once Luther had spent some days in the cloister's guesthouse, had reaffirmed his commitment to join the Order, and had been judged to be an acceptable candidate with no obvious blemish in his background or character, he was admitted to the novitiate, receiving the tonsure and monastic garb and moving inside the cloister.

Like other novices, Luther received a Bible, which he was to read, meditate upon, and memorize. However, unlike other novices, Luther immersed himself in the red leather bound Bible

---

[1] *W A* 54, 179-187; *Luther's Works*, vol. 34: *Career of the Reformer IV*, ed. by Lewis W. Spitz (Philadelphia: Muhlenberg Press, 1960), 327-338.

he received. According to a *Table Talk* account of 1531, Luther reported that "he made himself so familiar with it [the Bible] that he knew what was on every page, and when some passage was mentioned he knew at once just where it was to be found."[2] Although this account may reflect some exaggeration, there is no denying Luther's extraordinary knowledge of the Bible. Other sources substantiate that Luther was fascinated by the Bible and that he devoted unusual energy to it from the moment it came into his hands. Scholars debate to what degree this interest had already developed during Luther's university days and through his contacts with humanism. Engaged though Luther was by the Bible, he was not allowed to retain the copy he had been given past his year as a novice, since it was passed on to the next novice. Luther was expected to read and study other texts in preparation for the priesthood and advanced degrees in theology.

At least some of Luther's brothers in the Order were convinced that he devoted altogether too much time to the life of the mind and not enough to what they regarded as true learning, imbibing the spirit of the Order. They urged him to put down the books and take up the "sack upon his back," to learn the true spirit of humility and poverty.[3] They also set him to cleaning the latrines.[4] One can almost hear those older voices saying that such "book learning" was well and good, but one

---

[2] *WA TR* 1, 44, 24-26; *LW* 54, 14.

[3] *WA TR* 5, 99, 20-24; Brecht, *Martin Luther: His Road to Reformation*, 90-91. See further Junghans, *Der junge Luther und die Humanisten*, 172. Junghans suggests that Johann von Staupitz, the vicar general of the Augustinians in Saxony, recognized Luther's plight and was sympathetic to it, given his own goal of furthering the study of the Bible within the cloister. Yet advanced theological study did not free Luther to concentrate upon the Bible, since the course of study necessitated that he become familiar with the medieval commentaries, along with the Bible. Junghans draws the analogy that just as Luther's studies in the liberal arts had prevented him from reading as much of the poets as he would have liked so his theological studies prevented him from concentrating upon the Bible.

[4] Brecht, *Martin Luther: His Road to Reformation*, 91.

needed to bring the biblical words to life through prayer and work, the ancient Benedictine idea of *laborare est orare*.

There is no reason to think that Luther was not in fact receptive to those voices—although he was also unable to quell his curiosity and love of learning. He had, after all, joined the Augustinians to follow Christ in the most single-minded way possible with the goal of thereby saving his soul. He embraced with fervor the Augustinian life with its rhythm of meditation, prayer, work, and—in his case, as he was ordered by his superiors—study.

As was noted in the preceding chapter, we do not know precisely why Luther chose the Augustinians. He had the option in Erfurt of joining several different orders, the Benedictines, Dominicans, Franciscans, Carthusians, and Servites.[5] Todd suggests that Luther's choice was based on the reputation of the Order and the "likelihood of further university work to come."[6] Luther may have come to an appreciation of the Augustinians during his university days. Two of their members held positions within the theological faculty. Their respect for humanism might also have been known to him. As Oberman and Brecht suggest, Luther may have been drawn to the Augustinians by their openness to nominalism, the school of thought in which Luther had been trained while an arts student.[7] Oberman suggests as well that Luther may have been attracted by the rigor of the Order, while Brecht notes that the Carthusians too would have

---

[5] There is some discrepancy concerning the number of orders in Erfurt. Boehmer in *Der junge Luther* states that in 1505 there were five other cloisters besides that of the Augustinians in Erfurt (p. 41) while James Atkinson in *Martin Luther and the Birth of Protestantism* states that there were five cloisters including that of the Augustinian Hermits (p. 57). The debate appears to center on the question of the status of the Servites.

[6] Todd, *Luther*, 27.

[7] Oberman notes that "though the Augustinians had decided for the via antiqua in their statutes, in practice they granted freedom of choice." *Luther*, 130. Brecht, *Martin Luther: His Road to Reformation*, 51.

offered Luther the possibility of an ascetic life.[8] The voices of Luther's friends may have influenced him, for if they could not deter him from joining the religious life, they could at least persuade him to join a religious order where his fine mind could continue to develop, and where there were already some strong connections with the university, as evidenced by Paltz and Nathin on the teaching faculty, and by the warm relationship that existed between the cloister and the humanistically inclined Eberbach family. However, convincing as these reasons may be, we simply do not know what ultimately led Luther to choose the Augustinians. Brecht properly reminds us that Luther was renouncing the world and its ambitions as he made his decision and was not seeking new ways to achieve academic success or gain a theological doctorate.[9] Nonetheless, for a young man who was making a major change of direction in his life it must have been a comfort to know that the life within the walls of the cloister was well-respected by the outside community and that the members of the Order, especially those who taught in the university, were esteemed both for their piety and their learning.

Although some of Luther's fellow Augustinians may have been concerned about his extraordinary zeal, manifested in various ways, from self-mortification to an obsessive desire to devote himself to the Bible, their concerns were in no way serious enough to prevent his rapid progress within the Order. In September of 1505 he became a novice, and a year later he made his final profession. He was then ordered by the prior, Father Winand von Diedenhofen, to prepare himself for the priesthood. This preparation involved several steps, progressing from subdeacon to deacon and ultimately to priest. We do not know precisely when Luther completed these various steps toward ordination, but his ordination itself occurred in the spring of 1507 with his first mass on May 2.

His training, taken under the direction of the distinguished teacher Johannes Nathin, who held a chair in the theological faculty of the university, was largely practical in nature. Obviously he had to learn the steps in the celebration of the mass and to memorize the words that were to be said, since

---

[8] Oberman, *Luther,* 130; Brecht, *Martin Luther: His Road to Reformation,* 51.

[9] Brecht, *Martin Luther: His Road to Reformation,* 51.

correct performance was essential for the miracle of Christ becoming present in the mass to occur. He also learned something of the other duties of a priest such as hearing confession, but the mass was his foremost study. His main text for this subject was the *Sacri canonis missae expositio*, the Canon of the Mass, by the Tübingen theologian Gabriel Biel. The work was very highly regarded, and Nathin had himself studied with Biel, the foremost late medieval exponent of nominalism. Luther appears to have been deeply influenced by his reading of the book, commenting in 1538: "Gabriel [Biel] wrote a book on the canon of the mass which I once thought was the best [on the subject]. When I read it my heart bled."[10] Biel's work, written in typical scholastic fashion, included many authorities and covered various topics, "such as indulgences, veneration of the saints, the presence of Christ in the sacrament, or the Lord's Prayer, or equally practical questions pertaining to the ceremony of the mass. ... He quoted copiously from the Bible, the church fathers, and the scholastics as authorities."[11]

Biel's work was intended to prepare a person for the responsibilities of the priesthood. In the case of Luther, however, the work served to heighten the concerns and doubts he already had about his worthiness and ability to perform the mass. He joined those doubts with a conviction that only by an absolutely perfect performance of the mass in an absolutely pure state could he as a priest earn merit before God. This dual emphasis on unworthiness and perfection is clearly reflected in Luther's letter of invitation to his old friend and mentor Father Braun of Eisenach to attend his first mass:

> God, who is glorious and holy in all his works, has deigned to exalt me magnificently—a miserable and totally unworthy sinner—by calling me into his supreme ministry, solely on the basis of his bounteous mercy. Therefore I have to fulfil completely the office entrusted to me so that I may be acceptable (as much as dust can

---

[10] *WA TR* 3, 564, 5-6; *LW* 54, 264.

[11] Brecht, *Martin Luther: His Road to Reformation*, 71.

be acceptable to God) to such great splendor of divine goodness.[12]

Although Luther may have experienced his doubts and anxieties in an unusually heightened way, he later came to learn that he was not unique, but he did not know this at the time, and he appears to have been overwhelmed by a sense of fear and loneliness.[13]

Whatever doubts may have lingered in Luther's heart after his first mass—and certainly his father's reminder of the importance of obedience to parents did not help—he nonetheless continued to be regarded highly by his superiors and to be selected for new opportunities. The monastic training that Luther had received to this point had been largely practical in nature—Biel's work on the mass, as we have seen; the monastic hours and the texts which accompanied them; and simply learning the routine that he was to follow as friar and as priest. His superiors now determined that Luther was to receive advanced academic training. Given the credentials with which Luther entered the cloister, his obvious intellectual ability, and his intensity, this decision was not surprising.

---

[12] *WA Br* 1, 10-11; *L W* 48, 3. On the demands that Luther felt placed upon himself with regard to proper performance of the mass and achieving a state of holiness before performing it, see the excellent discussion by Brecht, *Martin Luther: His Road to Reformation*, 72-76. Biel's instructions regarding the obligations of a priest exacerbated rather than eased the requirements that Luther felt God had put upon him. As John Todd notes, "One thing Biel emphasized, like all expositors of the Mass, was the need for purity of heart in the priest, in him who dispensed this sacrament of the divine life. ... Biel reached the point where he could say that absolute love of God for God's sake, or above everything, even though a tough assignment, is within reach of natural man; grace is not the root but the fruit of the preparatory good works which a Christian can do by himself." *Luther*, 37 and 38. For Luther's changing understanding of God's work in bringing man to salvation, as reflected in his writings through 1519, see Marilyn J. Harran, *Luther on Conversion: The Early Years* (Ithaca and London: Cornell University Press, 1983).

[13] Brecht, *Martin Luther: His Road to Reformation*, 74.

The stages of that training were clearly delineated. Although he was a student in the advanced faculty of theology of the university, because the Augustinians had a *studium generale* in Erfurt, one of two in the entire region of Saxony, Luther could continue his studies within the cloister under the direction of Father Nathin who held a chair in theology on the university faculty.[14] The first stage was the attaining of the *baccalaureus biblicus,* a degree which Luther obtained in March of 1509. According to Heinrich Boehmer, over a twenty-month period he would have studied a variety of texts, including the *Glossa ordinaria,* a biblical commentary; the *Collectorium* of Gabriel Biel, the *Quaestiones* of Pierre d'Ailly and Ockham, along with some smaller writings by Ockham.[15] However, Luther was not able to concentrate uninterruptedly upon his theological studies. In the same way that he would have lectured in the arts faculty if he had pursued his advanced studies in law, he was now obliged to fulfill that responsibility while in the theological faculty. The only difference was that he could lecture within the cloister, since it had the privilege of teaching as a *studium generale.* Helmar Junghans suggests that he probably lectured to about a dozen of his fellow Augustinians.[16] Beginning in the fall of 1508, he was charged with new responsibilities that included a change in location, from the well-established University of Erfurt to the new University of Wittenberg.

Once again sources are lacking to explain precisely why Luther, then at a very early stage of his monastic career, was chosen to take on this significant teaching responsibility, occupying—even as a substitute—one of the two chairs for which the Augustinians were responsible at the new university. Perhaps Luther's name was suggested by Jodocus Trutfetter, his former professor in the arts, who had accepted a call to the new university. Certainly the change was regarded only as a temporary one, to allow the holder of the chair in moral

---

[14] Reinhard Schwarz, *Luther,* vol. 3, part 1 of *Die Kirche in ihrer Geschichte: Ein Handbuch,* ed. by Bernd Moeller (Göttingen: Vandenhoeck & Ruprecht, 1986), 17.

[15] Boehmer, *Der junge Luther,* 47.

[16] Junghans, *Der junge Luther und die Humanisten,* 94; Oberman, *Luther,* 139.

philosophy, Father Wolfgang Ostermayr, to prepare for his doctoral exams.[17] No one, either at Erfurt or at Wittenberg, would have had any premonition that this dual training at two universities would lead to unexpected difficulties when Luther was later recalled to Erfurt.

His duties included lecturing on Aristotle's *Nichomachean Ethics* four times a week and supervising disputations three times a week while at the same time continuing his own advanced studies.[18] With the attainment of the *baccalaureus biblicus*, his workload increased even more as he was now required to offer brief commentaries or lectures on certain biblical texts selected by his superiors. We know something of the frustration that Luther felt from a letter that he wrote on March 17, 1509 to his mentor and friend Braun, in which he proclaimed the wish that he could exchange his studies in philosophy for theology. Even in 1509 Luther meant something very specific by theology. In his words, it was the theology which "seeks the marrow from the bone," phrased differently, a theology which goes to the very core, and by that Luther undoubtedly meant the Bible.[19]

Whatever Luther's own desires may have been, he was directed to prepare himself for the next academic step, that of *sententarius*. In Erfurt he would have been required by the statutes of the university to have been a *baccalaureus* for two years, but Wittenberg seemed to have had no such requirement, and so, undoubtedly at the order of Johann von Staupitz, the head of the order in Saxony, Luther immediately proceeded to this next stage of study.[20] Gaining this second degree required that he master the first two books of Peter Lombard's *Sentences*, the book that had comprised the foundation for all theological study since the twelfth century. The *Sentences* constituted a source book on all theological points, bringing together texts from both the Bible and the church fathers. Following the practice of the time, once Luther began his lecturing on these

[17] Brecht, *Martin Luther: His Road to Reformation*, 92-93.

[18] Boehmer, *Der junge Luther*, 55.

[19] *WA Br* 1, 17, 43-44.

[20] Brecht, *Martin Luther: His Road to Reformation*, 92.

two books, he added his own comments in the margins. These marginal comments along with those he made in works he read by Augustine upon his return to Erfurt, *The City of God* and *On the Trinity*, offer signposts pointing to new directions in Luther's thought. Perhaps influenced by his earlier humanist studies, Luther praised the way Lombard emphasized the church fathers, especially Augustine.[21] The marginal notes reflect a desire to go directly to the biblical text without proceeding through the intermediary of philosophy, especially when that philosophy was Aristotle. However, the notes also demonstrate that Luther still held true to the nominalism in which he had been trained.[22]

We do not know precisely when Luther earned the next degree of *sententiarius*, but we do know that upon his return to Erfurt his fellow Augustinians had second thoughts about the rapid progress of their young colleague. He had gained the *baccalaureus biblicus* in short order, and under the more lenient rules of Wittenberg he had not been obliged to remain in that status for two years as Erfurt required. He now claimed to have accomplished the preparation for the degree of *sententiarius*.

Not surprisingly, there was considerable resentment of a young man who had joined the Order four short years before and who was so rapidly approaching the apex of theological study. Apparently there was a significant dispute regarding whether or not Luther should be allowed to lecture on the *Sentences*.[23] Nonetheless, in the long run Luther's supporters

---

[21] Junghans, *Der junge Luther und die Humanisten*, 106.

[22] See the very helpful discussion of these marginal notes in Brecht, *Luther: His Road to Reformation*, 94-95. On Luther's notes to the *Sentences*, see Paul Vignaux, *Luther: Commentateur des Sentences*, Etudes de philosophie medievale, no. 21 (Paris: J. Vrin, 1935), and Junghans, *Luther und die Humanisten*, 94-239 passim.

[23] The absence of sources regarding this stage of Luther's career leads to disagreement among scholars regarding where and when he received the degree of *sententiarius*. For example, John Todd writes: "However, on his return, the University authorities were understandably cool about the young man who had left Erfurt only thirteen months previous, with no theology degree, and came back not only with his Bible 'Baca', but with his application already well advanced for the final degree of Sententiarius; they refused to

prevailed, and he was allowed to begin his lectures. However, in the dispute regarding this degree Father Nathin apparently omitted having Luther swear the usual oath promising that he would not receive the doctoral degree anywhere other than Erfurt. While this omission would allow Luther to fulfill with a clear conscience (at least in regard to his Erfurt obligations)

---

proceed with it. In fact they were out of order, and were obliged in the end to proceed with granting a degree already inaugurated by Wittenberg." *Luther,* 53. However, Heiko Oberman states: "The first stage on the long road to the doctoral degree in theology was initiated under Johannes von Staupitz as dean on March 9, 1509. Luther was now 'admitted to the Bible.' ... The next step followed in the autumn, just before he was recalled to Erfurt: he acquired the rank of *sententiarius,* which entitled him to give lectures on the doctrines of the Church." *Luther,* 145. Schwarz notes the difficulty in ascertaining when Luther received the degree and adds that Luther had already accomplished the required disputation for the degree before leaving Wittenberg in the fall of 1509. *Luther,* 17. Boehmer also affirms that Luther had fulfilled the disputation requirement but had not yet been able to give his inaugural lecture when he was recalled to Erfurt. *Der junge Luther,* 54-55. Erich Kleineidam who has thoroughly researched the records of the University of Erfurt states that Luther became a *baccalaureus sententiarius* in Erfurt upon his return from Wittenberg. *Universitas Studii Erffordensis II,* 197. Scholars also dispute the role played by Johann Nathin within the controversy. James Atkinson states that Nathin intervened on Luther's behalf. *Martin Luther,* 62. Boehmer too argues that it was Nathin who persuaded his faculty colleagues to accept the work that Luther had accomplished and to allow him to give his inaugural lecture, thereby securing the degree. *Der junge Luther,* 56. Todd meanwhile writes that "some kind of contretemps occurred at the ceremony itself. ... Father Nathin, the Augustinian theologian, came forward and started to read from a large sheet all the requirements to be filled by a candidate, evidently implying that he was doubtful whether Luther had fulfilled them all. ... But Father Nathin represented only one, authoritarian, element of the Erfurt establishment. The ceremony was duly completed." *Luther,* 53. It seems more likely that Nathin intervened on Luther's behalf since later the two would stand together in representing the Erfurt cloister's opposition to Staupitz's plan to merge the reformed and unreformed houses in Saxony.

Staupitz's demand that he prepare himself for the doctorate, it would leave some very hard feelings in Erfurt. Those feelings were very much in evidence when none of the Erfurt cloister attended the doctoral ceremony when he was awarded his degree in Wittenberg. It is worth noting that the first dispute in which Luther found himself embroiled was an academic one, indeed an academic bureaucratic one, not unlike the kinds of discussions that occur in universities today regarding acceptance of courses and units from other institutions.

In short order, however, Luther found himself enmeshed in an even more significant controversy. Engaged though he was in his lectures and studies, Luther was once again called to interrupt his work, this time on business for the Order. He was by no means the central player in this new drama, being commanded only to serve as companion to the brother who journeyed to Rome to represent the cloister's opposition to the plan of vicar general Johann von Staupitz to integrate the reformed and unreformed congregations. Given the rigor with which Luther pursued his own monastic vocation, we can assume that he was supportive of the cloister's position.

If we look at Luther's journey as an educational adventure, the results do not seem to have been very significant. It is often remarked that Luther never commented in lectures, letters, or talks about the various sights he must have observed, the great art and architecture of the past and the masterpieces that were being created while he was there. If only Luther had walked in to observe Michaelangelo painting the Sistine Chapel! However, such a meeting did not occur, and Luther seems to have been far more impressed by the well-organized and clean Roman hospitals than by any other sights. Lest one draw too many conclusions from this absence of remark and derive from it the conclusion that Luther was not in fact influenced by the humanist spirit of the time, scholars have pointed to the fact that Erasmus too remained silent about the sights of Rome. What we do know is that Luther went to Rome full of piety, wishing that his parents were dead so that he could earn merit for them through masses and acts of worship in the holiest of Christian cities. He was dismayed to discover how little piety was in fact evident.

The most important outcome of the trip was that the Erfurt cloister did not win its plea. Hostility within the Erfurt cloister toward Staupitz's plan continued, but by all accounts Luther and his colleague Johann Lang had a change of heart or at the very least felt themselves obliged to fulfill their vow of obedience to their superior now that the cloister's plea had been denied. Once again we have no sources to tell us precisely how unpleasant life in Erfurt then became for Luther and Lang. Nor do we know how well Staupitz knew Luther at that time and therefore how sympathetic he was toward his situation. Given the speed with which Luther achieved his theological degrees and the hostility that engendered among at least some in the Erfurt cloister, it is possible that Luther was already viewed as a special protégé of Staupitz. The situation appeared to require action on Staupitz's part, and so in the summer or early fall of 1511 he ordered Luther's transfer to the Wittenberg cloister.[24]

If it was Erfurt that provided Luther with his educational roots, it was Wittenberg that afforded him the chance to branch out in new directions, to grow, mature, and become an altogether new variety of scholar, professor, and pastor. The contrast between the well-established city of Erfurt with its great church spires, its many cloisters, its lively academic and economic life, and the muddy town of Wittenberg—capital of electoral Saxony though it was— must have been striking.[25] No one disputes that life in Wittenberg was nothing to boast about; the disagreement concerns how bad it really was.

Helmar Junghans notes that already in the sixteenth century there was debate regarding whether Wittenberg was an influential or an unimportant town at the time when Luther returned there.[26] E. G. Schwiebert cites two different sources, one Evangelical and the other Catholic. The Evangelical, Friedrich Myconius, described Wittenberg in the early 1500s as

---

[24] Brecht states that it was the Erfurt monastery that decided to transfer Luther and Lang as punishment for their disloyalty. See *Luther: His Road to Reformation,* 105.

[25] E. G. Schwiebert offers a more positive view of Wittenberg, at least in terms of its size: "In size Wittenberg compares quite favorably with other sixteenth-century cities of Germany. ... Wittenberg compared quite favorably in size with Dresden, Meissen, and Torgau ... but was smaller than Leipzig, Erfurt, Muehlhausen, or Magdeburg." *Luther and His Times,* 209; 210.

[26] Helmar Junghans, *Wittenberg als Lutherstadt* (Berlin: Union Verlag, 1979), 74.

"a poor, unattractive town with small, old, ugly, low, wooden houses, more like an old village than a town."[27] The Catholic, Johann Cochläus, described the Wittenberg of 1524 in even more bleak terms, but his description was colored by his antagonism toward Luther and the reform movement:

> A miserable, poor, dirty village in comparison with Prague, ... it is not worthy to be called a town in Germany. ... It is not an enjoyable place; it is very dirty; in fact, what would there be in Wittenberg were it not for the castle, the Stift, and the University? ... Its market place is empty, its town is without better citizens. The people dress as those of a lower middle class. There is great poverty in all the homes of the town.[28]

Wittenberg was not in the best geographical location to enjoy prosperity. The south was more economically vital with its "mines and production of textiles," while Wittenberg was surrounded only by farms.[29] Luther later admitted that farming in the area was difficult: "Our land is very sandy, in fact none other than mere stones, for it is not a fertile soil; yet God gives us daily from these stones good wine, delicious cereals; but because this miracle happens constantly, we fail to appreciate it."[30] Nor was Wittenberg in an ideal position as a center of trade. Records from 1500 indicate that the town had 2,146 inhabitants and 392 houses; in 1513 about the same number, with either 382 taxable property owners, according to Boehmer, or 356, according to Brecht.[31] On the whole, Wittenberg "was a

---

[27] Cited in Schwiebert, *Luther and His Times*, 206.

[28] Cited in Schwiebert, *Luther and His Times*, 206.

[29] Brecht, *Martin Luther: His Road to Reformation*, 110.

[30] Cited in Schwiebert, *Luther and His Times*, 207.

[31] Schwiebert, *Luther and His Times*, 210; Boehmer, *Der junge Luther*, 50; Brecht, *Martin Luther: His Road to Reformation*, 110. Within the number of 382 taxable persons, Boehmer reports that there were 172 *Brauerben*, persons who had the right to brew beer; 184 *Budelinge*, small householders (meaning huts), and 26

city of local industry with guilds of shoemakers, clothiers, butchers, and bakers. Later, next to the booksellers, the wealthiest were the tailors."[32] By the time Luther was ordered to Wittenberg, and especially by the time of his second stay there in 1511, Wittenberg was in the midst of a significant development phase, with many new buildings being constructed.[33] This extensive building program owed its origins to Elector Frederick the Wise, who hired the master builder Konrad Pflueger to construct a new castle and with it a new church.[34]

It somehow seems appropriate that Luther would develop his theology and pedagogy on the frontier, "on the edges of civilization," as even Wittenberg's inhabitants referred to it. Luther himself thought of the town in this light and noted that "had it been founded a little more to the East, it would have been *in mediam barbariam*."[35] Yet if Wittenberg lacked the amenities of Erfurt it offered something much more important, a vital energy and a firm commitment on the part of Elector Frederick the Wise to make his new university a jewel in his crown and the centerpiece of his territory. From architects and artists to professors and printers, Frederick was willing to draw

---

Vorstädter, those living in the surrounding area. Brecht does not include the *Vorstädter* in his numbers.

[32] Brecht, *Martin Luther: His Road to Reformation,* 110.

[33] Schwiebert, *Luther and His Times,* 208.

[34] Heinrich Heubner, "Die Stadt Wittenberg und die Universität," in Leo Stern et al., *450 Jahre Martin-Luther-Universität Halle Wittenberg,* Bd. I: *Wittenberg 1502-1817* (Halle-Wittenberg: Selbstverlag der Martin Luther Universität Halle-Wittenberg, 1945-52), 149.

[35] *WA TR* 2, no. 2800 b and *WA TR* 3, no. 3433, cited in Grossmann, *Humanism in Wittenberg,* 36. Grossmann's excellent work provides the basis for much of the subsequent discussion in this chapter and is strongly recommended for anyone who wishes a more detailed discussion of the foundation of the university, its faculty and curriculum, and the political and social milieu within which it operated.

from his own treasuries to enhance the reputation of his university. In the process, he linked the fate of his university—and in the long run of his territory—to the theology of a young Augustinian friar. Thanks to the work of Luther and his colleagues, over a period of some five decades, Wittenberg would become the foremost center of printing in all of Germany—producing more books than such larger cities as Strasbourg and Basel.[36]

Although Wittenberg was not very culturally advanced at the beginning of the sixteenth century, it had a long history, with its name appearing in written records of the late twelfth century, and for a time, during a period of about a hundred years from the 1320s to the 1420s, Wittenberg was the main residence of the electors.[37] Although Wittenberg then lost that status, it nonetheless remained the largest town in electoral Saxony. With the rule of Frederick the Wise in 1486, the town began to enjoy a liveliness and prosperity it had never known, as Frederick centered his attention upon building a university that would bring honor to his family and his territory.[38]

His enthusiasm for establishing a university was an outgrowth of his own ambitious nature (although in other ways, such as fighting for more territory, Frederick was decidedly unambitious) and love of culture, and the political circumstances and climate of the time.[39] The division of Saxony that resulted in the electoral holding being connected to Thuringia rather than to Meissen meant that Frederick lacked a university within his territory, since Leipzig lay outside of his territory and Erfurt fell under the jurisdiction of the Archbishop of Mainz—although, as the tumult of 1509 and 1510 demonstrates, there were at least some who would have preferred the elector over the archbishop in governing the disputed city with its famous university.[40]

---

[36] Heubner, "Die Stadt Wittenberg und die Universität," 150.

[37] Grossmann, *Humanism in Wittenberg*, 37-38.

[38] Grossmann, *Humanism in Wittenberg*, 20 and 38; Schwiebert, *Luther and His Times*, 200-201.

[39] Grossmann, *Humanism in Wittenberg*, 23.

[40] Grossmann, *Humanism in Wittenberg*, 14, 17.

There were other political factors that encouraged Frederick to found his own university. Emperor Maximilian expressed openly his wish that each electoral territory should have its own university, although it is clear that Frederick's decision preceded the call by the emperor.[41] Lacking a university meant that his position was inferior to that of the ruler of ducal Saxony. Nor did he enjoy the presence within his territory of a body of experts, in theology, and medicine, and most especially law, with whom he could easily consult. Although by no stretch of the imagination could Frederick be labeled a humanist, he was influenced by the humanist ideas of the time. He had some education, and he knew enough to know that he wanted to encourage learning within his territory. According to Grossmann,

> Frederick learned Latin well, but not enough to speak it fluently. ... Of the classical authors he recalled in later times he had studied mostly Terence and Cato whose sayings were similar to German proverbs. Frederick also understood some French, but no Italian.[42]

More importantly, Frederick had the knack of finding the right people to advise him in establishing a university and enhancing his territory's reputation as a site of culture and learning. Although there were several key figures involved in the early years of the university, there are two in particular who stand out for their importance not only to Frederick's efforts and to the founding and furthering of the university, but for the role they would play in Luther's career. These two, the Augustinian Johann von Staupitz and the humanist, tutor, and court

---

[41] Grossmann writes that "as early as 1493 Frederick the Wise was apparently considering the plan for a university in his lands. In a will drawn up at Torgau before embarking on his journey to the Holy Land, he established six scholarships for poor students, to be used at Erfurt or Leipzig, until a university should be established in his own lands. Thus he anticipated by two years Maximilian's recommendation that each elector should have a university in his territory." *Humanism in Wittenberg,* 40.

[42] Grossmann, *Humanism in Wittenberg,* 24.

chaplain Georg Spalatin were men of vision and understanding who were committed to helping Frederick realize his goal.

As did many others in the humanist camp, Spalatin changed the name which he was given at birth, Georg Burckhardt, to one more to his liking, Spalatin, after the town of Spalt, located near Nuremberg, where he was born in 1484.[43] Despite his illegitimate birth, Spalatin was able, much like Erasmus who shared the same disadvantage, to gain success through education. He studied at Erfurt and Wittenberg, where he came under the influence of the humanist Nicholas Marschalk and eventually became part of the group around Mutian Rufus.[44] Mutian became his mentor, and through his efforts Spalatin received a teaching position at a monastery in Georgenthal near Gotha, where he was also ordained.[45] Frederick the Wise turned to Mutian in 1508 for a recommendation of a tutor for his nephew and heir, John Frederick.

Like Luther, once engaged by Frederick, Spalatin remained in his service the rest of his life. His service was extraordinarily multifaceted, going far beyond his initial duties as tutor. He became translator, court historian, secretary, founding director of the university library, chaplain and confessor, and all around advisor, although technically his portfolio included only ecclesiastical and university matters.[46] In short, Spalatin became Frederick's right hand man and his most influential advisor. As we will see, his most important role was as the intermediary between Luther and Frederick the Wise. Strange as it may seem given their proximity to one another, Frederick and Luther never talked face to face. Thus, Spalatin's role in

---

[43] Brecht, *Martin Luther: His Road to Reformation,* 113; Boehmer, *Der junge Luther,* 134; Grossmann, *Humanism in Wittenberg,* 20. On Spalatin, see Irmgard Höss, *Georg Spalatin 1454-1545: Ein Leben in der Zeit des Humanismus und der Reformation* (Weimar: Hermann Böhlhaus Nachfolger, 1956).

[44] Grossmann, *Humanism in Wittenberg,* 21.

[45] Brecht, *Martin Luther: His Road to Reformation,* 113.

[46] Grossmann, *Humanism in Wittenberg,* 21; Brecht, *Martin Luther,* 113; Boehmer, *Der junge Luther,* 134.

representing the beliefs, needs, and desires of the two was absolutely key to the relationship between Luther and Frederick that began when Staupitz persuaded Frederick to pay the costs associated with Luther's candidacy for the doctoral degree and ended only with Frederick's death in 1525. Spalatin was the key figure behind the scenes.

Although Spalatin first became a member of the court some six years after the founding of the university, he quickly became a vital force in the university's promotion. For example, it was Spalatin to whom Frederick assigned in 1512 the task of beginning the university library.[47] His humanist training, his prior experience as the librarian at the monastery in Georgenthal, and his cordial association with Mutian to whom he turned for advice and contacts, made him an ideal candidate for this position. There is every reason to think that the library was a high priority for Frederick and therefore for Spalatin. Christoph Scheurl, who played a vital role as rector and professor from 1507 until his departure to Nuremberg in 1511, wrote that his friend "Spalatin was so extremely busy collecting books that he could 'scarcely breathe between sweatings'."[48] Their humanist interests are reflected in the types of purchases they made. Grossmann draws upon invoices from the early days of the library in 1512–13 to conclude that Spalatin emphasized certain areas:

> Bibles, Bible commentaries and sermons, the writings of the Church Fathers, the Greek and Latin classics, the works of humanists, grammars and language manuals, works on church history and secular history, scholastic treatises and books on science and law. Of the 153 books, 18 are by classical authors and 23 are writings of

---

[47] Grossmann, *Humanism in Wittenberg,* 106. Grossmann's research in the correspondence of Spalatin and the printer Aldus Manutius leads her to conclude that Spalatin and Frederick pursued the building of their new university library with extraordinary vigor.

[48] Schwiebert, *Luther and His Times,* 245; Grossmann, *Humanism in Wittenberg,* 60-72 passim.

humanists. ... Not a single work by Aristotle is listed in the invoices.[49]

This was precisely the kind of library Luther would need as he sought to develop his understanding of the biblical text and the church fathers. Already in Erfurt, shortly before his transfer to Wittenberg, Luther was referring to Greek and Hebrew in his marginal comments to the *Sentences*. Most scholars agree that his linguistic skill was then very basic, but his comments demonstrate the direction in which he was heading and his desire to learn more.

Spalatin, himself among the university's first students, proved to be an immense influence from the time when he joined the court in 1508 until his death in 1545. It was Johann von Staupitz, however, whose recommendations and support were especially important to Frederick during the crucial first years of the university. Much has been written about Staupitz, his theology, and the influence he had on the man whom he would choose to be his successor in the chair in Bible, Martin Luther.[50]

---

[49]Grossmann, *Humanism in Wittenberg*, 109; Junghans, *Wittenberg als Lutherstadt*, 57 concludes that Spalatin was above all interested in works of value to the humanists, including philological works "on the Hebrew, Greek and Latin languages."

[50] See David Steinmetz, *Misericordia Dei: The Theology of Johannes von Staupitz in Its Late Medieval Setting*, Studies in Medieval and Reformation Thought, vol. 4 (Leiden: E. J. Brill, 1968) and *Luther and Staupitz: An Essay in the Intellectual Origins of the Protestant Reformation*, Duke Monographs in Medieval and Renaissance Studies, no. 4 (Durham, N.C.: Duke University Press, 1980); Heiko A. Oberman, *Forerunners of the Reformation: The Shape of Late Medieval Thought Illustrated by Key Documents* (New York: Holt, Rinehart and Winston, 1966), 175-203. Regarding the difficulties in ascertaining the precise nature of and influences upon Staupitz's theology, Steinmetz comments: "The question of the relationship of Staupitz to the theological traditions of his own order, to which he was exposed to a greater or lesser degree, and the role which those traditions played in the relationship of Staupitz to Luther, has remained one of the interesting, if unsolved, problems of Luther research. Was there a revival of Augustinianism in the Augustinian Order, which exercised an important influence through Staupitz on the theological development of the young Luther? As

The Augustinian Hermits had long resided in Wittenberg. Beginning in 1359, the Augustinians situated at the cloister of Herzberg journeyed to Wittenberg in search of alms, and by 1414 they had established an alms house in the town, although their monastery and presence in numbers would be tied to the founding of the university in 1502.[51] The Augustinians were not, however, the first mendicants in Wittenberg. They had been preceded by the Franciscans, whose foundation in the town dated from 1261, and they were followed by the Antonites, whose vocation was care of the sick.[52] Operating from their monastery in Lichtenburg, between Torgau and Wittenberg, the Antonites established a chapel in Wittenberg in 1460.[53] As Frederick began to formulate his plans for a university, he turned to the Franciscans and the Augustinians to supply the professors he needed. Both orders responded positively, and the Augustinians proposed that Johann von Staupitz, who was himself a Saxon noble and prior of the house in Munich, be transferred to Wittenberg to assume responsibility for overseeing the development of an Augustinian house and facilitating its contribution to the university.[54] The Augus-

---

straightforward as this question appears, it has proven unbelievably complex and difficult to answer." *Luther and Staupitz,* 12-13.

[51] Junghans, *Wittenberg als Lutherstadt,* 43.

[52] Junghans, *Wittenberg als Lutherstadt,* 43; Schwarz, *Luther,* 24. Scholars dispute the date of the founding of the Franciscan house in Wittenberg. Junghans (p. 12) and Schwarz (p. 24) indicate that the cloister was founded by the wife of Albrecht I in 1261 as a pious response to his death. Grossmann, however, indicates that it was established in 1328. *Humanism in Wittenberg,* 37.

[53] Schwarz, *Luther,* 24.

[54] Brecht states that "Staupitz probably intended to make this monastery the real institution of theological education for the reform congregation [thus displacing Erfurt]. There were constantly between fifteen and twenty brothers from other places staying in the monastery to continue their studies. During the time of its existence, no fewer than fourteen Augustinian Hermits obtained the licentiate or doctor of theology degree." *Martin Luther: His Road to*

tinians were charged with providing two professors, one in theology who was to be Staupitz himself and the other in moral philosophy in the arts faculty. It was this position that Luther held on an interim basis when he was called to replace Ostermayr in the fall semester of 1508.

Staupitz contributed much more than his knowledge in theology, although that knowledge was by no means insignificant. He had earned his doctorate at the University of Tübingen in 1500. Staupitz must have thought highly of his Tübingen experience, for he was a strong voice in assuring that the new Wittenberg University modeled its statutes after that university, and he persuaded a number of Tübingen scholars, including such men as Sigismund Epp, who became the first dean of the arts faculty, and Wolfgang Stähelin, who assumed the same position within the law faculty, to travel from the well-regarded university in southwestern Germany to the wilds of the east.[55] Staupitz also followed the Tübingen pattern of allowing for more than a single philosophical school, rather than adhering as did Leipzig or Erfurt to a single one.[56] Thomism or the *via antiqua* was represented by Martin Pollich von Mellerstadt, the first rector of the university, and later by Andreas Bodenstein von Carlstadt, who would eventually convert to Luther's reform and then proceed to more radical positions.[57] Scotism was represented first by Sigismund Epp, and after 1511 by Nikolaus von Amsdorf, Staupitz's nephew.[58]

Reformation, 121. Max Steinmetz adds that, during the years Staupitz was vicar general, some 100 Augustinians matriculated at Wittenberg and approximately 17 were admitted into the senate of the theological faculty. "Die Universität Wittenberg und der Humanismus (1502-1521)," *450 Jahre Martin-Luther-Universität Halle-Wittenberg*, 107.

[55] Grossmann, *Humanism in Wittenberg*, 44.

[56] Brecht, *Martin Luther: His Road to Reformation*, 120.

[57] Grossmann, *Humanism in Wittenberg*, 42; 69.

[58] Steinmetz, "Die Universität Wittenberg und der Humanismus (1502-1521)," 112. Steinmetz notes that Epp left Wittenberg returned to Tübingen in 1504, and that Scotism never attained the stature of Thomism in Wittenberg. Brecht, *Martin Luther: His Road to*

The *via moderna* or nominalist school was not represented until 1507 when Jodocus Trutfetter, Luther's professor, was wooed away from Erfurt to Wittenberg.[59] However, he did not stay long.

In her detailed study of the phases in the early history of the university, Maria Grossmann challenges the rosy picture which suggests that almost from the beginning the different schools were not only tolerated but welcomed.[60] Max Steinmetz adds that Wittenberg reinterpreted the statutes of Tübingen so that inclusion of the two *viae* meant initially Thomism and Scotism, not Thomism and Scotism as one *via* and Occamism or nominalism as the other.[61] As today, institutional reality does not always reflect the constitution and bylaws. Grossmann points out that the Thomist Mellerstadt was far from happy to have the esteemed nominalist, Trutfetter, in his academic territory, challenging his position. When Trutfetter returned in 1510 to Erfurt, his "place in Wittenberg University was not filled, and the Thomists and Scotists were again in exclusive control of the philosophical faculty. His place as archdeacon in

---

Reformation, 120. On Amsdorf, his friendship with Luther, and his contributions to the Evangelical Reformation, see Robert Kolb, *Nikolaus von Amsdorf (1483-1565): Popular Polemics in the Preservation of Luther's Legacy* (Nieuwkoop: B. de Graaf, 1978). Brecht notes (p. 120) that Amsdorf formally joined the theology faculty after he received his licentiate in theology in 1511, but he had been at Wittenberg since its inception, first as an arts student and then as a theology student. Kolb, *Nikolaus von Amsdorf*, 27.

[59] Grossmann, *Humanism in Wittenberg*, 68.

[60] Grossmann, *Humanism in Wittenberg*, 69. Steinmetz notes that the statutes of the arts faculty from November 25, 1508 refer for the first time to three scholastic ways, and he suggests that the inclusion of nominalism resulted from a desire to attract new students in the face of declining enrollments. Admissions propaganda to the contrary, the University remained steadfastly devoted to the *via antiqua* until the changes in curriculum connected to Luther's reform movement. "Die Universität Wittenberg und der Humanismus," 108-109.

[61] Steinmetz, "Die Universität Wittenberg und der Humanismus," 108.

the cathedral chapter was taken by Carlstadt, the Thomist, another victory for the *via antiqua*."[62] Although balance and representation may have been Frederick's and Spalatin's ideal, it did not become a reality. We may even question how high a priority balance was since Trutfetter's position was left unfilled.

They were more successful in giving a certain humanist spirit to the institution from its beginnings, although scholars debate how pervasive this was.[63] We have seen that even in Erfurt,

---

[62]Grossmann, *Humanism in Wittenberg*, 69.

[63] Schwarz, for example, reports that Staupitz and Mellerstadt worked together to ensure that from its beginnings the university was open to humanism. *Luther*, 24. While noting that the *humaniora* were listed as subjects to be taught in the foundation document of the university, Grossmann argues against drawing any radical conclusions from this fact: "Frederick the Wise certainly did not intend his new center of learning to become a rallying point for men opposed to the scholastic and religious traditions. Yet, for all the traditional structure, a number of signs point towards the dawn of a new era." *Humanism in Wittenberg*, 45. Max Steinmetz agrees that Wittenberg should not be viewed as a humanist institution, but he notes that humanists did have the right to teach [a standing that should not be underestimated in its significance since it allowed humanists to devote their time to scholarly pursuits rather than to waging political battles]. "Die Universität Wittenberg und der Humanismus," 108. In the same volume Kurt Aland argues that in comparison with other universities, Wittenberg was not at the forefront, but in fact lagged far behind. He notes that even a university like Leipzig which was far from being at the cutting edge of humanist studies, showed humanist influence from the middle of the fifteenth century onward. "Die Theologische Fakultät Wittenberg und ihre Stellung im Gesamtzusammenhang der Leucorea während des 16. Jahrhunderts," *450 Jahre Martin-Luther- Universität Halle-Wittenberg*, 163. John Todd to the contrary writes: "The Elector and Staupitz went out of their way to organise a modern university. There were lectures in Greek from the start. The modernist school of Occamites was not to dominate." *Luther*, 50. Indeed, it was anything but the case that nominalism dominated— the struggle was to have it included. Brecht reports that Greek began to be taught in 1513 (*Martin Luther: His Road to Reformation*, 120), but Grossmann reports only that "some study of Greek persisted in the

although there were some tensions between scholastics and humanists, there was initially a symbiotic relationship, with humanists writing elegant prefaces to scholastic tomes by Trutfetter and Arnoldi, while scholastics sought to integrate some aspects of humanist linguistic and textual study into their own work. The professors allowed the humanists to have some hours and rooms in which to lecture. By building the *humaniora* into the university charter, even though thorough coverage could not be accomplished from the beginning, Wittenberg made an explicit commitment to humanism. At the same time, Wittenberg certainly pursued a moderate path, similar to that of Tübingen, with humanist courses not included in the required arts curriculum.[64]

Although Frederick was genuinely interested in many aspects of humanism, particularly art and music, there was another factor that influenced his decision. No one in academic administration will be surprised at what that was—and it may even be reassuring to know that such concerns were not foreign to the sixteenth century. In short, the driving force was the need for strong enrollments. When enrollments dropped as the initial student enthusiasm to visit a new university waned and after the university was forced to move temporarily to Herzberg because of an outbreak of the plague, the authorities knew that they needed to follow an effective recruitment strategy.[65] In an age before college "view books" and videotapes offering tours of classrooms filled with happy students, a faculty member in the arts named Andreas Meinhardi was requested to prepare a work that would convince prospective students of the advantages of study at Wittenberg. His mission was to portray

---

years preceding the arrival of Melanchthon in 1518." (*Humanism in Wittenberg*, 48). Grossmann credits Nikolaus Marschalk who enrolled at the university at its opening in 1502 and remained until 1505 with furthering the study of Greek. His work was then continued by "Trebelius, Carlstadt, Tileman Conradi, Johann Lang, Johannes Rhagius Aesticampianus and finally Melanchthon." 48.

[64] Steinmetz, "Die Universität Wittenberg und der Humanismus," 112.

[65] Grossmann, *Humanism in Wittenberg*, 56.

both the university and the town in such glowing terms that the reputations of both would rise.[66]

The resulting *Dialogus* recounted a conversation between a young man on his way to study in Cologne and another on his way to the new university of Wittenberg.[67] All of the descriptions and conversations are directed toward convincing prospective students inclined toward humanist studies that their future lies in Wittenberg. As Grossmann describes, the university and its surroundings were "clothed in classical robes" and portrayed as representing the height of classical culture.[68] She concludes that "such a picture leaves little, if any, space for scholasticism."[69] At least to prospective students, the Wittenberg propagandists tried hard to portray the university as being on the curricular cutting edge.

The first rector of the university, Martin Pollich von Mellerstadt, although not a humanist, was certainly open to humanist ideas, and had even been the central figure in a literary society, the *Sodalitas Polychiana*.[70] Pollich had been

---

[66]Grossmann, *Humanism in Wittenberg*, 56-60.

[67]Grossmann, *Humanism in Wittenberg*, 57.

[68]Grossmann, *Humanism in Wittenberg*, 59.

[69]Grossmann, *Humanism in Wittenberg*, 60.

[70]Grossmann, *Humanism in Wittenberg*, 38. Brecht stresses the role that Mellerstadt as the first rector played in assuring humanism's place. *Martin Luther: His Road to Reformation*, 119. Schwiebert offers a more negative assessment of Mellerstadt, arguing that during his time as rector "many able liberal, Humanistic spirits, such as Herman von Busche, Nicolaus Marschalk, and Petrus of Ravenna, remained but a short time in Wittenberg." *Luther and His Times*, 269. Theodor Grüneberg in his chapter, "Martin Pollich von Mellerstadt, der erste Rektor der Wittenberger Universität," proposes that in his younger days Pollich devoted himself to humanistic studies and to building associations with such leading lights as Conrad Celtis, but as he grew older, he retreated more into the scholastic teachings of his youth and did not lend the support that he might have as rector to the humanists. *450 Jahre Martin-Luther-Universität Halle Wittenberg*, 87-88.

educated at Leipzig, where he matriculated in 1470, earning his B.A. two years later, and his M.A. three years after that.[71] He then studied medicine, and it was first as a physician that Pollich was engaged by Frederick. He entered his service in 1482 and accompanied him on pilgrimage to the Holy Land in 1493.[72] As the university's first rector, Pollich devoted himself to attracting excellent faculty, although he seems to have been more successful in drawing established scholars and promising beginners, especially humanists, than he was in keeping them at Wittenberg.[73]

Others, particularly Christoph Scheurl, who joined the faculty in 1507, were more successful than Pollich in furthering humanist studies. Grossmann regards Scheurl as the one who effectively initiated a new era in humanist studies at the university, and Steinmetz refers to him as the "soul of humanism" at Wittenberg.[74] In a variety of roles, as rector, professor of law and dean of the law faculty, lecturer on the classics, and writer, Scheurl was an enthusiastic proponent of the university and classical studies during his five years there. It was Scheurl to whom Frederick turned for new statutes for the university in 1508, statutes that were largely modeled on those of Tübingen and that conveyed an ideological openness, allowing for teaching by Thomists, Scotists, and Occamists.[75]

Humanism was also furthered through the addition of such faculty as Otto Beckmann, who became professor of Latin grammar and whose own education was influenced by the leading proponent of the *Devotio moderna*, Alexander Hegius, in

---

[71] Grüneberg, "Martin Pollich von Mellerstadt," 88.

[72] Grüneberg, "Martin Pollich von Mellerstadt," 90; Brecht, *Martin Luther: His Road to Reformation*, 119.

[73] Pollich seems to have gained a reputation as an effective administrator but a difficult colleague, according to Grüneberg, "Martin Pollich von Mellerstadt," 90.

[74] Grossmann, *Humanism in Wittenberg*, 60; Steinmetz, "Die Universität Wittenberg und der Humanismus," 120.

[75] Grossmann, *Humanism in Wittenberg*, 68.

Deventer, where Erasmus also studied.[76] Beckmann sought to find points of legitimate linkage between humanism and scholasticism and embodied a spirit of openness to different schools of thought.[77] Humanist studies, and particularly the study of Greek, received a boost when Johann Lang was transferred with Luther from Erfurt to Wittenberg. Lang took over the chair in moral philosophy for which the Augustinians were responsible and which Luther had held temporarily as a replacement for Father Ostermayr.

As Grossmann emphasizes, it was Frederick the Wise who pledged his new university to humanism and who provided the resources to make his promise a reality. The openness to humanism, including study of both classical languages and texts, provided a conducive and supportive environment for the more dramatic curricular reforms of Luther, Carlstadt, and Melanchthon, although such ideas were certainly not part of Frederick's original plan.

As Wittenberg was unusual in its commitment to teaching the *humaniora* from its very inception, there were also some unusual aspects to the way the university was founded. Frederick was committed to increasing the wealth of his realm, both intellectual and physical. Thus, he embarked on a large scale building and rebuilding campaign, beginning with his castle and the castle church, and progressing to buildings for the university. As part of the agreement that was reached with the Augustinians regarding their teaching at the university, Frederick contributed heavily—some 400 gulden in 1507 and 1508—to the building of the monastery, which contained on its first floor living and sleeping quarters, probably about 40 cells for the friars, and classrooms on the second floor.[78] He also was intent on beautifying his surroundings, bringing to

---

[76] Steinmetz, "Die Universität Wittenberg und der Humanismus," 114.

[77] Grossmann, *Humanism in Wittenberg*, 72-73; Brecht, *Martin Luther: His Road to Reformation*, 120.

[78] Junghans, *Wittenberg als Lutherstadt*, 57; Brecht, *Martin Luther: His Road to Reformation*, 122; Schwiebert, *Luther and His Times*, 221.

Wittenberg such renowned artists as Albrecht Dürer and Lucas Cranach.[79]

We have no way of knowing if Frederick had developed a "strategic plan." Did he believe that through an initial investment of capital in both "brick and mortar" and professionals he would attract more people and trade to his territory, and especially to Wittenberg? The problem, of course, was the usual one of money. Frederick was one of the most powerful and respected of the territorial princes, a fact that is duly emphasized in every history book as being key to Luther's survival after the Diet of Worms in 1521, but his ambitions, at least in terms of building, education, and the arts, exceeded his means.[80] To build his university he needed not only the support of the Augustinians and Franciscans in providing professorial manpower, but of the pope in supplying ecclesiastical income. This was the normal practice for universities.

Frederick surely recognized from the start the need for the pope's financial support if his dream of a university was to be realized. Scholars differ in their assessment of just how significant it is that Frederick did not in fact begin the university approval process in the usual manner by seeking papal permission. Instead, he appealed first to the emperor Maximilian I, who responded affirmatively with a letter of charter dated July 6, 1502. Junghans links this decision to Frederick's desire to educate capable lawyers for the administration of his territory—very much a secular aim—and so he began the approval process on the secular front, with the emperor rather than with the pope.[81] Grossmann concludes that Frederick's break with tradition "rested ... on a new view of the territorial state, seen as an independent entity. ... Wittenberg thus became the first German university founded without the permission of ecclesiastical authorities and hence

---

[79] For a discussion of Frederick's support of the arts, see Grossmann, *Humanism in Wittenberg*, 116-131. Grossmann also notes that Frederick so loved music that "he maintained at court an orchestra, under the direction of Conrad von Ruppisch, which accompanied him even to the imperial diets," 27. No wonder he had budget problems.

[80] Grossmann, *Humanism in Wittenberg*, 34.

[81] Junghans, *Wittenberg als Lutherstadt*, 52.

without recourse to the traditional benefices."[82] While agreeing that the way Frederick proceeded was unusual, Brecht argues against reading too much significance into his decision, noting that by "the beginning of 1503 Frederick the Wise had already obtained confirmation, at least in a preliminary way, from papal legate Raimund Peraudi for his new university."[83] By this interpretation, Rome's red tape rather than a political decision may have been responsible for the order of events.

Whatever the cause, Frederick did not allow the absence of a papal charter to stand in the way of the opening of his university. He and his brother Johann sent letters of invitation on August 24 for the inauguration of the university on October 18, 1502. The university opened under the protective eye of its patron saint, St. Augustine—a choice for which Staupitz may have been responsible—and with the distinguished humanist Hermann von dem Busche giving the inaugural address. The university was also blessed with a name that would have appealed to any budding humanist: *Leucorea* from the Greek words *leukos* for white and *oros* for mountain.[84] What other German university could make such a claim! In 1507 the pope gave his blessing to the enterprise, thereby granting the university permission to draw upon the benefices of the *Allerheiligenstift* or All Saints' Foundation for the salaries of one professor in civil law, three professors in canon law, and three

---

[82]Grossmann, *Humanism in Wittenberg,* 41. Max Steinmetz points to Staupitz's extensive involvement in the founding of the university as a sign that Frederick had no intention of breaking with the tradition of ecclesiastical involvement and influence upon universities. At the same time, he concurs with the assessment of Erich Haupt that the manner in which the university was founded is a sign of the beginning of the process by which universities were to be regarded as institutions of the state rather than of the church. "Die Universität Wittenberg und der Humanismus," 106 and 107. In the same volume, Hans Hartwig concurs with the assessment that the founding of the university marks the beginning of the secularization of higher education. "Die Verfassung der Universität Wittenberg, ihre ursprüngliche Form und deren Grundlagen," 94.

[83] Brecht, *Martin Luther: His Road to Reformation,* 118.

[84]Junghans, *Wittenberg als Lutherstadt,* 52.

theologians.[85] The elector subsequently "increased the foundation by six new canonries, from which the teachers of the philosophy faculty were to be compensated."[86] Thus, although later rather than sooner, the university was able to gain the crucial ecclesiastical approval and funding it needed.

Perhaps anticipating the more dramatic breaks with tradition that lay in its future, the new university also broke new ground in governance. Traditionally, the chancellor was appointed by the church and was a person of considerable power. For example, the Archbishop of Mainz was chancellor of the University of Erfurt. The chancellor and the vice-chancellor he appointed exercised decisive power over the administration of the university. At Wittenberg, however, the role of chancellor was limited to such functions as providing the official permission for granting of degrees, or attending the promotion ceremonies.[87] Demonstrating again the increasing dominance of secular power, real authority within the university during its first years lay with four men, the "*studii generales reformatores,*" who were appointed from the faculty by the elector.[88] From this group, the rector was elected biannually, but his authority stemmed more from his membership in the "*reformatores*" than from his office as rector. The new university also broke with tradition in not stipulating that the rector must be a cleric, although the old spirit lived on in the requirement

---

[85] Brecht, *Martin Luther: His Road to Reformation*, 118-19.

[86] Brecht, *Martin Luther: His Road to Reformation*, 119.

[87] Hartwig, "Die Verfassung der Universität Wittenberg, ihre ursprüngliche Form und deren Grundlagen," 96. Grossmann finds considerable significance in the fact that the chancellor was only a "minor ecclesiastical officer, Goswin of Orsoy, *praeceptor* of the Antonines, at Lichtenberg. He never gained much influence, most of his duties in the period 1502-1513 being taken over by Martin Polich von Mellerstadt, the vice-chancellor, who became one of the most influential men in the university." She cites this as a sign of the growing power of the secular authorities. *Humanism in Wittenberg,* 41.

[88] Hartwig, "Die Verfassung der Universität Wittenberg, ihre ursprüngliche Form und deren Grundlagen," 97.

that the rector be unmarried—a practice that ended with the naming of the married Philipp Melanchthon as rector in 1523.[89] This group was responsible for the curriculum, for assigning teaching responsibilities to the docents, and for arbitrating disputes among the professors—in other words, for all the decisions that truly affected the daily life of the university.[90]

The absence of a papal charter in 1502 did not deter a positive student response to the opening of the new university. Students who previously had traveled to Erfurt or Leipzig now found themselves with a new option, and the university's openness to the "new learning" of humanism proved attractive to many. The university boomed with 1,204 matriculations from the opening of the university through 1505.[91] During the same period, Tübingen, for example, had only 444 enrollments; Wittenberg occupied fourth place in enrollments among German universities, behind only Cologne, Erfurt, and Leipzig.[92] At least initially Frederick's recruitment strategy worked; unfortunately, the effects were not lasting, and, the university's leaders were soon heavily promoting their humanist orientation as a means of drawing students. Nonetheless, along with those early strong enrollments came a positive response from another quarter, one that would prove to be decisive not only in the development of the university but in the spread of Luther's ideas.

The promise of students and professors wanting books, as well as a library that was growing, drew printers to

---

[89] Hartwig, "Die Verfassung der Universität Wittenberg, ihre ursprüngliche Form und deren Grundlagen," 98 and 100.

[90] Hartwig, "Die Verfassung der Universität Wittenberg, ihre ursprüngliche Form und deren Grundlagen," 97.

[91] Stern et al., *450 Jahre Martin-Luther-Universität Halle-Wittenberg*, table 20. Utilizing the *Album Academiae Vitebergensis*, Schwiebert reports that "the first few semesters show a heavy enrollment: 416, 258, 132, and 158 respectively." *Luther and His Times*, 255.

[92] Stern et al., *450 Jahre Martin-Luther-Universität Halle-Wittenberg*, table 20.

Wittenberg.[93] They were undoubtedly also drawn by the university's and the elector's commitment to humanism. In these early years of the university, there were five printers at work, the most important and successful of whom was Johannes Rhau-Grunenberg, who became the publisher of Luther's works. During the crucial first years of the university, especially from 1507-1512, as the curriculum evolved in an increasingly humanist direction, the printers responded quickly to the need for new texts and editions. For example, Grossmann reports that "in 1509 a new translation of Aristotle's *De Anima* by the Greek scholar Johannes Argyropylos was published in Wittenberg, which, being in modern Latin, could be used by the Wittenberg professors with greater ease than earlier translations. Chilian Reuter had it printed as a textbook for use in his philosophy course in 1509."[94] Over a fifty-year period the small town of Wittenberg literally became the publishing capital of all of Germany.[95]

It was to this lively intellectual environment that Luther was recalled by Staupitz in 1511. At first his duties lay solely within the monastery where he became the official preacher. In May 1512 at the chapter meeting in Cologne his election as subprior was approved, and he was given responsibility for overseeing the education of the young friars. The monastery at Wittenberg, as at Erfurt, housed a *studium generale,* and it seems likely that Staupitz intended for the Wittenberg house to become one of special academic distinction.

Precisely when Staupitz decided Luther was to become a candidate for the doctorate with the goal of taking over Staupitz's own chair in Bible is unclear, although it seems that he first informed Luther of his wish while the two were sitting together in the garden (the place where the friars gathered

---

[93] On the development of printing in Wittenberg from 1502 to 1517, see the excellent discussion by Grossmann, *Humanism in Wittenberg,* 86-99. Grossmann rightly points to the reciprocal relationship between the printers and the humanists, 99. The one printer who devoted himself to printing scholastic texts did so poorly that he left Wittenberg.

[94] Grossmann, *Humanism in Wittenberg,* 73-74.

[95] Heubner, "Die Stadt Wittenberg und die Universität," 150.

together outside since there was no cloister) after Luther's return to Wittenberg. We do not know just when Staupitz became well acquainted with Luther. He had been present in Wittenberg and teaching at the university during Luther's first stay, and, of course, it was Staupitz who was responsible for the decision to call him and six of his fellow Augustinians there in the first place, even as he must also have acquiesced in Luther's return to Erfurt. Since Luther was continuing to pursue his theological studies while also teaching in the arts faculty, he studied with Staupitz, but we have no reports from Luther as to what was involved in that study and what degree of contact he had with his professor, who must have been absent from Wittenberg on business for the Order at least some of the time. Some scholars, such as Heiko Oberman, argue that dating from Luther's first stay in Wittenberg, Staupitz not only had his eye on Luther but had determined that he, along with Wenczeslaus Linck, was to prepare for the doctorate.[96] Other scholars, such as James Atkinson and John Todd, argue that Staupitz— even assuming he had made such a decision—had certainly not articulated it to Luther at that time.[97]

His difficulty in carrying dual responsibilities as professor and vicar general of the Augustinian Hermits brought Staupitz to the decision to find a successor for himself at Wittenberg. Luther was that man. And, at least initially, Luther was

---

[96] Oberman, *Luther*, 145.

[97] The moment in which Staupitz informs Luther of his decision that he should seek the doctorate has become the stuff of myth and legend, particularly since Luther himself helped to highlight the drama of the event. Atkinson writes: "At Wittenberg, Staupitz informed Luther that he intended him to become a doctor and a preacher. Under the famous pear tree in the garden ... he persuaded the reluctant Luther to assume the office of preacher and to acquire the degree of doctor of theology, remarking darkly that this would provide him with the opportunity of saying what he wanted to say." *Martin Luther and the Birth of Protestantism*, 67. Todd reports: "After the main meal each day the friars would walk up and down outside in good weather. ... One such midday, Father Staupitz was sitting outside silently under the pear tree. At last he made Father Martin sit down and said to him that he was to arrange to take a Doctorate. Martin nearly fainted." *Luther*, 60-61.

anything but happy about it. To modern students pursuing graduate study, it may seem difficult to understand why Luther who had already achieved two advanced degrees in theology would have been so reticent about proceeding to the next stage. His entire career to that point, both before and after he joined the Augustinians, had demonstrated his willingness to be on the "fast track." Unlike the modern Ph.D. candidate, Luther was not required to write a dissertation or to take a special examination. Instead, the doctorate was a validation of his previous accomplishments, as well as a judgment upon his character.

In the sixteenth century the doctorate was regarded quite differently than it is in the late twentieth. Even of those gaining the *sententiarius*, relatively few went on to the doctorate. There are a number of reasons for this situation. Certainly one of the principal ones was cost, since there were special fees associated with the degree which one had to agree to meet. These costs—for the degree itself, for the doctoral ring, for the festivities that surrounded this most awesome of all academic attainments—were not insignificant. As a friar, without any money of his own, Luther certainly could not look forward to gaining the doctorate on his own initiative. There was also a sense of propriety about when one went forward for such a high honor. For example, the distinguished Augustinian Johann von Paltz matriculated at Erfurt in 1462 and received his B.A. in 1464; he earned the doctorate only in 1483 while the bishop who ordained Luther to the priesthood, Johannes Bonemilch von Laasphe matriculated in 1462, received his B.A. in 1465, and the doctorate in 1491.[98] Luther's professor, Bartholomäus Arnoldi von Usingen, received his B.A. in 1486; his M.A. in 1491, and his doctorate in 1514, two years after Luther received his.[99] While Arnoldi may have been unusually old when he received his degree, Luther was certainly unusually young.

As he tried to talk Staupitz out of his decision, Luther appealed to his youth as a reason why he did not deserve such

---

[98] Kleineidam, *Universitas Studii Erffordensis II*, 282; 284.

[99] Kleineidam, *Universitas Studii Erffordensis II*, 298.

an honor.[100] Indeed, he appealed to every reason he could possibly think of, including the fact that he was already overworked as subprior.[101] But none of his pleas worked. Staupitz would neither be persuaded nor deterred. Whether his insistence was caused by his conviction that this was the right step for Luther or because he himself could no longer handle the demands of two positions, or both, we will never know. Because Luther came to look upon Staupitz as a mentor and because he gained much from Staupitz's theology and pastoral insights, many scholars have credited Staupitz with unusual insight into the intense and brilliant young man who stood before him.[102] For example, in his classic biography *Here I Stand: A Life of Martin Luther*, Roland Bainton writes: "The chair designed for him was the one which Staupitz himself had occupied, the chair of Bible. One is tempted to surmise that he retired in order unobtrusively to drive this agonizing brother to wrestle with the source book of his religion."[103] Whatever the

---

[100] According to Luther, there were at least some who were persuaded by the age issue and believed that he was far too young for the doctorate. *WA TR* 1, 129, 21-130, 8; *LW* 54, 320: "In Paris nobody is awarded a degree in theology who hasn't worked in that field for ten years. In Erfurt only fifty-year-olds were made doctors of theology. Many took umbrage at my getting the doctorate at the age of twenty-eight, when Staupitz drove me to it."

[101] *WA TR* 1, 442, 9-12. In this account Luther reports that Staupitz said that the doctorate would give him something to do. *WA TR* 2, 379, 7-19 and 20-24, 2255 a and b offer this same remark, and 2255 a includes Staupitz's famous answer to Luther's protest that the work would kill him, noting that God could make good use of him in heaven if that occurred. *WA TR* 3, 13, 30-35 offers a briefer version of the same retort while *WA TR* 5, 98, 21-29 conveys a longer version of Staupitz's rebuttal as does *WA TR* 5, 654, 34-36 and 655, 1-8.

[102] For example, Luther credits Staupitz with telling him that one must turn one's eyes to Christ, and notes that Staupitz was the one who began the teaching of the gospel. *WA TR* 1, 245, 9-12; *LW* 54, 97.

[103] Bainton, *Here I Stand*, 60. It is probably unwise to yield to this temptation, for Staupitz was truly overwhelmed by his myriad of responsibilities, the one set which mandated that he travel from monastery to monastery, address specific problems and grievances,

reason and whether Luther liked it or not, he was bound by obedience to comply.

Yet Staupitz's desire could not be immediately accomplished, since he too had no funds with which to pay the costs of Luther's promotion. Not surprisingly, he turned to Frederick, and also not surprisingly, Frederick wanted something for his money, namely, the assurance that the young Augustinian would remain a professor at Wittenberg for the rest of his life. As Luther's superior, Staupitz could make such a promise for him; so the deal was struck, and the steps toward the awarding of the degree began. First, of course, the Augustinians had to approve, and that was accomplished at the general meeting in Cologne in May 1512, the same meeting at which Luther was confirmed as subprior and teacher in the *studium generale*.[104] Considerable time lapsed between this approval and the next step, securing the necessary 50 gulden from Frederick to pay the costs of the promotion. That occurred only in October 1512 when Staupitz and Luther went to Leipzig to obtain the needed funds from the prince's treasury.[105] With the funds in place, the academic steps followed, the application for the degree and the receiving of the license. In many cases, even after the chancellor granted the license, there might be a substantial interval, probably in most cases due to the lack of funds for the promotion costs. To cite again the example of Luther's professor Bartholomäus Arnoldi von Usingen, he secured the license in the winter semester of 1512, but was promoted only about two years later, in October 1514.[106]

In October 1512 the chancellor gave Luther the license to proceed, "at which time Luther had to swear to obey the Roman Church and to promote peace among the scholars."[107] Now the ceremony itself could unfold, beginning on October 18

---

and make necessary personnel and other decisions, while the other set required that he remain in Wittenberg.

[104] Brecht, *Martin Luther: His Road to Reformation*, 126.

[105] Brecht, *Martin Luther: His Road to Reformation*, 126.

[106] Kleineidam, *Universitas Studii Erffordensis II*, 298.

[107] Brecht, *Martin Luther: His Road to Reformation*, 126.

in the afternoon, with disputations and a speech by the dean of theological faculty. The next morning at 7 a.m. was the real graduation ceremony, with Luther swearing an oath to obey the authorities of university and church and not to teach any strange doctrines or ideas. The dean then conferred upon him the degree with all its rights and privileges. He also received the symbols of his new office and work, a closed and open Bible, a red beret, and his doctoral ring. Luther had to deliver an address or perhaps a sermon, and then there were disputations with the new doctor judging who won. Afterwards, there was a festive meal to celebrate the occasion. Even after all these ceremonies, there was one more set of requirements to fulfill, those associated with gaining admittance to the faculty senate. This required swearing an oath to follow the statutes and to promote the welfare of the theological faculty.[108] Only now did Luther truly enter into a new arena of university life.

For all his qualms, Luther energetically engaged his new duties, preparing his first set of biblical lectures. His joy was marred to some extent by the fact that Erfurt launched a series of complaints against him, largely stemming from the claim that he had broken his oath not to receive his doctorate anywhere other than Erfurt. However, Luther had in fact done nothing wrong—even if his action was unusual—since he had received his *baccalaureus biblicus*, his first theological degree, in Wittenberg, and in the confusion concerning whether or not he was properly qualified for the second degree of *sententiarius*, no oath had been administered. Luther had, in fact, openly informed both university and cloister of what was happening, indicating that he was acting out of obedience to his superiors in proceeding for the degree, and inviting them to the ceremonies.[109] None of them attended.

As Luther found himself a few years later in the eye of the hurricane unleashed by his biblical scholarship, he gained great comfort from the fact that he had been called against his will to become a doctor of theology. In 1530, he proclaimed: "I shall be a doctor ... and that name they shall not take from me till the Last Day, this I know for certain," and two years later he pronounced: "I have often said and still say, I would not

---

[108] Brecht, *Martin Luther: His Road to Reformation*, 127.

[109] *WA Br* 1, 18; *LW* 48, 6-7.

exchange my doctor's degree for all the world's gold. For I would surely in the long run lose courage and fall into despair if ... I had undertaken these great and serious matters without call or commission."[110] Luther was convinced that it had been God acting through Johann von Staupitz who had called him to the doctorate and to a life of preaching and teaching. In retrospect, Luther was certain God knew what would come from Luther's honest and faithful fulfilling of his vocation, even if Luther himself did not.

In the last chapters we have walked with Luther as a schoolboy striving to perform so perfectly he would avoid his teacher's rod and gain his father's esteem, and as a successful student of the arts, fulfilling his and his father's dreams for success. We have also traveled with him as he journeyed down a different and unexpected road that led him to the cloister of the Augustinian Hermits in Erfurt, to the study of theology, and eventually to a new monastery and a new university on the edges of civilization. We have done so because Luther's education furnished the storehouse upon which he would draw for his preaching and teaching the rest of his life. From the study of Latin and Greek to the fables of Aesop to the nominalism of Occam and Biel to the writings of Augustine, and above all the texts of the Bible, throughout the rest of his life Luther would continue a dialogue with the texts and ideas he had learned at Mansfeld, Magdeburg, Eisenach, Erfurt, and Wittenberg. Some he would place at the core of the new curriculum; some he would reject.

As we will see in the next part of the story, Luther influenced education in much of the western world for centuries to come. His ideas were in large part the result of the education he received and his response to it, sometimes positive, as in the case of humanism, and sometimes negative, as in the case of an Aristotle he found an intrusive part of the curriculum. At a new university that already had broken with tradition on several fronts Luther found the support to launch a reform of church, school, and society. Little did Staupitz and Frederick know

---

[110] *WA* 30 II, 640, 16-18; *Luther's Works*, vol. 35: *Word and Sacrament I*, ed. E. Theodore Bachmann (Philadelphia: Fortress Press, 1960), 194 and *W A* 30 III, 522, 2-5; *Luther's Works*, vol. 40: *Church and Ministry II*, ed. Conrad Bergendoff (Philadelphia: Fortress Press, 1958), 387-388.

what amazing and dramatic results would come from their decision of 1511.

4

Martinus Luther Doctor S Theologie Vocatus

From the moment he received the doctorate, promising to fulfill a life-time commitment to teach at the University of Wittenberg, Martin Luther's future appeared firmly anchored in *stabilitas*. In return for Frederick's paying the costs of his promotion, Luther agreed faithfully and diligently to fulfill his professorial duties.

To a striking degree, during all the turbulence and tumult that would be unleashed by his performance of those professorial duties, Luther remained faithful to that promise. Until his death in 1546, his home remained Wittenberg, the small town on the edge of civilization. Frustrated and angry as he sometimes became, and threaten though he might to depart, Luther never did. Even when his own safety was at stake, as it was during episodes of the plague, Luther remained in Wittenberg. He was convinced that God had called him there, and God would do with him according to His will.

John Todd captures the spirit of the intense relationship between Luther and Wittenberg: "Wittenberg was the making of Martin. It produced many different Luthers: the Religious Superior, the theology lecturer, the popular preacher, the spiritual guide, the University man, and Luther the man, universal friend and acquaintance and, soon now, author."[1] Yet the opposite is also true, for just as Wittenberg was the making of Luther, so was Luther the making of Wittenberg. He transformed the town on the edge of civilization into the center of the movement to reform the church.

---

[1] Todd, *Luther*, 81.

Luther never wavered in his belief that God had called him to the doctorate and to his vocation as professor. After his name, Luther added the title *Doctor S Theologie vocatus* (along with his designation as an Augustinian) in the letter to Archbishop Albrecht of Mainz that accompanied his 1517 theses on indulgences.[2] Luther's sense of calling certainly did not originate with his challenge to the church hierarchy. It guided his first lectures on the Psalms, and it shaped all that he did from podium and pulpit for the rest of his life. When challenged that his authority was limited to his parish and university, Luther replied that his calling as *doctor theologiae* extended to all the church. During the dramatic events of 1517–21, Luther remained firmly devoted to his university, from spearheading curricular reform to protesting the university senate's actions to pleading for a higher salary for an esteemed colleague. His vocation as *doctor theologiae* connected all the specific, and sometimes mundane, aspects of his work at the University of Wittenberg with the larger concerns of church and society. Thus, this chapter focuses upon Luther as the young professional, with obligations that extended from the university classroom to the cloister and the community. These responsibilities sometimes pulled Luther in different directions. As he often lamented, there were not enough hours in the day to do all that was required of him. How did the transformation from successful student to provocative professor come about?

Initially Luther's concerns centered on preparing his lectures and proving that Staupitz's and the elector's trust had not been misplaced. Scholars disagree on precisely when Luther began his duties and on which biblical book he lectured first.[3] If Luther

---

[2] *WA Br* 1, 112, 70f. Leif Grane, *Martinus Noster: Luther in the German Reform Movement 1518-1521*, Veröffentlichungen des Instituts für Europäische Geschichte Mainz, Abteilung Religionsgeschichte, vol. 155 (Mainz: Verlag Philipp von Zabern, 1994), 19; Schwarz, *Luther*, 45.

[3] Martin Brecht reports that Luther apparently did not begin his lecturing until about a year after receiving the doctorate with the first known lectures the ones "on the Psalms. ... It is not known whether another series of lectures preceded these in 1512/13." *Martin Luther: His Road to Reformation*, 127; 129. Heiko Oberman offers the same conclusion, *Luther*, 162, while James Kittelson argues: "He began his lectures, perhaps on Genesis, the following Monday,

did in fact begin his lectures immediately after receiving his doctorate, neither his lecture notes nor those of his students have survived. Our sources for Luther's teaching career as a doctor of theology begin with his first course of lectures on the Psalms, the *Dictata super Psalterium*, which he began in August of 1513 and continued perhaps until late October 1515.[4] These lectures and the following ones on Paul's letter to the Romans have been the subject of intense scholarly scrutiny and debate regarding when Luther came to his "reformatory" insight. Regardless of when one dates that insight and whether one regards it as the result of a gradual process or a more dramatic breakthrough, both sets of lectures give eloquent testimony to Luther's extensive preparation. He utilized the best scholarly tools available and engaged body and soul in intensive meditation on the text, seeking to draw forth God's meaning.[5]

Luther proceeded in the traditional manner, the way that he had been taught, as he prepared and presented his lectures. He offered his students both interlinear glosses, brief discussions of words, with particular emphasis on grammar or philology, followed by somewhat more lengthy explications drawing on the church fathers and tradition.[6] Student note-taking was facilitated by a printed biblical text which Luther had prepared for them, with ample space for notes between the lines and in the margins. The glosses were followed by *scholia*, longer expositions of particular texts. Luther utilized, as he was expected to do, the exegetical methodology in which he had been trained, interpreting according to the fourfold meaning of allegorical, literal (or grammatical-historical), tropological, and

---

October 25, at 7 a.m." *Luther the Reformer*, 85. James Atkinson offers the same conclusion, *Martin Luther and the Birth of Protestantism*, 68.

[4] The precise date when Luther concluded the Psalms lectures is also uncertain. See Brecht, *Martin Luther: His Road to Reformation*, 129.

[5] Brecht describes Luther's attitude in approaching the biblical text as an intense process of listening and questioning in which one is "confronted by it." *Martin Luther: His Road to Reformation*, 131.

[6] Gritsch, *Martin—God's Court Jester*, 10; Schwiebert, *Luther and His Times*, 283.

anagogical.[7] He consulted the commentaries of Nicholas Lyra and Paul of Burges, and the most recent humanist tools available, including the *Psalterium Quintuplex* of one of the leading humanists, Lefevre d'Etaples.[8]

Like any other young professor, Luther experienced both excitement and a bit of anxiety as he began his teaching career. Contrary to university practice today, Luther had wide latitude in deciding upon both the text on which he would lecture and the length of time his exposition would take. He was expected to lecture twice a week and so he did, appearing before his students at 6 a.m. in the summer semester and 7 a.m. in the winter.[9] Although this may seem to be a light teaching load—two hours of lecturing per week!—Luther was also responsible for supervising disputations. His university duties were paralleled by increasing responsibilities within cloister and community.

As Luther's obligations increased and pulled him in different directions, they also drew him toward a common concern. In various contexts, this concern focused upon what a person must do to be righteous before God. As he meditated on the biblical text, this question was central to his study, for it was also central to his own intensive spiritual quest. As a doctor might seek a cure in the pages of a medical book, so the young theologian sought to find the remedy for his spiritual torment and confusion by pounding again and again upon the door of Scripture.

If we simply took at face value Luther's description of those early years of teaching and preaching, we would emerge with the portrait of a young man so obsessed with doubt and spiritual tribulations that he was of little use to himself or anyone else. But that picture would be very much in error. In reality Luther was still on the "fast track." Already in the fall

---

[7] Boehmer notes that in his exegesis of the Psalms the literal or grammatical-historical interpretation subsides into the background, in contrast to Luther's subsequent exegesis, since he interpreted the Psalms as a prophetic book, pointing to Christ. *Der junge Luther*, 108.

[8] Schwiebert, *Luther and His Times*, 282–83.

[9] Brecht, *Martin Luther: His Road to Reformation*, 129; Boehmer, *Der junge Luther*, 105.

of 1511 he had been named preacher in the monastery. At the Augustinian chapter meeting in Cologne in 1512 he was appointed subprior, and, more importantly, director of studies within the monastery. This position entailed guiding the studies of the young monks and overseeing their repetitions of their lessons, and most likely sharing with them the fruits of his own study. As Brecht observes: "In these years it was for the most part by him that the new theological generation of the reform congregation of Augustinian Hermits was educated, a seed which later would stand him and his cause in good stead."[10] As Trutfetter and Arnoldi had played a significant role in his education, so he was now doing for the next generation.

The Augustinians served the Wittenberg community, as well as the university. Although the precise date is uncertain, but from the end of 1514 at the latest, Luther was commissioned to preach in the City Church. Legally that responsibility rested with the cantor of the *Allerheiligenstift* or All Saints' Foundation, but he seemed not to have fulfilled his duty.[11] Boehmer estimates that this assignment would have obliged him to preach twice a week, probably about 170 times a year.[12] Given Luther's prominence within university and community, it is surprising that he is not included among the names of noteworthy professors in a list compiled by a Benedictine named Lange in 1514, a *"Who's Who* of German university life."[13]

The next chapter meeting in Gotha in May of 1515 brought Luther new responsibilities within the Order. He was elected district vicar for a term of three years, testimony to the Augustinians' confidence in him. This new assignment dramatically increased his already heavy work load, as he now

---

[10] Brecht, *Martin Luther: His Road to Reformation*, 155; Boehmer, *Der junge Luther*, 106.

[11] Brecht, *Martin Luther: His Road to Reformation*, 150; Boehmer, *Der junge Luther*, 106.

[12] Boehmer, *Der junge Luther*, 106.

[13] Atkinson, *Martin Luther and the Birth of Protestantism*, 88.

exercised supervision over eleven monasteries.[14] On more than one occasion he served as a court of appeal in difficult personnel matters. In addition, as part of his duties as district vicar, Luther assumed the role of controller or treasurer, supervising the monasteries' financial dealings. Some years later, Luther's wife, Katie, must have been amused to learn of this role since Luther was widely known for his generosity but not for his financial acumen. A letter written to Johann Lang at the monastery in Langensalza in late May 1516 suggests that he could be quite perceptive about financial matters and very cognizant of how easily costs in the monastery could soar when appropriate policies were not instituted and followed. Thus, he admonished Lang to

> draw up a special list, in which you record daily how much beer, wine, bread, meat, and, in short, how much of anything else may have been used in the guest house. ... If you do not find a more efficient form, then organize this list so that you write in different columns the following: on the day of this saint, or on this weekday, so much was consumed—for instance, so much wine, so much bread, etc., by this or that guest. ... Through such organization ... you will be able to see whether the monastery is a monastery rather than a tavern or hotel.[15]

His new assignments combined administrative and pastoral responsibilities. Some of these were quite a challenge for the young monk who was called upon to act with both wisdom and authority over much older men. For example, in September 1516 he found it necessary to ask the prior of the monastery in Neustadt/Orla to resign his office in order to end dissension within the house. Luther's letter to Michael Dressel demonstrates considerable sensitivity to his feelings, as well as

---

[14] In his letter of October 26, 1516, to Johann Lang in Erfurt, he writes that he is responsible for overseeing eleven monasteries. *WA Br* 1, 72–73. Brecht states that Luther was responsible for ten monasteries in Meissen and Thuringia. *Martin Luther: His Road to Reformation*, 156.

[15] *WA Br* 1, 42, 12–23; *L W* 48, 15.

an unwillingness to allow the dissension—no matter what its cause—to continue. To comfort Dressel he wrote:

> The following should console you. It is not enough that a man be good and pious by himself. Peace and harmony with those around him are also necessary. For the sake of preserving peace, the best undertakings must often be deemed unsatisfactory and be rightly condemned.[16]

These diverse obligations in university, community, and cloister provide the context for the well known letter that Luther wrote in October 1516 to his friend Lang, now prior in Erfurt. In that letter he detailed the demands enveloping him. These had become so extensive that it was now almost impossible for him to devote any time to his spiritual life. The pressure Luther felt is evident from his opening words:

> Greetings. I nearly need two copyists or secretaries. All day long I do almost nothing else than write letters; therefore I am sometimes not aware of whether or not I constantly repeat myself. ... I am a preacher at the monastery, I am a reader during mealtimes, I am asked daily to preach in the city church, I have to supervise the study [of novices and friars], I am a vicar (and that means I am eleven times prior), I am caretaker of the fish [pond] at Leitzkau, I represent the people of Herzberg at the court in Torgau, I lecture on Paul, and I am assembling [material for] a commentary on the Psalms. ... The greater part of my time is filled with the job of letter writing. I hardly have any uninterrupted time to say the Hourly Prayers and celebrate [mass]. Besides all this there are my own struggles with the flesh, the world, and the devil. See what a lazy man I am.[17]

In the midst of these manifold obligations Luther completed his lectures on the Psalms and began a new series in spring 1515 on Paul's letter to the Romans. As he prepared these lectures, Luther struggled to understand how a Christian—indeed how

---

[16] WA Br 1, 58, 37–40; L W 48, 22.

[17] WA Br 1, 72, 4–13; L W 48, 27–28.

Luther himself—might fulfill God's expectations. How could he meet God's demand for righteousness? He had already been struggling with this question in his lectures on the Psalms, the *Dictata*. As he had pondered the Psalms, he had found a partial answer to his question in humility, which he increasingly came to see as God's work within the individual.[18] During some of Luther's worst bouts with despair, his mentor Staupitz urged him to trust in the wounds of Christ, advice that brought Luther some comfort.[19] However, none of his actions seemed to be enough. No matter how hard he worked, how much he struggled to be humble before God, to trust in Christ, and to conform to the nominalist dictum that if he would simply do his best, God would give him grace (*facere quod in se est, Deus non denegat gratiam*), he was never convinced that he had indeed done his best, and therefore he was never convinced he had done enough to gain God's grace.

Regardless of precisely when Luther's final moment of insight occurred, his lectures on Romans provided the context for a heightened struggle for reconciliation with God. In the famous passage written in 1545, a year before his death, he proclaimed:

> Though I lived as a monk without reproach, I felt that I was a sinner before God with an extremely disturbed conscience. I could not believe that he was placated by my satisfaction. I did not love, yes, I hated the righteous God who punishes sinners, and secretly, if not blasphemously, certainly murmuring greatly, I was angry with God, and said, "As if, indeed, it is not enough, that miserable sinners eternally lost through original sin, are crushed by every kind of calamity by the law of the decalogue, without having God add pain to pain by the gospel and also by the gospel threatening us with his righteousness and wrath!" Thus I raged with a fierce and troubled conscience. Nevertheless, I beat importunately

---

[18] I have discussed Luther's road to conversion, along with his developing understanding of *conversio* and other concepts in his lectures and sermons in *Luther on Conversion*.

[19] Luther noted several times his obligation to Staupitz, including *WA Br* 11, 67, 7 f.

upon Paul at that place, most ardently desiring to know what St. Paul wanted.[20]

That Luther continued to beat upon the biblical text for an answer to his anguish is of decisive importance for much that follows. It is key to understanding his theological breakthrough and his perception of how education occurs. The answer to his anguished search came through Scripture itself. Luther understood this answer not as the fruit of his own interpretation, but as the power of the Word that broke through the barrier of his interpretation. The teacher was taught by the text, a perception that would be central to Luther's concept of education.

In these lectures Luther moved away from the fourfold method of interpretation to an emphasis on the grammatical-historical. Thus, exegetical method no longer obstructed the Word in all its starkness and power from addressing him. He described his moment of understanding in these words:

> At last, by the mercy of God, meditating day and night, I gave heed to the context of the words, namely, "In it the righteousness of God is revealed, as it is written, 'He who through faith is righteous shall live.' " There I began to understand that the righteousness of God is that by which the righteous lives by a gift of God, namely by faith. And this is the meaning: the righteousness of God is revealed by the gospel, namely, the passive righteousness with which merciful God justifies us by faith, as it is written, "He who through faith is righteous shall live." Here I felt that I was altogether born again and had entered paradise itself through open gates. There a totally other face of the entire Scripture showed itself to me.[21]

In this text, written near the end of his life, Luther chose to portray his discovery as a dramatic moment of conversion, being "born again." However, his lectures and sermons from the time suggest that he experienced a process of understanding,

---

[20] W A 54, 185, 21–186, 2; L W 34, 336–37.

[21] W A 54, 186, 3–10; L W 34, 337.

with a striking moment of culmination to that process, probably in 1518, as Luther himself recounted.[22]

In the midst of his spiritual struggles, his lectures, sermons, and duties to his Order, Luther fulfilled another academic duty. He was called upon to supervise and sometimes to write the disputation theses which were an essential part of the degree process. These theses offer us another window on Luther's theology and show us the influence his theological questioning had upon his students. On September 25, 1516 Luther's student, Bartholomäus Bernhardi of Feldkirch, was called upon to prepare and defend a set of theses for the theological degree of *sententiarius*. Although Bernhardi was the author, the theses develop the same themes as in Luther's *Lectures on Romans*, challenging the nominalist assertion that a person can earn partial merit, *meritum de congruo*, by natural effort, and affirming that one is dependent upon God for righteousness.[23]

---

[22] Harran, *Luther on Conversion,* especially 151–93; Brecht argues on the basis of Luther's changed definition of righteousness that "the decisive breakthrough came in 1518." *Martin Luther: His Road to Reformation*, 229. Luther's writings of 1518–19 also demonstrate a clarity with regard to the process of conversion. In *Auslegung des 109 [110] Psalms*, Luther emphasizes the role of the Word in conversion that comes to a person's heart and awakens it. Luther asserts that unlike worldly lords, Christ does not use force to win obedience, but the power of the Word. *Luther on Conversion*, 170.

[23] Harran, *Luther on Conversion*, 146–50. See *W A* 1, 145–51, and the discussion of this disputation by Leif Grane, *Modus Loquendi Theologicus: Luthers Kampf um die Erneuerung der Theologie* (1515–1518), Acta Theologica Danica, vol. 12 (Leiden: E. J. Brill, 1975), 110–15. Grane notes that the theses are especially significant for the discussion which they opened in Wittenberg regarding Luther's theology, although we know relatively little about the shape of that discussion, 114–115. The fact that Bernhardi chose to write and defend these theses suggests that at least among some students there was already a lively discussion. Luther discussed the impact of the theses in *WA Br* 1, 65 (to Johann Lang, middle of October 1516), noting that some, in particular Luther's fellow professor Andreas Bodenstein von Carlstadt, were especially offended by his assertion that Augustine was not the writer of *De vera et falsa poenitentia* (*WA Br* 1, 65, 24–25; 29).

Although nothing compared to the storm that would arise a year later, the theses generated a few shock waves, principally among Luther's colleagues in Wittenberg, who questioned his authority on several points. Luther's distinguished senior colleague, the Thomist Andreas Bodenstein von Carlstadt, was especially incensed by his argument that Augustine was not the author of *De vera et falsa poenitentia.* Convinced that Luther was in error, Carlstadt proceeded to buy the work, read it, and set about proving him wrong. However, upon completion of his study, Carlstadt realized, much to his surprise, that his young colleague was correct. Whether he intended to do so or not, Luther was beginning to find himself the leader of a Wittenberg consortium, a group of professors and students critical of accepted authority and tradition.[24]

Luther was only thirty-two when the Bernhardi theses were debated. He had already begun to forge an independent attitude toward various authorities, from nominalism to mysticism to humanism, and to follow his own unique path that was guided above all by Scripture. That independence is perhaps what marks Luther as most unique. Others before him had rejected the easy marriage between scholasticism and humanism and proclaimed their loyalty to the men of letters against the "obscurantists." The Reuchlin affair had provided the rallying point for that battle. But Luther stood apart, even from his humanist colleagues, challenging all sources and methods with his questions, deriving in large part from his spiritual struggle to attain righteousness before God, but also from the struggles he saw going on around him, from the battle of ideas and authorities within the university to the quest within the parish to encourage true repentance rather than the easy purchase of indulgences.

Luther's independence of mind is strikingly manifested in two letters, less than a month apart, from early 1517. Both were to his friend Johann Lang, prior in Erfurt. In the first, dated

---

[24] Todd argues that already by the fall of 1516 "Luther had become the unacknowledged leader of what amounted to a campaign to change the syllabus. ... Dr. Luther, however, was not as yet seen by his colleagues as any kind of unique phenomenon, but simply as part of the *avant garde,* one of the followers of Erasmus, Reuchlin, and others who, throughout the European universities, were demanding new syllabuses in line with the 'new learning'." *Luther,* 86.

February 8, Luther told his friend of the letter he had written to his former professor and mentor Jodocus Trutfetter, a letter filled, as he phrased it, with

> serious questions regarding logic, philosophy, and theology; that is, it is full of blasphemies and revilings against Aristotle, Porphyry, the masters of the *Sentences* or, in other words against the hopeless studies which characterize our age. ... He is the most subtle seducer of gifted people, so that if Aristotle had not been flesh, I would not hesitate to claim that he was really a devil. Part of my cross, indeed its heaviest portion, is that I have to see friars born with the highest gifts for fine studies spending their lives and wasting their energies in such play-acting; in addition universities do not cease burning and condemning good books but produce, or rather dream up, bad ones.[25]

Luther's reference to the burning of good books probably refers to the attack on Reuchlin. His critique of the studies of his age resonates with that of the humanists. However, his critique focused not only upon the errors within the studies themselves, but the human cost of this misguided study. In much the same way, he would soon critique both the theology behind the indulgences and the cost to individuals who falsely placed their trust in them and who deprived themselves and their children in order to purchase them.

In the early days of reform, Luther's affiliation with the "new learning" benefited him and supplied him with energetic and committed supporters throughout Germany. Unsure of his young professor's credibility, Frederick the Wise sought the opinion of the great Erasmus about the young man who was eliciting such glowing praise and such damning criticism. While Luther identified himself enough with the movement to sign his name as the Greek "Eleutherius" in letters to his close friend, the humanistically inclined Spalatin, he soon stopped doing so.[26] More importantly, he utilized extensively humanist tools

---

[25] *WA Br* 1, 88, 5–8, 21; 89, 24–26; *L W* 48, 37–38.

[26] Most of the letters signed in this way are to Spalatin. For example, see *WA Br* 1, 118, 16 [to Spalatin, beginning of November 1517]; 134, 60 [to Spalatin, January 18, 1518]; 147, 95 [to Spalatin,

and sought to enhance his skills in Greek and Hebrew so that he could interpret directly the biblical texts. At the same time, he never thought that skill in using tools was equated with true understanding and wisdom.

In the second of the two letters to Lang, from March 1, 1517, Luther demonstrated his critical attitude toward humanism itself. He even articulated his independence toward the great Erasmus:

> I am reading our Erasmus but daily I dislike him more and more. Nevertheless it pleases me that he is constantly yet learnedly exposing and condemning the monks and priests for their deep-rooted and sleepy ignorance. ... Although I pass judgment upon him reluctantly, nevertheless I do it to warn you not to read everything, or rather, not to accept it without scrutiny, for we live in perilous times. I see that not everyone is a truly wise Christian just because he knows Greek and Hebrew.[27]

In two letters, written less than a month apart, Luther demonstrated his independence toward both of the great intellectual movements of his age, scholasticism and humanism, and established his growing originality as a thinker.

Some months earlier, in a letter to Spalatin of October 1516, written while Luther was completing his lectures on Romans, he dared to differ with Erasmus on his interpretation of Paul's understanding of righteousness. He appealed to Spalatin to convey his critique to Erasmus.[28] To those who might argue that Luther was being very brash indeed in criticizing the greatest of the northern humanists, he replied: "I do this out of concern for theology and the salvation of the brethren."[29] This dual focus, upon both theology and the salvation of individuals, was his

---

February 15, 1518]. The final letter signed in this form is to him and is dated August 28, 1518.

[27] *WA Br* 1, 90,15–17, 20–23; *L W* 48, 40.

[28] *WA Br* 1, 70–71; *L W* 48, 24–26.

[29] *WA Br* 1, 70, 41–71, 43; *L W* 48, 26.

center. It is reflected in the two key sets of theses from fall 1517, the first on scholastic theology and the second on indulgences.

Just as theological and human concerns were linked in Luther's mind, so too were his concerns about university and church. He would view the battles he would soon wage as two fronts in the same war. As Martin Brecht observes,

> Luther's theological work and teaching activity were not performed in an academic vacuum divorced from life. Education was directed to a person's entire being, including one's piety, and theological reflection took place for the sake of the church and in committed confrontation with its concrete structure.[30]

Luther's calling as doctor of theology mandated that he speak from both podium and pulpit.

In both university and church, he witnessed the same error, a desire to avoid facing God directly. Luther understood this attitude since he too knew the fear of God. Yet, ironically, this avoidance was the surest road to perdition. Both trusting in one's own efforts to gain merit and striving to become a theologian, not through knocking again and again upon the door of Scripture, but through the intricacies of logic and the appeal to Aristotle, led to failure. In both cases, the genuine questions were not asked and therefore the true answers would not be given. For, as Luther was learning, salvation comes about only by reliance upon faith and only after knowing and carrying the cross. In both church and university, people were being led astray, in the university by an emphasis on studies that were "play-acting" and in the church by a stress on indulgences that masqueraded for true repentance. In both cases, these masks—which Luther was intent on ripping off—camouflaged true Christianity and drove souls to perdition.

Luther's bold effort to confront his colleagues and students with his growing realization of the gulf separating God and man, a gulf that could not be overcome by effort or logic, took on even more urgency in the *Disputation against Scholastic*

---

[30] Brecht, *Martin Luther: His Road to Reformation*, 144. Eric Gritsch also notes the linkage between Luther's academic and ecclesiastical reforms. *Martin—God's Court Jester*, 22.

Theology of September 1517. Ironically, it was these theses, not the *95 Theses* of a month later, which Luther believed would raise a storm and would force his former professors at Erfurt to respond. Indeed, the theses—even though intended as ideas for debate—were remarkable, and there must have been one or two gasps from the assembly when young Franz Günther defended them to fulfill the requirements for the degree of *baccalaureus biblicus*. The theses apparently derived from Luther's efforts over those months to complete a commentary on Aristotle's *Physics*, a work that unfortunately has not survived. Nonetheless, the theses offer sufficient evidence of Luther's critical attitude.

Two themes within the theses are especially striking, not only in themselves but as the foundation for Luther's subsequent theological development. He already knew that human efforts to achieve salvation do not work. Therefore, he forcefully attacked the intrusion of Aristotle into theology. In theses 43 and 44 he proposed: "It is an error to say that no man can become a theologian without Aristotle. This is in opposition to common opinion. Indeed, no one can become a theologian unless he becomes one without Aristotle."[31] Likewise, the effort to do theology as a logician, to construct a "logic of faith," is a false enterprise. In short, Luther concluded thesis 50 in terms that could not be more absolute: "Briefly, the whole Aristotle is to theology as darkness is to light. This in opposition to the scholastics."[32]

Just as Aristotle impedes the pursuit of true theology, so too does reliance upon human effort impede the way to salvation and lead either to false security or despair. Self-reliance only prevents one from approaching God. Thus, drawing upon Augustine, Luther wrote: "It is false to state that the will can by nature conform to correct precept. This is said in opposition to Scotus and Gabriel. ... Man is by nature unable to want God to be God. Indeed, he himself wants to be God, and does not want God to be God."[33] Luther had now come to the crux of the

---

[31] *W A* 1, 226, 14–16; *Luther's Works,* vol. 31: *Career of the Reformer I,* ed. Harold J. Grimm (Philadelphia, Fortress Press, 1957), 12.

[32] *WA* 1, 226,26–27; *L W* 31, 12.

[33] *W A* 1, 224, 17–18; 225, 1–2; *LW* 31, 9 and 10.

problem. The theology he had been taught was intended to convince him that he needed only to follow to the best of his ability the road laid out before him, and he would succeed. God would accept his work and regard it as meritorious. Salvation would be his. But Luther knew differently. As the theses demonstrate, even if he was still unsure of what God expected from him, he knew one thing: "Hope does not grow out of merits, but out of suffering which destroys merits. This in opposition to the opinion of many" [thesis 25].[34]

By his or her own will, a person can do nothing to prepare for grace and earn salvation: "The best and infallible preparation for grace and the sole disposition toward grace is the eternal election and predestination of God" [thesis 29].[35] Yes, Luther's colleagues might have replied, but that surely doesn't mean that a person is to do nothing. Luther's response was that one could certainly pray, could humbly beseech God, while knowing that "doing all that one is able to do can[not] remove the obstacles to grace. ... In brief, man by nature has neither correct precept nor good will."[36] A person can neither know the good nor will to do it. He or she only wills to do that which pleases him or her. Deluded by the mask of sin, a person has no idea where to turn. In other words, "we are not masters of our actions, from beginning to end, but servants. This in opposition to the philosophers."[37] The only hope is the grace of God. If natural will, in contrast to what Luther had learned from Gabriel Biel, can only lead a person astray, then hope lies only in a will directed by God. Thus, Luther affirmed: "The grace of God is given for the purpose of directing the will, lest it err even in loving God. In opposition to Gabriel."[38] And what might the proof of that redirected will be? As Luther now knew,

---

[34] *W A* 1, 225, 15–16; *L W* 31, 10.

[35] *W A* 1, 225, 27–28; *LW* 31, 11.

[36] *W A* 1, 225, 35–36; *LW* 31, 11 [thesis 33]. The well-known formula of the scholastic doctors was, *Facere quod in se est deus non denegat gratiam.*

[37] *W A* 1, 226, 6–7; *L W* 31, 11 [thesis 39].

[38] *WA* 1, 228, 20–21; *L W* 31, 15 [thesis 90].

"To love God is at the same time to hate oneself and to know nothing but God."[39]

These early theses reflect beliefs that Luther would hold throughout his life, absolute dependence upon grace and the insufficiency of human effort to attain salvation. They also demonstrate his theological approach, an approach focusing on irreconcilable opposites. For Luther, the choices were clear— Aristotle or the Bible; self-love or love of God; trust in oneself or trust in God; reliance upon the treasury of merits or upon the way of the cross. Martin Brecht argues these theses represent "not the program for a new theology, but the final break with the false Aristotelian course of traditional scholasticism. ... It was a theology that was completely critical, and not yet constructive."[40] Yet, while the theses were largely negative and critical, the juxtapositions that Luther posed also constitute building blocks in his developing theology. The theses provide a basis for understanding Luther's heated conflict with Erasmus over the free or enslaved will, and his equally intense dispute after his return from the Wartburg with Andreas Carlstadt, when he argued that reform could only proceed when people truly understood why. To thrust upon them a new set of beliefs and directives was only to replace one false mask with another and to impede their progress toward God.

Hoping to keep the lines of communication open with his former teachers and friends, Luther sent the theses to Erfurt, but, to his surprise, there was no response. Nor was there any response from the distinguished humanist and former Wittenberg dean and professor Christoph Scheurl in Nuremberg. Luther had requested that Scheurl forward the theses to the theologian Johannes Eck in Ingolstadt.[41] In Wittenberg the theses were viewed as another step in the process of curricular reform and as elements of a constructive theology. Some four months before the Günther theses with their direct attack on Aristotle, Luther had written his friend Lang:

---

[39] W A 1, 228, 29; L W 31, 15 [thesis 95].

[40] Brecht, *Martin Luther: His Road to Reformation*, 173.

[41] Boehmer, *Der junge Luther*, 138.

Our theology and St. Augustine are progressing well, and with God's help rule at our University. Aristotle is gradually falling from his throne, and his final doom is only a matter of time. It is indeed amazing how the lectures on the *Sentences* are disdained. Indeed no one can expect to have any students if he does not want to teach this theology, that is, lecture on the Bible or on St. Augustine.[42]

A month before, in April, Andreas Carlstadt, now a fervent participant in the process of curricular reform, had prepared some 151 theses challenging scholastic theology. Luther was delighted that his older colleague had seen the light, and he sent a copy of the theses to Scheurl, exclaiming: "Not the paradoxes of Cicero, but of our Carlstadt, no instead, of Augustine."[43] Luther's excitement about this theology is manifested in the closing sentence of the paragraph. "Blessed be God who once again commands the light to shine from the darkness."[44] Not all aspects of this Pauline theology were clear to Luther. However, he grasped enough to know that it alone could draw people from despair to hope, from darkness to light.

We can imagine the energy and excitement that were present at the University of Wittenberg in those hopeful days of fall 1517. The theological faculty was unified, from the Scotist Amsdorf to the Thomist Carlstadt. Their ideas were permeating the other faculties as well. From Frederick's perspective, much was going well with his university, although some problems merited his attention. In September 1517 Frederick sent two representative to the university to do the modern equivalent of an accreditation report. The visit was prompted by the fact that several law professors were not fulfilling their obligations to lecture, a recurring problem in spite of the elector's admonitions.[45] As a result of that visit curricular reform along

---

[42] *WA Br* 99, 8–13; *L W* 48, 42.

[43] *WA Br* 1, 94, 17–18.

[44] *WA Br* 1, 94, 26.

[45] Walter Friedensburg, *Geschichte der Universität Wittenberg* (Halle: Verlag von Max Niemeyer, 1917), 109–110.

humanist lines received a boost. In 1518 the elector approved new lectures on Pliny and Quintilian, as well as mathematics. Perhaps most importantly, Greek and Hebrew were to be taught.[46] Recognizing the problem of underprepared students, a *paedagogium* was established, with instruction in Latin, Greek, and Hebrew.[47] For a time two masters in the arts faculty were assigned to oversee the students, but this was reduced to one in the 1536 statutes, perhaps reflecting the admission of better prepared students.

The student response to the humanist curriculum was enthusiastic. They crowded into the lectures that focused upon classical texts and the Bible and avoided those on Aristotle and the *Sentences*. As with most curricular reforms, however, not everything was entirely coordinated, and Luther informed Spalatin in September 1518 that it was unfortunate that students were still obliged to take the old, required courses and to pass examinations in areas that were no longer seen as vital parts of the curriculum. He complained,

> This is the problem: since now by God's grace the best lectures flourish and the students are astonishingly eager for Scripture and unadulterated theology, it seems hard to them to have to neglect the best courses because of other courses required for graduation, or at least to have to carry a load that is far too heavy and composed of both kinds of courses.[48]

Effecting change meant creating faculty consensus, no small accomplishment as anyone who has sought to bring changes in general education knows! Significant changes also required the elector's approval, especially since they usually involved more expense. The key person in this regard was Spalatin with whom Luther engaged in an increasingly active correspondence.

---

[46] Friedensburg, *Geschichte der Universität Wittenberg*, 112; Brecht, *Martin Luther: His Road to Reformation*, 275–282; Friedrich Paulsen, *Geschichte des gelehrten Unterrichts*, vol. I (Leipzig: Verlag von Veit & Comp., 1919), 117.

[47] Friedensburg, *Geschichte der Universität Wittenberg*, 114.

[48] *WA Br* 1, 196, 22–26; *LW* 48, 82.

It was in the midst of this lively curricular reform, a month after the Theses against Scholastic Theology, that Luther turned his attention another matter that deeply concerned him. This concern arose from his duties as preacher at the City Church. It was but another aspect of the problem he had addressed in his earlier theses, namely a false trust in human effort to prepare the way for salvation. In this instance, the problem was very practical. As Luther preached a life of repentance and the cross from the pulpit of the City Church, he found seated before him parishioners who much preferred the less troublesome method of purchasing indulgences. Frederick the Wise had forbidden the sale of the new papal indulgence within his lands, not of course because he opposed indulgences—Frederick was no theologian—but because he was well aware that the new sale offered competition to his own relic collection and the salvific benefits it provided. Guided solely by pastoral concern, Luther had no idea of the politics behind the indulgence as he formulated theses for debate. He seems honestly to have believed that if the abuses in the sale of indulgences, the promotion of them at the expense of the true preaching of the gospel, were called to the attention of the appropriate ecclesiastical authorities, principally bishop Jerome and archbishop Albrecht of Mainz, then the matter would be corrected.

There was a great deal he did not know, as he recalled in the *1545 Preface to the Complete Latin Writings* when he professed:

> Hence, when in the year 1517, indulgences were sold ... in these regions for most shameful gain—I was then a preacher, a young doctor of theology, so to speak—and I began to dissuade the people and to urge them not to listen to the clamors of the indulgence hawkers; they had better things to do. I certainly thought that in this case I should have a protector in the pope, on whose trustworthiness I then leaned strongly. ... Soon afterward I wrote two letters, one to Albrecht, the archbishop of Mainz who got half of the money from the indulgences, the pope the other half—something I did not know at the time—the other to ... Jerome, the bishop of Brandenburg. I begged them to stop the shameless blasphemy of the quaestors. ... I developed the idea that indulgences

should indeed not be condemned, but that good works of love should be preferred to them.[49]

For Luther the theses, although intended as topics for debate, stated what he now understood to be the foundation of Christian life. How could anyone disagree with such statements as these: "When our Lord and Master Jesus Christ said 'Repent' [Matt. 4:17], he willed the entire life of believers to be one of repentance" or "Those who believe that they can be certain of their salvation because they have indulgence letters will be eternally damned, together with their teachers"?[50]

Little did Luther know what "heresy" he would be accused of unleashing when he affirmed, "The true treasure of the church is the most holy gospel of the glory and grace of God," not the treasury of indulgences.[51] In closing he railed against those who misled Christians into a life of secure comfort when their very salvation was at stake. Thus, he proclaimed:

> Away then with all those prophets who say to the people of Christ, "Peace, peace," and there is no peace! [Jer. 6:14]. Blessed be all those prophets who say to the people of Christ, "Cross, cross," and there is no cross! Christians should be exhorted to be diligent in following Christ, their head, through penalties, death, and hell; and thus be confident of entering into heaven through many tribulations rather than through the false security of peace [Acts 14:22].[52]

Brecht posits that at the time Luther formulated the *95 Theses* he was not yet "'evangelical."[53] He did not yet articulate the concept of justification by faith. However, he unmistakenly

---

[49] *WA* 54, 180, 5–16; 19–29; *L W* 34, 329–30.

[50] *WA* 1, 233, 10–11; *L W* 31, 25; *W A* 1, 234, 39–40; *L W* 31, 28 [theses 1 and 32].

[51] *WA* 1, 236, 22–23; *LW* 31, 31 [thesis 62].

[52] *W A* 1, 238, 14–21; *LW* 31, 33 [theses 92–95].

[53] Brecht, *Martin Luther: His Road to Reformation,* 221.

conveyed that the true treasure of the church is the Gospel and that nothing must obstruct the preaching of the Word of God. Although there are still hints of a theology of humility, exemplified by the struggle to live according to the cross, there is also recognition that salvation lies with God, not with human effort or papal dispensation. The theses reflect Luther's profound concern regarding the practical effects of the indulgences upon his congregation. Not only was the Word of God displaced in favor of indulgence sermons, but Christians were neglecting those in need. Indeed they deprived their families so they could purchase an indulgence. They chose to place their trust in indulgences rather than in the Gospel. Yet, ironically, "papal indulgences are useful only if they do not put their trust in them, but very harmful if they lose their fear of God because of them."[54]

Luther's letter to the archbishop was no less direct than the theses themselves. It too stressed his pastoral concern. He wrote:

> I bewail the gross misunderstanding among the people which comes from these preachers and which they spread everywhere among common men. Evidently the poor souls believe that when they have bought indulgence letters they are assured of their salvation. They are likewise convinced that souls escape from purgatory as soon as they have placed a contribution into the chest. ... O great God! The souls committed to your care, excellent Father, are thus directed to death.[55]

Little did Luther then know how naive he was in his belief that the indulgence promotion was an aberration. It in fact represented papal financial policy.

In earlier hagiographic works about Luther, the posting of the *95 Theses* was portrayed as a dramatic event, with the young, slightly haggard, young professor striding across the courtyard to hammer his theses upon the door of the church.[56]

---

[54] *W A* 1, 234, 34–35; *L W* 31, 29–30 [thesis 49].

[55] *WA Br* 1, 111, 17–21, 24–25; *L W* 48, 46.

[56] There has even been scholarly debate regarding whether or not Luther posted the theses for debate. See Erwin Iserloh, *The Theses*

In fact, the posting was anything but dramatic. Placing notices and topics for debate upon the door of the Castle Church was routine (much like a college bulletin board). The theses attracted so little attention among the students that there was in fact no debate. If Luther had been surprised at the lack of response to the *Theses against Scholastic Theology,* he was astounded when he learned that the copy of the new theses he had sent to his acquaintance Scheurl in Nuremberg had been hastily reprinted, with numbers added for the convenience of the reader.[57] Luther had expected a response to the theses of a month earlier, and he had even anticipated a lively debate and exchange of letters, but he had in no way anticipated what the *95 Theses* elicited.

If the students had initially been slow to respond to the invitation to debate, their interest increased rapidly when they learned of the attention the theses were gaining elsewhere in Germany. Luther had the full support of his colleagues. He was even allowed to draft the letter in his defense to the elector, which was then signed by the faculty.[58] Like Luther, the faculty regarded the theses as another round in the university reforms in which they were engaged. Their young colleague was simply applying his understanding of the biblical text to a practical pastoral problem. The gospels and the letters of Paul spoke of repentance and acts of love, not of indulgences.

Although there was strong support for Luther within the university, he had reason to be concerned about the theses' effect on relations between Saxony and Mainz. What Luther had not realized was the political dimension of the issue. In a letter to Spalatin largely devoted to answering his questions about the value of dialectic, he offered heartfelt remarks about the potential for conflict between the elector of Brandenburg and Frederick the Wise:

> I am not distressed ... that [my enemies] are speaking so badly of me, or that they stamp our Elector as the author of my theses. I fear only that this affair might create

---

Were Not Posted: Luther Between Reform and Reformation (Boston: Beacon Press, 1968).

[57] Todd, *Luther,* 110.

[58] Schwiebert, *Luther and His Times,* 302.

hostility between our great rulers, should perhaps the
Sovereign of Brandenburg, out of vengeance, permit
something similar to happen as we have recently heard
about *Schenke*.[59]

While Luther's exact reference is unknown, his intention is clear
enough. He regretted that his theses (in which he obviously had
no pride of authorship!) might lead to conflict between the
political authorities. At the same time, he expressed no desire
to retract the theses. Nor would he do so in the ensuing days
when the Dominicans, at the instigation of the indulgence
preacher Johann Tetzel, pressured the papal court to have
Luther tried as a heretic. In those intervening months between
the printing of the theses and the call for a trial in Rome, he had
much more important issues on his mind.

His life continued to be occupied with the university and the
Order. In April 1518 he attended the chapter meeting of the
Augustinians in Heidelberg. As the district vicar concluding his
term in office, it would have been unthinkable for him not to be
there. Unlike earlier meetings he had attended as a promising
but largely unknown young friar, this time he was given official
letters of introduction by Frederick the Wise to protect him on
his journey.

Luther's mentor and superior, Johann von Staupitz, went
out of his way to give him a chance to present himself and his
ideas, inviting him to draw up and present theses which his
student Leonard Beier defended. Such a presentation of theses
was a normal part of the proceedings at the chapter meetings.
One monk was selected beforehand to present theses that
represented Augustine's theology in whose honor the Order was
named.[60] If there was an expectation that Luther would speak
about indulgences, his listeners were disappointed. Not
surprisingly, however, he sounded many of the same notes that
he had in the earlier theses concerning scholastic theology.

James Kittelson suggests that at this time in "late April 1518
… Luther had made no connection between the day-to-day
practice of ordinary Christians and the theology he had been

---

[59] *WA Br* 1, 149, 4–9; *LW* 48, 56 [February 22, 1518].

[60] Kittelson, *Luther the Reformer*, 110.

developing while lecturing to his students."[61] Although that connection may not be explicit in the Heidelberg theses, it is certainly implicit. Composed of two parts, theological and philosophical, the theological theses stressed the juxtaposition between the works of man and those of God. Luther had critiqued indulgences precisely because people placed their reliance upon them and found them more attractive than the works of love to which Christians are called. He wrote: "Although the works of man always seem attractive and good, they are nevertheless likely to be mortal sins. Although the works of God always seem unattractive and appear evil, they are nevertheless really eternal merits" [theses 3 and 4].[62] He challenged the Nominalist stress on human effort preparatory to grace, proclaiming:

> The person who believes that he can obtain grace by doing what is in him adds sin to sin so that he becomes doubly guilty. ... It is certain that man must utterly despair of his own ability before he is prepared to receive the grace of God [theses 16 and 18].[63]

Indulgences were but another example of the misguided effort to earn grace.

In his philosophical theses Luther limited the reliance upon human works in another way, by placing severe restrictions upon the use of Aristotle. He stated: "He who wishes to philosophize by using Aristotle without danger to his soul must first become thoroughly foolish in Christ" [thesis 29].[64] Just as one can only purchase indulgences without danger when one does not rely on them, so can one utilize Aristotle wisely only when one knows Christ.

With the benefit of hindsight, we can see both how far Luther had come in his theological development and how far he had yet to go. While the Heidelberg theses contain themes that

---

[61] Kittelson, *Luther the Reformer*, 113.

[62] *W A* 1, 353, 19–22; *LW* 31, 39.

[63] *WA* 1, 354, 11–12; *LW* 31, 40.

[64] *W A* 1, 355, 2–3; *L W* 31, 41.

will be constants in the reformer's theology, such as the difference between the works of God and man, and the distinction between the genuine theologian who speaks of suffering and the cross and the false theologian of glory [theses 19 and 20], other central points, including justification by faith, are not yet explicitly formulated. The theses continue to emphasize humility as preparation for grace, even though it is insufficient to bring about righteousness.[65] In the proof to thesis 16 he noted:

"Through the law comes knowledge of sin" [Rom. 3:20], through knowledge of sin, however, comes humility, and through humility grace is acquired. Thus an action which is alien to God's nature results in a deed belonging to his very nature: he makes a person a sinner so that he may make him righteous.[66]

Luther wrote to Spalatin a few weeks after returning to Wittenberg that he had utilized the trip home from Heidelberg to try to mend fences with those in Erfurt. His efforts had proven fruitless, at least as far as Trutfetter was concerned. He lamented,

My theology is like rotten food to the people from Erfurt. Especially the Doctor from Eisenach has condemned all my statements; he has written me a letter in which he has accused me of being an ignoramus in dialectic, not to speak of theology. ... Nevertheless I did have a face-to-face conference with the Doctor from Eisenach. ... But it is vain to tell a story to someone who is deaf. ... I worked harder with Doctor Usingen than with anyone else in

---

[65] On the concept of humility, see Reinhard Schwarz, *Vorgeschichte der reformatorischen Busstheologie,* Arbeiten zur Kirchenge-schichte, vol. 41 (Berlin: Walter de Gruyter, 1968) and Rudolf Damerau, *Die Demut in der Theologie Luthers,* Studien zu der Grundlagen der Reformation, vol. 5 (Giessen: Wilhelm Schmitz), 1963.

[66] *WA* 1, 361, 2–5; *LW* 31, 51. For a discussion of Luther's understanding of the alien and appropriate works of God, see Harran, *Luther on Conversion,* especially 155–57.

order to persuade him (for he was my traveling companion in the wagon). But I don't know if I accomplished anything. I left him pensive and wondering. How terrible, to grow old in false suppositions![67]

The letter demonstrates his genuine sympathy and concern for his former professor, Arnoldi von Usingen, who was struggling to understand something that seemed so difficult to him and so obvious to Luther. Luther also perceived the growing generational divide:

On the other hand the thinking of the young men—in fact, of all youth—differs by two whole octaves from the old. I have great hope that as Christ went over to the Gentiles when he was rejected by the Jews, so now too his true theology (which these opinionated old men reject) may pass over to the younger generation.[68]

Luther had reason to be pleased with his reception among the young. Enrollments at the University of Wittenberg were on the rise, due to the reformed curriculum and his growing reputation. He had been received very positively in Heidelberg by the younger members of his own Order, and men like the Dominican Martin Bucer.[69] Bucer wrote immediately after the meeting to his friend and fellow humanist Beatus Rhenanus in Basel. He conveyed his very favorable impression of Luther:

I will oppose to you a certain theologian ... who has been heard by us in the last few days, one who has got so far way from the bonds of the sophists and the trifling of Aristotle, one who is so devoted to the Bible, and is so suspicious of antiquated theologians of our school ... that he appears to be diametrically opposed to our teachers. ... He agrees with Erasmus in all things, but with this

---

[67] WA Br 1, 173, 29–35, 40–174, 42; L W 48, 61–63.

[68] WA Br 1, 174, 44—7; L W 48, 63.

[69] Reinhard Schwarz reports that in these years Wittenberg was the most vital of the German universities. A town of 2500 now had to find ways of coping with a student body of 600. *Luther*, 56.

difference in his favor, that what Erasmus only insinuates he teaches openly and freely. ... He has brought it about that at Wittenberg the ordinary textbooks have all been abolished, while the Greeks and Jerome, Augustine and Paul, are publicly taught.[70]

Yet, if his reception by the young filled him with hope, he must have felt an intense sadness as he realized that reconciliation with his Erfurt mentors seemed increasingly unlikely. An event that occurred a few weeks before his journey to Heidelberg may also have given him cause to reflect on the unpredictability of the young.

Luther's Wittenberg colleagues and those with whom he corresponded understood the theological reasons for his critique of indulgences. Others judged him to be representing the humanist cause. Still others, less well informed, viewed the matter as merely another squabble between mendicants, in this case between the Augustinians, represented by Luther, and the Dominicans, represented by the indulgence seller, Johann Tetzel. Such an interpretation was given further credence by the Dominicans' immediate intercession on behalf of their besieged colleague.

In January 1518 at the chapter meeting of the Dominicans in Frankfurt an der Oder, Tetzel was made a doctor of theology. As at Luther's doctoral ceremony, Tetzel was called upon to participate in a disputation. In this case, the theses were formulated in direct opposition to Luther's 95 Theses by the Leipzig theologian Konrad Wimpina, who had his own reasons for disliking anyone representing the University of Wittenberg.[71] That might have ended the matter. The Dominicans' representative, Tetzel, was now on an academic par with his Augustinian critic. However, Tetzel decided to have the theses printed and distributed for sale in Wittenberg. Without Luther's knowledge, students threatened the bookseller and burned the

---

[70] Cited in Schwiebert, *Luther and His Times,* 328–29.

[71] Schwiebert, *Luther and His Times,* 323. See Grossmann, *Humanism in Wittenberg,* on Wimpina's earlier attack on Wittenberg, rooted in his antagonism toward humanism and Martin Polich von Mellerstadt, the first rector of the University of Wittenberg, 43–44.

copies in the marketplace. In a letter to his friend Lang, Luther described what occurred:

> Then some students bought copies of the *Theses*, and some simply seized them, and, having given notice to all who wished to be present at the spectacle to come to the market place by two o'clock, they burned them without the knowledge of the Elector, the town council, or the rector of the university, or of any of us. Certainly we were all displeased by this grave injury done to the man [who brought the theses] by our students. I am not guilty, but I fear the whole thing will be imputed to me.[72]

Luther was understandably concerned about Frederick's reaction to such lawlessness. He also recognized that such a fervent student response could result in unpredictable and potentially violent activities.[73] Such upheaval could place in jeopardy all that he and his colleagues were building.

In spite of the excitement caused by the theses and by his journey to Heidelberg, Luther never lost sight of his goals for the University. His first letter to Spalatin after Heidelberg was the occasion for yet another plea on behalf of the University: "Finally I hope and ask of you not to forget our University; that is, that you be concerned for the establishment of a chair in Greek and a chair in Hebrew."[74] His request may be read as reflecting his allegiance to humanism and its emphasis on the classical languages. By now, however, Luther had an even more

---

[72] Preserved Smith and C.M. Jacobs, ed., *Luther's Correspondence and Other Contemporary Letters*, vol. 1 (Philadelphia, 1913), 75. Cited in Schwiebert, *Luther and His Times*, 324; *WA Br* 1, 155, 31–36. The *WA* editor indicates in his introduction that the theses were burned by Erfurt students, but the text of the letter does not so indicate.

[73] Schwiebert suggests: "There is good reason to believe that Luther was not as displeased as he inferred about the student action." *Luther and His Times*, 324. Given Luther's fear of tumult and association of it with the devil, I would argue that his words should be taken at face value.

[74] *WA Br* 1, 174, 48–49; *LW* 48, 63.

pressing reason. This reason stemmed from his awareness of the radical divergence between the man-made theology of his time and the theology of the Bible. Education in the fullest sense could only occur when the young men he was teaching were able to read and interpret the biblical words for themselves. As Luther pondered his growing distance from his own mentors, he realized that his students too must have the tools to proclaim their independence. Yet, if Luther was both insistent and optimistic that Spalatin would answer his pleas, his colleagues were much less so. Nonetheless, they were soon to be surprised as the elector demonstrated his commitment to the University by once again loosening his purse strings to fulfill their request.

In spring 1518 as Luther prepared his response to the attack on his *95 Theses*, the *Resolutions Concerning the 95 Theses;* wrote his lectures on the letter to the Hebrews, and fulfilled his regular responsibility of preaching at the City Church, he remained focused on curricular reform. It was a time for celebration. Within the arts faculty, the lectures on Aristotle were now to be presented on the basis of the best available texts in translation. Luther's former student, Bartholomäus Bernhardi of Feldkirch, was given the assignment of lecturing in this new manner upon both the *Physics* and *Metaphysics* of Aristotle. As Friedensburg observes, the trend was to put the schools and their way of lecturing more and more into the background.[75] The liberal arts could now be taught in such a way that young men were adequately prepared for theological study.

The elector's decision to hire professors in Greek and Hebrew excited the faculty with hopes of bringing the University into the first rung of humanistic institutions. Naturally, they wanted the elector to recruit the most distinguished candidates possible. In Hebrew, to begin teaching already in the winter semester of 1517-1518, Aesticampianus, Johannes Rhagius, a distinguished scholar already advanced in years, was selected. Unfortunately, he soon became so caught up in the spirit of the University reform that he tried to avoid his primary teaching assignments in order to lecture on Jerome and Augustine, displeasing both Luther and Spalatin.[76]

---

[75] Friedensburg, *Geschichte der Universität Wittenberg,* 112.

[76] Friedensburg, *Geschichte der Universität Wittenberg,* 113–14; Brecht, *Luther: His Road to Reformation,* 276.

The appointment of a Greek scholar was far more fortuitous. Rarely has any search yielded a more superb candidate. Ironically, he was not the candidate whom Luther initially preferred, Petrus Mosellanus of Leipzig. Philipp Melanchthon, the grandnephew of the distinguished Hebraist Johannes Reuchlin of Tübingen, was only twenty-one when he was appointed as professor of Greek. We do not know if Melanchthon considered the position at a still young and undistinguished institution as a mere stepping stone to a more renowned university. He proved, however, to be as loyal to Wittenberg as Luther, and he became Luther's most faithful and effective colleague.

Luther was won over by Melanchthon as soon as he presented his inaugural lecture on August 29, 1518. His enthusiasm for his young colleague is evident in his letter to Spalatin:

> Four days after he had arrived, he delivered an extremely learned and absolutely faultless address. All esteemed and admired him greatly, so you need not worry on what grounds you should recommend him to us. We very quickly turned our minds and eyes from his appearance and person to the man himself. We congratulate ourselves on having this man and marvel at what he has in him.[77]

Indeed, Luther was so convinced that they had the ideal person that he proclaimed: "I certainly do not wish to have a different Greek instructor as long as he is alive."[78] His only concern was that Melanchthon's constitution might not be up to his many responsibilities. He also worried that he might be wooed away by another university that could offer a more generous salary. Even though he had known Melanchthon only a few days, he pleaded with Spalatin to make certain that the elector treated him as generously as possible:

> Therefore, my dear Spalatin, to speak freely, as with my dearest friend, see to it that you people [at the court] do

---

[77]WA BR 1, 192, 12–16; L W 48, 78.

[78]WA Br 1, 192, 18–19; LW 48, 78.

not undervalue Melanchthon because of his person or age. This man is worthy of every honor. I do not want us and our University to expose ourselves as country-bumpkins, from which our enemies could make such a splendid story at our expense.[79]

Luther's worries were not without foundation, since Ingolstadt, where Reuchlin had received a position, soon sought to recruit Melanchthon to their faculty. Attractive as the idea must have been to Melanchthon to be once again by the side of his distinguished relative and mentor, he chose to remain in Wittenberg. Although his own desires might lead him to Ingolstadt, God's will had called him to Wittenberg.[80]

Melanchthon proved immediately to be an extraordinarily popular professor. In early December 1520, Spalatin could report to the elector that he had attended Melanchthon's lecture the day before, along with between five and six hundred students.[81] Luther's lectures in the higher faculty of theology also continued to draw a great number of listeners, nearly four hundred, according to Spalatin, including the rector, the canon at Altenburg and other distinguished people.[82]

Melanchthon's influence soon extended beyond the arts faculty. While Luther provided the impetus for reform and focused his attention primarily on the theological curriculum, Melanchthon linked those reforms to ones in the liberal arts. As Benrath describes, Melanchthon and Luther began from two different points, the one "below" from the arts faculty and the other "above" from the higher faculty of theology, with the two reform plans then joining and reinforcing one another.[83] With

---

[79] WA Br 1, 26–30; L W 48, 79.

[80] Friedensburg, *Geschichte der Universität Wittenberg*, 121.

[81] Walter Friedensburg, *Urkundenbuch der Universität Wittenberg, Teil 1: 1502–1611*. Geschichtsquellen der Provinz Sachsen und des Freistaates Anhalt, Bd. 3 (Magdeburg: Selbstverlag der Historischen Kommission, 1926), 109.

[82] Friedensburg, *Urkundenbuch der Universität Wittenberg*, 109.

[83] Gustav Adolf Benrath, "Die deutsche evangelische Universität der Reformationszeit," in Hellmuth Rössler und Günther Franz, ed.,

Greek as the center of Melanchthon's teaching, he lectured widely, from Homer to Paul's letter to Titus.[84] He received the degree of *baccalaureus biblicus* in 1519, and from that time on his lectures covered biblical texts, as well as classical ones.[85] When necessary, following the death of Aesticampianus, he even taught Hebrew.[86] Luther's initial concern that Melanchthon would be asked to do too much was well-founded.

Melanchthon's growing reputation as an extraordinary teacher, Luther's renown, and the new, explicitly humanist curriculum, generated increased enrollments for the University. Frederick must have been convinced that his money was being well spent. From the year beginning Easter 1517 through Easter of the following year, some 242 new students matriculated at the University, and over the next three years the numbers increased to 274, 459, and 579.[87]

This positive turn of events brought with it new problems, as both students and professors struggled to find housing. Prices rose with the increased demand.[88] As a result, tensions between town and gown heightened. Luther and other faculty leaders sought to control student conduct, prohibit rowdiness, and further an environment conducive to serious study, but they were not always successful. Dress codes and the all important prohibition on the carrying of weapons were sometimes observed in the breach. Somewhat later, in 1520 Luther himself came into conflict with students over their violation of the

---

Universität und Gelehrtenstand 1400-1800, vol. 4 in Deutsche Führungsgeschichten in der Neuzeit (Limburg/Lahn: C.A. Starke Verlag, 1970), 70. Friedensburg, *Geschichte der Universität Wittenberg,* 181; Karl Hartfelder, *Philipp Melanchthon als Praeceptor Germaniae* (Nieuwkoop: B. de Graaf [reprint 1889 edition], 441.

[84] Friedensburg, *Geschichte der Universität Wittenberg,* 119.

[85] Friedensburg, *Geschichte der Universität Wittenberg,* 119-20.

[86] Friedensburg, *Geschichte der Universität Wittenberg,* 125.

[87] Friedensburg, *Geschichte der Universität Wittenberg,* 147.

[88] Friedensburg, *Geschichte der Universität Wittenberg,* 150.

elector's command concerning weapons.[89] He ascribed their disobedience to the work of the devil, who sought through this means to bring the Word now being openly proclaimed into disrepute. However much admired Luther was by the students, he never played up to them, and they, in turn, could be quite vocal—and almost violent—in their criticism of him.

In addition to conflicts between town and gown, there were disputes among students. From its beginnings, Wittenberg had avoided the division into geographical "nations" typical at some other universities, but that did not mean that matriculation erased long standing animosities among students from different areas with different customs. Nor did students in the different faculties always get along, and the new building that Frederick planned was in part intended as a way of separating arts from law students.[90] However, the building did not go according to plan and for a time remained only partially completed, due to a lack of financial resources on the part of both elector and university. Demands on Frederick's purse increased in other areas as well. New courses required new books for the library. In the midst of these challenges, he could not help but be concerned about the storm of ecclesiastical censure that was developing around his star professor. What would this mean for his university?

The specific events that transpired during those years between the publishing of the 95 Theses and Luther's condemnation by the Diet of Worms are well known. Had it not been for Frederick's unswerving support, there is little doubt that Luther would have followed in the footsteps of Jan Hus and died as a heretic, burned at the stake. Luther certainly recognized the pressure that was being brought to bear on the elector. He was willing to do whatever the elector willed of him. In November of 1518, he wrote Spalatin:

> I daily expect the condemnation from the city of Rome; therefore I am setting things in order and arranging everything so that if it comes I am prepared and girded

---

[89] WA Br 2, 142–43; L W 48, 167–69. See also Brecht, Martin Luther: His Road to Reformation, 295.

[90] Friedensburg, Geschichte der Universität Wittenberg, 149.

to go, as Abraham, not knowing where, yet most sure of my way, because God is everywhere.[91]

In those ensuing months, in addition to his normal lectures and sermons, and an increasingly heavy correspondence, Luther sought to explain his critique of the indulgences and the theology behind them. By the end of 1518, he had published his *Explanations to the 95 Theses*, had responded to the Dominican theologian Sylvester Prieras' *Dialogus*, and had met with the papal legate, Cardinal Cajetan, at the Diet of Augsburg. This meeting left him uncertain of his future. He was convinced both that it was quite likely bleak and that it was in God's hands. Meanwhile, he continued to dedicate himself to educational reform.

In December 1518 Luther wrote Spalatin a letter devoted entirely to his thoughts about curricular reform. He recommended that various courses be eliminated, including one on Thomas Aquinas' commentary to Aristotle's *Physics*, and he looked forward to

such time as the Chair of the Scotistic Sect—that equally useless and unfruitful occupation of gifted men—is also abolished. In this way the subtle hair-splitting finally may perish altogether, and genuine philosophy, theology, and all the arts may be drawn from their true sources.[92]

His focus on the university curriculum continued in the days following his meetings with Karl von Miltitz and during the strange period after the death of Emperor Maximilian when Pope Leo X appealed to Frederick for support in opposing the election of Maximilian's grandson, Charles I, as emperor. In a letter of February 7, 1519 Luther pleaded again for permission to eliminate "those courses by which precious hours are wasted and ... the substitution of better ones, especially a course on Ovid's *Metamorphoses*."[93] In the context of discussing the proposed debate at Leipzig between Johannes Eck and

---

[91] *WA Br* 1, 253, 8–11; *LW* 48, 94.

[92] *WA Br* 1, 262, 10–13; *L W* 48, 96.

[93] *WA Br* 1, 325, 5–7; *L W* 48, 107.

Carlstadt, Luther pleaded once again for a raise for the deserving Melanchthon.

Knowing what momentous events were unfolding, we may find it hard to believe that in those days Luther continued to be so concerned with curricular reform. Even in the midst of responding to the critics, Luther continued his focus on the well-being of the University. In early March 1519, he voiced his concern that Melanchthon was being overloaded with courses, including those on Aristotle's *Physics* that were unworthy of his intellect and that should be stricken from the curriculum.[94] In November, he recommended a potential candidate for the position in Hebrew to the elector, and in March of 1520 he urged Spalatin to expedite matters.[95]

Luther's students tell us that in the midst of the turmoil and tumult revolving around the *causa Lutheri*, he remained a devoted and effective teacher. Luther's rejection of the fourfold method of interpretation in favor of a more straightforward grammatical-historical one that no longer divided the exposition into glosses and scholia also enhanced the clarity and effectiveness of his lectures.[96] One of his students, Georg Benedict, who attended lectures at Wittenberg from 1518-23, recorded this impression of him:

> He was a man of middle stature, with a voice which combined sharpness and softness; it was soft in tone, sharp in the enunciation of syllables, words and sentences. He spoke neither too quickly nor too slowly, but at an even pace, without hesitation, and very clearly, and in such fitting order that each part flowed naturally out of what went before. He did not expound each part in long labyrinths of words, but first the individual words, then the sentences, so that one could see how the content of the exposition arose, and flowed out of the text itself. ... He had his lecture material always ready to

---

[94] *WA Br* 1, 359–60; *L W* 48, 112.

[95] *WA Br* 1, 551 and *WA Br* 2, 72; *LW* 48, 132 and 154.

[96] Brecht, *Martin Luther: His Road to Reformation*, 286–291; Gerhard Ebeling, *Luther: An Introduction to His Thought*, trans. R.A. Wilson (Philadelphia: Fortress Press, 1972), 51.

hand, conclusions, digressions, moral philosophy and also antitheses: and so his lectures never contained anything that was not pithy and relevant.[97]

Luther's commitment to his vocation as professor demonstrates his trust in God, his affirmation of his vocation, and his recognition of the value of education. No more young men should be led astray and deprived of true learning.

Meanwhile events were taking Luther down a path that would cause him for a time to be absent from his beloved university. The Leipzig Debate with Eck in late June and early July of 1519 made Luther aware of precisely how far he had come. In the course of the debate and much to his own surprise, he admitted that on several matters he sided with the condemned heretic Jan Hus. Not only had Luther condemned indulgences and the false spiritual security to which they led, but he had come to look anew at the sacraments. With the Bible as his touchstone, he found evidence for only three sacraments, not seven. He argued that these three had in large part been perverted by the Romanists. Whether Luther knew it or not, he had come to the parting of the ways with the church of his time, and although he would always see himself as the true Catholic with the hierarchy of the church as the heretics, those in power would see matters differently.

By the end of 1520 many of the reforms that Luther had sought for the University had been accomplished, although reform of both curriculum and University statutes would continue over the next decades. Many of the lectures that Luther believed had wasted his own time and those of so many others had been abolished. They had been replaced by ones that focused upon the classical and biblical texts. The curriculum now stressed the learning of languages, and there were new courses in such areas as mathematics and history. Many students had been drawn to the new curriculum in both the arts and theology. However, as it became increasingly clear that Luther would sooner or later be condemned, rulers grew concerned about permitting their young men to study at a place

---

[97] *W A* 57, lxxvi. Cited in Gordon Rupp, *Luther's Progress to the Diet of Worms* (New York: Harper & Row, 1964), 44. See Brecht, *Martin Luther: His Road to Reformation*, 297, and Harran, *Luther and Learning*, 42–46; Boehmer, *Der junge Luther*, 366.

regarded at least by some as a cradle of heresy. Although the enrollments increased until the Diet of Worms in 1521 at which Luther was condemned, they declined significantly thereafter, when it was unknown if Luther was living or dead, or if alive, if he would ever be able to return to his university.[98]

Luther's scholarly work brought him to center stage in Germany, and with him his University. His discoveries came as he prepared his courses; as he reflected upon the University curriculum and realized that it not only wasted students' time, but, more importantly, that it had both the wrong subjects and the wrong methods at its core. His critique of scholastic theology and of the false attitude and actions it caused was driven by the twofold concern he articulated in a letter of October 1516: "I do this out of concern for theology and the salvation of the brethren."[99] With the gradual support of colleagues like Amsdorf and Carlstadt and with the tremendous boost brought by the young, brilliant and energetic Philipp Melanchthon, the reform of the University, both in the arts and in theology, made significant progress.

Luther, who had done so much to further curricular reform, especially within the theology curriculum, found curricular abuses paralleled by ecclesiastical ones. The *Disputation against Scholastic Theology* and the *95 Theses* were two sides of the same coin. Formulated in 1517 by a young professor seeking his own salvation, the theses had become transformed by 1520 into a call for a reform that would go beyond university and parish to encompass all aspects of society. What began in the pulpit and podium of a small university town on the edge of civilization would now encompass all of Germany. Luther was about to become teacher to the nation.

---

[98] Friedensburg reports that from 1516–25 the University had 3,500 matriculations, but over the next decade only 400. *Geschichte der Universität Wittenberg*, 242.

[99] *WA Br* 1, 70, 41–71, 43; *L W* 48, 26.

5

Martin Luther
"Docendi sunt christiani"

In the last chapter we traced Martin Luther's journey from student to professor. From his university podium he was now called to a much larger stage. His role would be that of teacher to the nation. The words he had proclaimed in the *95 Theses*, "docendi sunt christiani"—"Christians are to be taught"— became his charge. He never lost sight of the absurdity and "foolishness" of a lowly monk taking on such awesome duties. At the same time, as a doctor of Holy Scripture he had been called by God to this role.[1]

In this chapter we will look more closely at Luther's ideas on education as expressed in several works from the decade 1520–30. Many questions confronted him: Who should be educated and in which subjects? What constituted a genuine Christian education? What should the schools accomplish? What should the universities? With support from his young colleague Philipp Melanchthon, Luther answered these questions. Indeed, in several instances, Melanchthon took the lead, earning the title of *praeceptor Germaniae*. In a later chapter we will examine the implementation of their educational ideas, along with their successes and failures.

In the response to his *95 Theses* and subsequent writings, Luther discovered that many people, from princes to peasants, agreed with his critique of the church. However, there was far less agreement on how the situation should be altered, and even less willingness to take on the slow and difficult process of

---

[1] *WA* 6, 404, 31--05, 3; *Luther's Works*, vol. 44: *The Christian in Society* I, ed. by James Atkinson (Philadelphia: Fortress Press, 1966), 124. Eric Gritsch recognizes the significance of the role of fool and court jester in Luther's concept of vocation in *Martin—God 's Court Jester*.

creating new structures and practices. Indeed, even more disturbing, some used the confusion to their own advantage. Meanwhile the papacy and higher clergy demonstrated themselves unwilling to engage in reform. Destroying the old was far easier than building the new—or reaching consensus on what the new should be. This was also true in education. And, Luther knew, no task was more crucial to both secular and spiritual realms.

Reform of the church was inseparable from the reform of education. As Eric Gritsch observes, "worship and education are interrelated and are grounded in the doctrine of baptism."[2] The concept of the priesthood of all believers demolished the hierarchy the papacy had created between "spiritual" and secular offices. It opened many new opportunities for concerned lay people to become actively involved in reform of both church and schools. A man of his age, Luther did not, however, wish for such reform to proceed without order or to be initiated by those lacking proper authority. The idea of democratic reform from the "bottom up" was foreign to Luther and many of his time. When he saw reform and rebellion originating from the masses, he promptly condemned it as the devil's work.

Within an amazingly short time after the publication of the 95 Theses, Luther was faced with a formidable dual challenge— to keep the momentum of reform going and to see that the proper authorities guided it, those to whom God had given the authority. The many facets and dimensions of this dual challenge are revealed in his programmatic writings of 1520–30, beginning with the treatise To the Christian Nobility of the German Nation.

In that work Luther sought to educate the leaders of Germany about reform. An eloquent teacher, Luther engaged his readers' attention by thematically contrasting appropriate and inappropriate actions. He informed them of the misdirected

---

[2] Gritsch, Martin—God 's Court Jester, 179. Of the many works on Luther's theology and pedagogy, see especially Ivar Asheim, Glaube und Erziehung bei Luther: Ein Beitrag zur Geschichte des Verhältnisses von Theologie und Pädagogik (Heidelberg: Quelle & Meyer, 1961) and Helmut Liedtke, Theologie und Pädagogik der Deutschen Evangelischen Schule im 16. Jahrhundert (Wuppertal: Aloys Henn Verlag, 1970).

actions of the papacy and urged those in authority to change directions. One example demonstrates his approach:

> Now the Romanists turn all that upside down. They take the heavenly and kingly form from Christ and give it to the pope, and leave the form of a servant to perish completely. ... At Rome Christ counts for nothing, but the pope counts for everything. ... The Romanists themselves devised the saying, 'The nearer Rome, the worse Christians'.[3]

Reform assumed such urgency because young people were being misled. They were not receiving the care and attention crucial to their formation as Christians. Indeed, Luther believed that those in power were failing to fulfill their primary obligation—"The care of young people ought to be the chief concern of the pope, bishops, the ruling classes, and of the councils."[4]

Both duty and freedom were at stake. The failure of the authorities to do their duty meant that Christian freedom would continue to be suppressed. Guided by a "believing understanding of the Scriptures, ... it is the duty of every Christian to espouse the cause of the faith, to understand and defend it, and to denounce every error."[5] A "believing understanding of the Scriptures" was the foundation for reform and for Luther's pedagogy. It depended both upon the Word being preached and the listener approaching it with faith. It also connected to something Luther now sought to build, a shared or community understanding.

To assure those in positions of secular authority that they had the freedom to act, Luther targeted the three "walls" of the Romanists. They had used these "walls" to defend their authority and to prevent others from challenging their actions. In attacking them, Luther drew upon Scripture and the practices of the early church. He attacked the papal position that the temporal powers have no jurisdiction over the spiritual, that

---

[3] *W A* 6, 434, 13–15; 436, 34; 437, 6–7; *L W* 44, 165, 169; 170.

[4] *W A* 6, 468, 23–24; *L W* 44, 216.

[5] *W A* 6, 412, 28–31, 37–38; *L W* 44, 135; 136.

only the pope may interpret Scripture, and that only he may call a council. Connecting all these defenses was the claim for the special rights and privilege of a spiritual class—the clergy— who are of a higher status than the laity. These hierarchical claims are demolished by the simple fact that all Christians share the same baptism and therefore are all equally members of the spiritual estate. The difference among Christians exists only in their callings: "We all have one baptism, one gospel, one faith, and are all Christians alike; for baptism, gospel, and faith alone make us spiritual and a Christian people. ... All Christians are truly of the spiritual estate, and there is no difference among them except of office."[6] With that foundation, freedom prevails, and those who have been placed in positions of authority may act with Scripture as their guide without fear of reprisals.

Concern for building leaders in church and state led Luther to turn to the reform of the universities. As we have seen, Luther led the reform at the University of Wittenberg. This curricular reform had to be extended to other institutions. If the errors of the past were not to be perpetuated among new generations, then change was urgent. Luther underscored the importance of the universities. They educate the leaders of society, those who become the jurists, educators, and pastors of tomorrow. Thus, Luther proclaimed that "there is no work more worthy of pope or emperor than a thorough reform of the universities. And on the other hand, nothing could be more devilish or disastrous than unreformed universities."[7] If the pope would not begin the process, Luther and his colleagues from Wittenberg would.

As the foremost authority and heart of the curriculum, Scripture was at the center of Luther's vision of the university. Scripture is the core of the curriculum, not only in theology, but in the arts faculty as well. Failure to train students in Scripture undermines the very purpose of the university, to "turn out men who are experts in the Holy Scriptures, men who can become bishops and priests, and stand in the front line against heretics, the devil, and all the world."[8] Products of more secular

---

[6] W A 6, 407, 17–19, 13–15; L W 44, 127.

[7] W A 6, 458, 37–40; L W 44, 202.

[8] W A 6, 462, 6–8; L W 44, 207.

institutions, we may have difficulty accepting Luther's mandate that Scripture be the center of the curriculum. But we can respond empathetically to his effort to establish a curriculum of values that met society's needs. As we today struggle to find shared values around which we can unite, we can understand Luther's effort to do the same. He found that only a curriculum with Scripture at its core gave education meaning. Indeed, he argued that without that core the university cannot help but become corrupt—and a corrupt institution can only produce corrupt representatives. When the universities further corruption and lead students away from God rather than toward Him, by their neglect of Scripture they become nothing other than "wide gates to hell."[9]

Luther was not speaking metaphorically. By replacing Scripture with Aristotle, the universities were no less of a threat to Christianity than a papacy that had become the representative of Antichrist. As a result Luther advocated that "Aristotle's *Physics, Metaphysics, Concerning the Soul,* and *Ethics,* which hitherto have been thought to be his best books, should be completely discarded along with all the rest of his books that boast about nature."[10] Other works, such as the *Logic, Rhetoric,* and *Poetics,* could be retained since they are useful "in training young people to speak and to preach properly."[11] Likewise, the languages, Latin, Greek, and Hebrew, were to be taught, along with mathematics and history.

Luther turned next to the upper faculties of medicine, law, and theology. He left it to the medical faculty to reform their own curriculum, while he took "responsibility" for directing the reform of law and theology. Both are at the very core of society, with law guiding behavior and ordering society, and theology centering people upon the life of faith and obedience to God. In law, Luther advocated radical reform, urging that "it would be a good thing if canon law were completely blotted out, from the first letter to the last, especially the decretals. ... The study of

---

[9] *W A* 6, 462, 9–10; *L W* 44, 207.

[10] *W A* 6, 457, 36–38; *L W* 44, 200.

[11] *W A* 6, 458, 26–28; *LW* 44, 201.

canon law only hinders the study of the Holy Scriptures."[12] As in the arts, Scripture is the central value in Luther's pedagogy. Not only had canon law displaced Scripture, it had displaced temporal law as well, leading to a dual system of codes that generate untold confusion, confusion that Luther saw as the devil's activity. While the Turks follow the straightforward path of law in the Koran, Christians are thrust into a wilderness of canon and temporal laws.

While canon law should be abolished, temporal law should be simplified. For "the secular law ... has become a wilderness. ... There is far too much of it. ... Would to God that every land were ruled by its own brief laws suitable to its gifts and peculiar character."[13] Luther advocated a return to simplicity so that people are truly able to know the good from the bad. The law should function again as a schoolmaster and guide for a just and Christian society.

As a theologian who struggled to come to his own understanding of God and His expectations, it is not surprising that Luther was especially outraged over those studies that deluded the young and deterred them from a study of the Bible. The inappropriate and inconsequential have again misplaced the appropriate and significant, with dire consequences for society. First and above all, the Bible should be the core of theological study. Instead it had been relegated to a preliminary or preparatory role while the *Sentences* occupy a far more significant place. As Luther wrote,

> The sentences ought to be the first study for young students of theology, and the Bible left to the doctors. But today it is the other way around. The Bible comes first and is then put aside when the bachelor's degree is received. The sentences come last, and they occupy a doctor as long as he lives.[14]

In yet another striking example of inappropriate and misdirected practices, those who bear the title of doctor of Holy

---

[12] *W A* 6, 459, 2–6; *L W* 44, 202.

[13] *W A* 6, 459, 30–32; 38–39; *L W* 44, 203; 204.

[14] *W A* 6, 460, 7–10; *L W* 44, 204.

Scripture teach anything but Scripture. Fortunately, even from such misguided teaching doctors of theology emerge, since more than human effort is involved: "Pope, emperor, and universities may make Doctors of Arts, of Medicine, of Laws, of the Sentences, but be assured that no man can make a doctor of Holy Scripture except the Holy Spirit from heaven."[15]

Much as Luther advocated reducing the number of laws, he urged a reduction in the number of works being published in theology. Here too more is not necessarily better, and the abundance of works impedes the study of Scripture. Even the church fathers should not displace Scripture, since they intended their writings "to lead us to the Scriptures ... but we use their works to get away from the Scriptures."[16] Instead, Scripture is the enduring vineyard in which Christians should labor and rejoice all their lives.

In his vineyard God calls people to different vocations and tasks. For some, those called by God to become pastors, teachers, lawyers, and doctors, for example, university education is appropriate and necessary. However, not all are called to these offices, and for them, Luther argued, university may not be appropriate. While such thinking might seem elitist, it in fact demonstrates a respect for all the different vocations to which God calls people and for which He gives them special abilities and gifts. Different gifts require different forms of nurturing. While all young people should go to school—the better to realize their vocations—their paths diverge thereafter with the universities the appropriate next step only for those who are the "most highly qualified ... who have been well trained in the lower schools."[17]

From the university, Luther turned to the schools. In an argument that would have vast consequences for society and that follows directly from his recognition that Scripture is the touchstone for all of Christian society, Luther advocated the formation of schools for all children, boys and girls. As in the universities, Scripture should be the central element of the curriculum in the schools. Luther even asks: "Is it not only right

---

[15] *W A* 6, 460, 28–31; *L W* 44, 205.

[16] *W A* 6, 461, 8—9; *L W* 44, 205.

[17] *WA* 6, 461, 38–39; *LW* 44, 206.

that every Christian man know the entire holy Gospel by the age of nine or ten?"[18] Parents and secular authorities neglect their highest duty and, as a result, the "young people of Christendom languish and perish miserably in our midst for want of the Gospel, in which we ought to be giving them constant instruction and training."[19] Those in authority must remedy this situation and provide schools in every town and village.

In schools, Luther maintained, the Gospel can be taught so that the next generation will not be duped and made victims of the papacy as Luther's generation had. Granted by God the responsibility of serving as pedagogue to Christians, the papacy transformed its teaching office into a school for sin. Instead of performing his proper duties, the pope has instead taught "Christians, especially the German nation, praised throughout history for its nobility, its constancy and fidelity, to be inconstant, perjurers, traitors, profligates, and faithless."[20] Now that the papacy has failed in its God given duty, that obligation falls to the secular authorities. They should lead the people by their example and turn the nation toward the Gospel.

To the Christian Nobility constitutes the first salvo in the effort to reform all aspects of German society, with education at the center of that effort. In the broadest terms, it presents a road map for the nobility as they struggle to move from the old to the new. It leaves a multitude of questions unanswered or unresolved, questions that would be addressed by Luther and his young colleague Melanchthon in many writings, sermons, and tracts over the next decades. Although Luther's starting point was theology and Melanchthon's the liberal arts, their goals intersected in their common vision of reviving German education.

Melanchthon's inaugural address two years earlier at the University of Wittenberg had convinced Luther of their shared vision. Clyde Manschreck describes Melanchthon's speech of August 29, 1518, *De corrigendis adolescentiae studiis*, as a

---

[18] *W A* 6, 461, 19–20; *L W* 44, 206.

[19] *W A* 6, 461, 33–35; *L W* 44, 206.

[20] *W A* 6, 453, 15–17; *L W* 44, 193–94.

"formula for improvement of studies."[21] Humanist in tone and content, the address demonstrated Melanchthon's openness to theology and its guidance of study in the arts. From his humanist and liberal arts perspective, Melanchthon analyzed the causes that had led to the loss of true learning in Germany. For the Greek scholar Melanchthon, not surprisingly, the loss of the knowledge of Greek was responsible. As he told his audience on that day, "the disciplines of the ancients ... [were] deserted when that brash manner of commenting and philosophizing prevailed, Greek was likewise despised, mathematics were deserted, and the sacred were cultivated more negligently."[22] The result was both corruption of church rites and the loss of good letters, either one of which, if still in its true state, could have helped to preserve and protect the other:

> For, on the one hand, the uncorrupt rites of the church could easily have restored the lapsing letters, and, on the other hand, with good letters, if any had been saved, it was possible to correct the ruined ethics of the church, to excite, to confirm, and to rally the flagging spirits of the people.[23]

Instead, "good letters have been exchanged for bad ones, old piety for human ceremonies, traditions, principles, tenets, chapters, extravagances, and glosses of secondary sources."[24]

---

[21]Richard Nürnberger, ed., *Melanchthons Werke*, vol. III: Humanistische Schriften, 2nd ed. (Gütersloh: Gütersloher Verlagshaus Gerd Mohn), 29–42. Clyde Leonard Manschreck, *Melanchthon: The Quiet Reformer* (New York and Nashville: Abingdon Press, 1958), 23. See also Max Dorn, "Melanchthons Antrittsrede von 1518, ein Bekenntnis und ein Appell zum Fortschritt," in *450 Jahre Martin-Luther-Universität Halle-Wittenberg*, vol. 1, 141–48.

[22]*Melanchthons Werke*, vol. III, 33, 16–19.

[23]*Melanchthons Werke*, vol. III, 33, 21–26.

[24]*Melanchthons Werke*, vol. III, 33, 26–29.

Melanchthon sought to restore good letters, to further a "renaissance through a study of original sources."[25] This renaissance of study would in turn "rejuvenate society and regenerate theology."[26] Above all, it would lead to the restoration of true Christianity. First, the studies currently taught must be pruned with an eye to their original purpose. Philosophy, in the mode of Socrates, must once again return to its source and be freed from the factions and opinions that have transformed it into a swamp of confusion that exhausts its students. Fortunately, in Wittenberg, Melanchthon already saw the signs of that return in the teaching of the classics, such as Quintilian and Pliny, as well as mathematics and poetry.

After gaining knowledge in grammar, logic, and rhetoric, as well as in Greek and Latin letters, students may pursue the study of philosophy. Homer, Vergil, and the *Laws* of Plato, provide the basis for understanding and discussing human behavior. No less important, Melanchthon stressed, is history, for "it says ... what is noble, what shameful, what useful, what not. No part of life, neither public nor private, can remain unaffected by it."[27] Indeed, Melanchthon could not praise history too highly: "I do not know if our world would suffer less harm without the sun, its soul, as it were, than without history, the principle of all civil activities ... every kind of art flows from history."[28]

The study, first of grammar, logic, and rhetoric, followed by classical letters, mathematics, and history, provides the best foundation for study of the sacred. One enters unwisely into this area if ill prepared. Only preparation in the languages of the Scriptures allows one to read the texts directly and clearly, unencumbered by a mask. Yet Melanchthon too perceived the limits of humanist tools. Even the best preparation in the classical languages is not sufficient without the guidance of the Holy Spirit. For, it is

---

[25] Manschreck, *Melanchthon*, 23.

[26] Manschreck, *Melanchthon*, 23.

[27] *Melanchthons Werke*, vol. III, 39, 15–18.

[28] *Melanchthons Werke*, vol. III, 39, 19–22; 24.

with the spirit as guide, as companion, one can come to
the sacred by way of cultivating our arts. ... Thus,
inasmuch as theology is partly Hebrew, partly Greek, for
we Latins drink of their brooks, other languages must be
learned, so that we do not deal with theologians as with
dumb masks. Then the splendor and peculiar
characteristic of the words will be revealed and become
manifest in the midday sun, the true and genuine sense of
the word.[29]

From the understanding of the letter, gained through the tools of
language, one can reason to the meaning, without the layers of
glosses and concordances and other impediments that have
obscured the Scriptures to this time. Then, as Melanchthon
affirmed, "when we have brought [our] minds to the fountain,
we shall begin to understand Christ."[30]

Lacking the tools, the Church has become misguided, as a
result corrupting "true and genuine piety with human
traditions."[31] It has become enamored of human works at the
expense of the divine. Although Melanchthon's address was
filled with classical references that are foreign to the prose of
Luther, humanist and theologian shared the same conclusion:
"After the comments of men began to please us, we, overcome
by the love of our works, partook beelphegor for manna."[32] In
short, "we began to be humans and not christs."[33] But now the
light has once more begun to shine and to overcome the
darkness that has inhabited men's minds since the loss of true
letters. Young men need only pursue the studies that are open to
them so that through the "propriety of language" they may
understand "the mysteries of the sacred. ... Therefore, take hold
of sound studies and ... dare to know; cultivate the ancient

---

[29] *Melanchthons Werke*, vol. III, 40, 5–6, 11–16.

[30] *Melanchthons Werke*, vol. III, 40, 19–20.

[31] *Melanchthons Werke*, vol. III, 41, 4–6.

[32] *Melanchthons Werke*, vol. III, 41, 6–8. See the Bible, Numbers 25:
1-5 for Melanchton's reference to Baal of Peor.

[33] *Melanchthons Werke*, vol. III, 41, 8–9.

Latins, embrace the Greeks, without which the Latin cannot be rightly pursued."[34] In terms reminiscent of Erasmus, Melanchthon ended his address on a note of hope, finding in Germany men who serve as examples of true learning and as stimuli to study. Thus, "Germany at various places is blossoming again ... and once brutal with barbarous disciplines [it] is ... being tamed."[35]

These two works, separated by two years—Melanchthon's to the faculty and students of Wittenberg, and Luther's to the nobility—differ in tone, format, and audience. Yet they share a common goal, the reform of the University. Luther asserted the responsibility of the secular leaders to root out the inappropriate, replace it with true learning, and perform their proper responsibility of shepherding the young. Melanchthon laid the foundation for those studies, linking Luther's return to the gospel with the "disciplines of the ancients."[36]

In the next years Christians failed to demonstrate the commitment to education that both men had so avidly sought. Indeed education was fundamentally threatened by the winds of change that Luther had unleashed. Recognizing that the church was no longer a source of lucrative careers, many parents regarded schooling beyond the rudimentary level as an unnecessary luxury that only delayed their sons' entrance into the world of commerce. Nobles and city councils recognized the financial advantages in the tumultuous situation by taking over church endowments for their own secular uses. And, perhaps most distressing to Luther, was the attack from within. Former allies such as Andreas Bodenstein von Carlstadt, the former dean of the theological faculty at Wittenberg and Luther's debate partner at Leipzig, and Thomas Muentzer, who had studied briefly at Wittenberg, rejected formal education in favor of "inspired learning" through the Holy Spirit.[37] In 1524,

---

[34] *Melanchthons Werke*, vol. III, 41, 37–38; 42, 5–7.

[35] *Melanchthons Werke*, vol. III, 42, 10–13.

[36] *Melanchthons Werke*, vol. III, 33, 7.

[37] *LW* 45, 343. Ernst Kähler, "Karlstadts Protest gegen die theologische Wissenschaft," *450 Jahre Martin-Luther-Universität Halle-Wittenberg*, vol. 1, 299–312.

Carlstadt resigned his academic position at Wittenberg, claiming that no Christian should bear any such title as "doctor."[38]

During Luther's period of enforced exile at the Wartburg from May 1521 to March of the following year, change had been anything but orderly and systematic. Without his guiding hand, the reform confusedly veered in different directions. The mass had been disrupted and Franciscans had been threatened by zealous students and townspeople.[39] Nor was there unanimity within the ranks of the faculty or between faculty and the elector. In the midst of such turmoil, education could not help but suffer. With the star of the university absent, many students departed. Others were called home by their parents who feared their sons' association with such a hotbed of heresy, while yet others found themselves deprived of support now that begging was no longer allowed.[40] Not only the University but the Wittenberg schools also suffered. One report even suggests that the schools, influenced by Carlstadt's anti-academic bent, were closed for a time, with the teachers turning against learning: "The schoolmaster George Mohr was even said to have advocated taking the children out of school. The building, in fact, was turned into a bakery shop (*Brotbank*) for a time. Not until late in 1523 was the school reopened under Pastor Bugenhagen."[41]

---

[38] Ronald J. Sider, *Andreas Bodenstein von Karlstadt: The Development of His Thought 1517–1525*, vol. 11 in *Studies in Medieval and Reformation Thought* (Leiden: E. J. Brill, 1974), 190–193; Ronald J. Sider, "Andreas Bodenstein von Karlstadt: Zwischen Liberalität und Radikalität," in Hans-Jürgen Goertz, ed., *Radikale Reformatoren* (Munich: C.H. Beck, 1978), 26.

[39] Martin Brecht, *Martin Luther: Shaping and Defining the Reformation 1521–1532*, trans. James L. Schaaf (Minneapolis: Fortress Press, 1990), 30.

[40] Brecht, *Martin Luther: Shaping and Defining the Reformation*, 40.

[41] Brecht, *Martin Luther: Shaping and Defining the Reformation*, 138.

The precarious state of reform in Wittenberg prompted Luther's return, even if his life was in jeopardy and the elector did not approve. In his famous *Invocavit* sermons he set the direction and strategy for reform, emphasizing unity and Christian love. By early 1524 the reformer could turn his attention once more to education and to the devil's efforts to undermine the progress of the Gospel. Indeed, Luther felt compelled to speak: "God has opened my mouth and bidden me speak. ... He who heeds me in this matter is most certainly heeding not me, but Christ."[42] Through the new preaching of the Gospel, parents had recognized how "un-Christian" schools and universities were and had withdrawn their children, an act that infuriated the devil. So, Luther observed, the devil took another tact, playing to the carnal desires of the people, he "goes to the other extreme and will permit no learning at all."[43] To alert his beloved Germans to this new challenge to the Gospel, Luther wrote in the first weeks of 1524 *To the Councilmen of All Cities in Germany That They Establish and Maintain Christian Schools,* published in February. It was marked by a sense of urgency: "O my beloved Germans, buy while the market is at your door; gather in the harvest while there is sunshine and fair weather; make use of God's grace and word while it is there!"[44]

Heinrich Bornkamm described this treatise as "far more than a program for the schools." He noted: "As sometimes happens in occasional writings—when motives of a great life work emerge enforced, enriched, and simplified by the demand for application—this little booklet is a brief summary of the thoughts that moved Luther during these years."[45] As in his 1520 tract to the nobility, Luther directed himself to the authorities, alerting them to the battle within their midst, and reminding them of how much was at stake. In a famous passage that rings as true today as it did then, Luther questions: "My

---

[42] *W A* 15, 27, 12–13; 28, 1–2; *LW* 45, 347; 348.

[43] *W A* 15, 29, 27–28; *LW* 45, 349.

[44] *WA* 15, 32, 4–6; *LW* 45, 352.

[45] Heinrich Bornkamm, *Luther in Mid-Career 1521–1530,* trans. E. Theodore Bachmann (Philadelphia: Fortress Press, 1983), 138.

dear sirs, if we have to spend such large sums every year on guns, roads, bridges, dams, and countless similar items to insure the temporal peace and prosperity of a city, why should not much more be devoted to the poor neglected youth?"[46] The authorities fail to recognize that the very survival of civic life is at stake, since the future depends upon well-educated and prepared citizens. As Brecht observes, Luther saw education as a "community responsibility," which if left unfulfilled would lead to destruction.[47] In another oft quoted passage, Luther reminded the council that a city's true wealth resides not in its "guns and armor" or in its material goods, its "mighty walls and magnificent buildings," but in its "able, learned, wise, honorable, and well-educated citizens."[48] Only such people know how to conserve and use wealth wisely. Luther reminded the authorities that God will not step in to perform "miracles" when people can solve their problems on the basis of the gifts that God has already given them—gifts that need only be cultivated by education.[49] The authorities bear a crucial and heavy responsibility. The welfare of society depends on their fulfilling their duty.

Important as government's role is, Luther recognized that the first steps in a child's education occur not within the civic context, but within the home. Parents have no higher duty than the care and nurturing of their young. However, not all parents are sufficiently well-intentioned or able to perform this duty to the greatest benefit of their offspring. For this reason, the civic authorities must intervene, to assure that all children receive adequate training. The most sensible way to accomplish this goal is through the hiring of a well-trained schoolteacher, who can instruct all the children and assure that no one is omitted. The alternative, if children are allowed to go uneducated, is grave indeed, since these children will grow up "to poison and pollute the other children until at last the whole city is

---

[46] W A 15, 30, 16–20; LW 45, 350.

[47] Brecht, *Martin Luther: Shaping and Defining the Reformation,* 139.

[48] W A 15, 34, 28–34; L W 45, 355–56.

[49] W A 15, 35, 18–19; L W 45, 356–57.

ruined."[50] Even more than the spiritual realm, the temporal realm is threatened by the loss of learning. Thus, Luther argued, even if education were not necessary "for the sake of the Scriptures and of God," it would be essential for the temporal estate, which "must have good and capable men and women, men able to rule well over land and people, women able to manage the household and train children and servants aright. Now such men must come from our boys and such women from our girls."[51] The founding and furthering of schools rests with the city councils since the princes are too busy in "cellar, kitchen, and bedroom."[52]

In his 1520 tract Luther had focused specifically on the reform of the universities. In the short term, that was where change had to begin. Yet, in the long term, the reform of education had to begin with the children. Thus, in writing to the councilmen, he concentrated on the grassroots of education, the schools and their curricula. Leaving it to others, especially Melanchthon, to establish the specifics, Luther provided a general framework for education within the schools, stressing, above all, the languages. Countering the anti-intellectualism of the "enthusiasts," Luther argued that the languages are the gateway to the gospel. In the words of one scholar, "not enthusiasm but grammar leads to a sound understanding."[53] Further study in the languages is especially necessary for those who are to become preachers, for "where the preacher is versed in the languages, there is a freshness and vigor in his preaching, Scripture is treated in its entirety, and faith finds itself constantly renewed by a continual variety of words and illustrations."[54] Loss of the languages means "the gospel must finally perish."[55] Besides the languages, singing, mathematics, and especially history were to be taught.

---

[50] WA 15, 34, 6–8; L W 45, 355.

[51] W A 15, 44, 28-31; LW 45, 368.

[52] W A 15, 45, 2-3; L W 45, 368.

[53] Bornkamm, *Luther in Mid-Career*, 140.

[54] W A 15, 42, 9-11; L W 45, 365.

[55] W A 15, 38, 31-32; L W 45, 360.

Like the humanists, Luther appreciated the role of history as pedagogue. In his Preface to *Galeatus Capella's History*, written a little over a decade after the tract *To the Councilmen*, Luther commended history. History teaches by example and brings to life the lessons of the philosophers. "Histories are, therefore, a very precious thing."[56] History demonstrates God's action in human affairs, His rewarding of the just and punishing of the evil. Only those who know the people and events who have gone before them, know their own role and place in history, or, as Luther phrases it to the councilmen, "their own place in the stream of human events."[57]

Luther argued that teaching methods as well as content needed to be reformed. Learning should be joyful. Teachers should not rely on floggings and threats designed to beat from their pupils their energy and playfulness. Nor should they stress rote memorization detached from purpose. Luther challenged teachers to channel children's youthful energy into excitement for their studies—"By the grace of God it is now possible for children to study with pleasure and in play languages, or other arts, or history."[58] Luther did not discuss specific pedagogical techniques, but he clearly saw the secret as lying within the disciplines themselves, and implicitly believed that poetry and history, along with the other arts, properly taught, would engage students more than the "philosophers and sophists" whom Luther had been forced to study.[59] A successful curriculum is diverse and recognizes the energy and playfulness of the young. Thus, children's attention is better engaged by a multiple-subject curriculum, with singing and languages and mathematics.

In a letter a few months earlier to the humanist Eobanus Hessus, Luther had sought to address his colleague's concern that the new theology was only leading to more barbarity and

---

[56] *W A* 50, 383, 8–9; *LW* 34, 275.

[57] *W A* 15, 45, 19; *L W* 45, 369.

[58] *W A* 15, 46, 4–6; *L W* 45, 369.

[59] *W A* 15, 46, 20; *L W* 45, 370.

the further neglect of studies.[60] Humanistic studies are absolutely essential for theology, for "there has never been a great revelation of God's Word unless God has first prepared the way by the rise and the flourishing of languages and learning."[61] Likewise, young people should study poetry and rhetoric, for these studies equip young people "for grasping the sacred truths, as well as for handling them skillfully and successfully."[62] In closing, Luther lamented that his many responsibilities prevented his own reading of the poets.

The single most important idea within Luther's tract to the councilmen is that *all* children should be educated. Luther recognized that for some parents offering their children this opportunity entailed sacrifice. Many parents could not spare their children from their work in home or fields for several hours of the day. Thus, seeking to include all children, he limited education to only one or two hours a day for boys, and an hour a day for girls. Believing that worthwhile and effective teaching and learning could now occur, even those few hours a day would yield greater accomplishments than when a boy "slaved away at his Donatus and Alexander for twenty or thirty years and still learned nothing."[63] Luther's proposal was a workstudy situation, in which children combined school with learning a skill or trade.

Luther's goal of inclusivity of all children is commendable and his recognition that many parents could not part from their children for long is realistic. At the same time, we may question whether his curricular plan of one or two hours of school a day allows for the realization of the educational goals that he envisioned, especially when schooling was limited to only a few years. Yet, what is most important is the foundation that Luther laid for the future—first, education for all; and second,

---

[60] *WA Br* 3, 49–50; *Luther's Works*, vol. 49: *Letters II*, ed. and trans. by Gottfried G. Krodel (Philadelphia: Fortress Press, 1972), 32–35. See also Bornkamm, *Luther in Mid-Career*, 137, and Brecht, *Martin Luther: Shaping and Defining the Reformation*, 138.

[61] *WA Br* 3, 50, 23f; *L W* 49, 34.

[62] *WA Br* 3, 50, 27–29; *L W* 49, 34.

[63] *WA* 15, 46, 25–26; *L W* 45, 370.

an education that was broad and humanistic. Society could only flourish with educated men and women. He encouraged advanced schooling for those who demonstrated themselves especially gifted.

To support these studies there must be good libraries, adequately funded by the civic authorities. Libraries exist to support the learning of languages and the arts. Luther firmly opposed those who aimed to build as extensive a library as possible. He argued instead for a judicious selection of those books that promote knowledge of the gospel and the arts, i.e. quality over numbers. Indeed, those books that Luther was convinced cause harm and drive people away from the Bible and the arts, such as the commentaries of the jurists and the *Sentences* commentaries of the theologians, should be removed. As he wrote, "I would discard all such dung, and furnish my library with the right sort of books, consulting with scholars as to my choice."[64] What does Luther mean by the "right sort of books"? Not surprisingly, his list includes copies of the Scriptures in various languages, the "best commentaries" (most likely meaning those closest in time to the texts themselves) in Hebrew, Greek, and Latin, and books that prepare one to study the Scriptures, those about language and those by the poets. Included also are volumes in the liberal arts, as well as various books in medicine and law. Receiving a place of special distinction within the library are "the chronicles and histories, in whatever languages they are to be had. For they are a wonderful help in understanding and guiding the course of events, and especially for observing the marvelous works of God."[65]

Living in a more religiously diverse and secular culture, we may differ with Luther's selection criteria and his omission of books in many fields. His purpose was not that of making all knowledge available to people to allow them to make their own choices. He did not regard knowledge as neutral in character. He believed there were books that further the cause of God and those which support that of the devil. Had Luther taken a more neutral position, including all available works, he would have seen himself as shirking his true responsibilities. From Luther's

[64] *W A* 15, 51, 27–52, 1; *L W* 45, 376.

[65] *W A* 15, 52, 11–14; *LW* 45, 376.

perspective—using our language—a failure to censure would have meant a failure to act as a responsible Christian and a deliberate siding with the devil, whose aims in this area were very clear to Luther. In the concluding lines of his tract, he acknowledged:

> Now that God has today so graciously bestowed upon us an abundance of arts, scholars, and books, it is time to reap and gather in the best as well as we can, and lay up treasure in order to preserve for the future something from these years of jubilee. ... It is to be feared ... that men will go on writing new and different books until finally, because of the devil's activity, we will come to the point where the good books which are now being produced and printed will again be suppressed, and the worthless and harmful books with their useless and senseless rubbish will swarm back and litter every nook and corner.[66]

Thus, while the worthwhile books must be protected and treasured, the "dung" must be expelled, lest it serve as a model and an inducement to others to write such works. Unlike the papal jubilees that encourage only greed and corruption, God has proclaimed in Germany a true jubilee year, filled to overflowing with a harvest of true learning. The challenge before the authorities is to preserve this rich harvest and to secure the seed for the future.

If Luther's hopes focused upon the coming Kingdom of God, his daily life focused very much on the here and now. Young men must be trained not only to preach the Gospel but to secure the temporal well-being of city and state. It was the responsibility of the councilmen to further both aims. Fortunately, Luther's call did not go unheeded. A number of city councils responded quickly.[67] School reforms occurred within Halberstadt and Gotha.[68] In 1525, at the invitation of

---

[66] W A 15, 52, 25–33; L W 45, 377.

[67] LW 45, 344.

[68] Brecht, *Martin Luther: Shaping and Defining the Reformation*, 141.

Count Albrecht of Mansfeld, Luther, Melanchthon, and John Agricola traveled to Luther's birthplace of Eisleben to establish a Latin school.[69] Nikolaus von Amsdorf founded a new school at Magdeburg, the Johannisschule, of which former Wittenberg student Caspar Cruciger became the first rector.[70] Nor did Luther shirk in his commitment to provide education for girls. On August 22, 1527 he wrote a former nun, Else von Kanitz, requesting that she come to Wittenberg to teach the girls, promising her a place at his own table, so that she need "have no worries" about her livelihood.[71]

Melanchthon also responded to the needs he saw within Wittenberg. Already in 1520 he had set up a private school within his home. Its primary goal was to prepare boys for university study. It also augmented Melanchthon's meager income, since he did not charge students fees for attending his lectures.[72] He may have tutored individual students in his home soon after his arrival in 1518.[73] Financial concerns, desperate as they were for a time, were obviously very much secondary, however, since Melanchthon maintained the school for some ten years. It may have been that for these students Melanchthon prepared two texts, the *Enchiridion elementorum puerilium* of 1524 and the *Institutio puerilis literarum Graecorum* of 1525, the first of which was a handbook for beginners in Latin and the second that performed the same function for those learning Greek.[74] Melanchthon utilized various techniques to engage the

---

[69] Brecht, *Martin Luther: Shaping and Defining the Reformation*, 141.

[70] Manschreck, *Melanchthon*, 133; Kolb, *Nikolaus von Amsdorf*, 37.

[71] *WA Br* 4, 236, 1–16; 7–8. Brecht, *Martin Luther: Shaping and Defining the Reformation*, 141.

[72] Robert Stupperich, *Melanchthon*, trans. Robert Fischer (Philadelphia: The Westminster Press, 1965), 69; Hartfelder, *Philipp Melanchthon als Praeceptor Germaniae*, 491–95.

[73] Hermann-Adolf Stempel, *Melanchthons pädagogisches Wirken* (Bielefeld: Luther Verlag, 1979), 39.

[74] Hartfelder, *Philipp Melanchthon*, 493.

active participation of his young students. For example, the boy who performed best in Latin earned the title *rex poeticus*, king of the poets, and occupied the place of honor at the meal table.[75] The boys also performed Latin comedies by Plautus, Terence, or Euripides, among others, to which guests were invited.[76]

Among the most prominent of the educational reforms was the new school established in 1526 in Nuremberg, which invited Melanchthon to give the inaugural oration. City officials had approached him earlier to accept the appointment as rector and professor of rhetoric at the prestigious new school, but Melanchthon felt obliged to remain in Wittenberg. He nominated Johannes Camerarius for the position.[77] However, he willingly accepted the invitation to speak at the dedication.

Melanchthon enthusiastically assured the magistracy of the value and wisdom of their investment. He reminded his listeners of the dangers confronting learning, including the desertion of the schools and the lack of support from public officials and rulers who "are in part so dull that they do not understand the worth of letters, in part so evil that they believe it to be advantageous to their despotic rule that all laws, religion, and civil discipline [are] abolished altogether."[78] In distinction from these misguided officials, are those of Nuremberg, who, following the example of the great city of Florence, have acted in defense of letters. They have realized that letters are essential to the preservation of both "religion and good laws." For, as Melanchthon assured his audience,

> If anyone thinks that genuine virtue can be acquired without teaching, he is very much deceived, nor is anyone sufficient enough to govern the state without the knowledge of those letters with which every principle of ruling states is maintained.[79]

---

[75] Hartfelder, *Philipp Melanchthon*, 493.

[76] Hartfelder, *Philipp Melanchthon*, 494.

[77] *Melanchthons Werke*, vol. III, 63.

[78] *Melanchthons Werke*, vol. III, 66, 1–5.

[79] *Melanchthons Werke*, vol. III, 69, 9–10.

Thus, although the officials may encounter both envy and hostility for their accomplishments, they could not be acting more wisely or as better stewards of the state. They assure that they will be succeeded by men well trained and committed to virtue. The Nuremberg magistrates are building the true defense to the state, better than any walls surrounding the city might be. As Melanchthon proclaimed, "no bulwarks or walls are stronger monuments than citizens endowed with erudition, prudence, and other virtues. The Spartan said that walls must be of iron not of stone. But I judge it to be defended not so much with weapons as with prudence, moderation, and piety."[80] Nuremberg's leaders have set a model for all of Germany and in the process guaranteed that their city will flourish. Following Nuremberg's lead, some 56 cities would appeal to Melanchthon for counsel and guidance in founding schools.[81]

While Luther must have been encouraged by the actions of cities such as Nuremberg, he continued to be deeply troubled by a lack of consistent grassroots involvement in reform. Many issues occupied him, of course, but education ranked high among them. In order better to understand where the need was greatest, Luther persuaded Elector John, successor to Frederick the Wise, to begin visitations, inspections of the parishes. These first surveys attested that both doctrinal confusion and a poor level of support for the clergy were endemic. In response, in 1527 Melanchthon, with assistance from Luther, compiled the *Instructions for the Visitors of Parish Pastors in Electoral Saxony*, to guide those who were regularly to visit the various regions. These visitors were to examine the financial affairs of each parish, as well as to assess progress in instituting religious reform. The publication of the *Instructions* was delayed due to a variety of circumstances, including a paper shortage.[82] When the document at last appeared it addressed diverse topics of belief and practice, from the proper teaching regarding penance to the office of superintendent in each parish.

---

[80] *Melanchthons Werke*, vol. III, 66, 28–33.

[81] Manschreck, *Melanchthon*, 143.

[82] Brecht, *Martin Luther: Shaping and Defining the Reformation*, 266.

The entire document is a "teaching" manual. Its purpose is to guide pastors in what and how they should teach the people, as well as the visitors in what they should examine. In addition, the *Instructions* sought to correct errors, as, for example, the idea that people need not be exhorted to contrition since God himself brings about contrition in people's hearts. Luther rebutted such an argument with the words that although "it is true that God works true contrition, ... he works it through the Word and preaching."[83] The tract offers a balance between insistence on those teachings that are central to the gospel and flexibility regarding those matters in which Christians have freedom. In fact, a central part of the tract discusses Christian freedom itself. Guiding the efforts of the two reformers was the desire to avoid confusion, recognizing that people are in different stages of the journey of faith. Thus, with regard to the use of Latin or German in the mass, they advised: "Some sing the mass in German, some in Latin, either of which is permissible. It would be reasonable and useful if we used German where most of the people do not understand Latin."[84] The spirit within this tract is much the same as that which Luther showed in his *Invocavit* sermons, a desire to bring about change through education, mandating conformity only where it was absolutely essential.

While the entire document focused on education in the general sense, one section constituted a curricular plan for the schools, encouraging attendance and describing the studies that were to be offered at each level. As Manschreck notes in his biography of Melanchthon, it is significant that the instructions on doctrine and practice were joined to a plan for the establishing of schools "for Melanchthon considered the churches and schools complementary parts in the Christian scheme."[85] The section begins with the familiar argument that parents are to be encouraged to send their children to school so that they might later be of service to both secular and spiritual offices. Recognizing that the schools still have many flaws,

---

[83] *W A* 26, 219, 18–19; *Luther's Works,* vol. 40: *Church and Ministry II,* ed. Conrad Bergendoff (Philadelphia: Fortress Press, 1958), 295.

[84] *WA* 26, 224, 12–14; *L W* 40, 300.

[85] Manschreck, *Melanchthon,* 138.

Melanchthon and Luther began by urging well-intentioned schoolmasters not to seek to accomplish too much. Latin is to be taught, "not German or Greek or Hebrew."[86] By seeking to teach their young students too much, the teachers overwhelm and confuse them. Rather than nurturing their students and gradually aiding them to construct a house of learning, such teachers are only interested in building their own reputations. Since children learn differently at different ages, Melanchthon and Luther urged that the children be divided into three divisions, according to their accomplishments. This was similar to the medieval practice that Luther had experienced. Although the precise criteria for the transition from one division to another are not spelled out, the implication is that progress is "competency based." No age parameters are set; the curriculum implicitly recognizes that children develop differently.

In the first division, children take their initial steps in learning how to read, beginning with the "alphabet, the Lord's Prayer, the Creed, and other prayers." From there, they progress to the work in which Luther himself was trained, the *Ars grammatica* of Donatus, along with Cato. The pedagogy that is to be followed is that of exposition by the teacher and repetition by the students, with the goals of learning to read and gaining a vocabulary. Children in this division also learn to write and begin their study of music, engaging in singing with those who are more advanced in their studies.

The curriculum of the second division builds upon that of the first, with more attention devoted above all to grammar. Students learn specific conjugations and declinations, along with syntax, derived from their reading of the *Fables* of Aesop, and later the plays of Terence and sections of the *Colloquies* of Erasmus. This learning is reinforced through study of the grammar book, *Paedagogia*, written by the humanist Peter Mosellanus. Rote learning is also crucial to this stage of study. The reformers insisted that children must "recite these grammatical rules from memory, so that they are compelled and driven to learn grammar well."[87] Such learning may not appear to be very different from that which Luther himself experienced and which he complained about so vigorously, but there is a

---

[86] *WA* 26, 236, 38; *L W* 40, 315.

[87] *W A* 26, 238, 22–23; *L W* 40, 318.

different pedagogy at work. There are also some differences in content, with the inclusion of more humanist works, such as those by Erasmus and Mosellanus. Nonetheless, the curriculum is certainly not a rejection of the past—in spite of Luther's negative comments about his own experiences! Repetition and reinforcement remain pedagogical techniques, just as they were for Luther. At the same time, this curriculum recognizes the need for variety to avoid boredom and to keep the attention of the young. Thus, the study of grammar is intermixed with singing, with the entertaining stories of Aesop, and with Christian instruction. The reformers explicitly directed teachers not to shift rapidly from book to book and not to try to proceed too rapidly, lest their students be overtaxed. They were firmly committed to students learning the fundamentals, above all, grammar, since without such a foundation "all learning is lost labor and fruitless."[88] Remarks that Melanchthon offered elsewhere suggest that he defined the study of language more broadly than might be assumed from the description in the *Instructions*. Stressing the necessity for learning the classical languages, Melanchthon argued: "Without an understanding of language, one cannot read the Old and New Testaments; and to understand languages one needs all sorts of related knowledge in history, geography, chronology, and other liberal arts."[89] Elsewhere Melanchthon suggested that language study encompassed far more than grammar and syntax:

> I always endeavor to introduce you to such authors as will increase your comprehension of things while they contribute toward enlarging your language. ... No one can speak well if he does not understand what he wishes to say, and again knowledge is lame without the light of speech.[90]

---

[88] *W A* 26, 238, 20–21; *L W* 40, 318.

[89] Manschreck, *Melanchthon,* 146, citing *CR* 11:130.

[90] Manschreck, *Melanchthon,* 148, citing E. R. Graves, *History of Education during the Middle Ages and Transition to Modern Times* (New York: The Macmillan Co., 1910), 243.

Religious instruction also should proceed at a rate where students can truly absorb and comprehend what is being taught. Thus, students are asked to recite the Lord's Prayer, the Creed, and the Ten Commandments, and the teacher is obliged to interpret and explain each, so that the children may learn what "is necessary for living a good life, namely, the fear of God, faith, good works."[91] Later on, children may memorize certain Psalms and proceed to a study of the gospel of Matthew, where grammar is again stressed. Those who are even more advanced may proceed to other writings, such as Paul's letter to Timothy or the Book of Proverbs, but in no instance are the students to be expected to read the more theologically difficult texts, such as the gospel of John.

For many students the second division completes their studies. Only those who excel progress to the third, where they study Vergil, Ovid, and Cicero. The boys are required not only to read and repeat the classics, but to create their own poems and letters, thereby increasing their vocabulary and skill in composition. At this level too, music is studied in the hour after noon, and, although it is not explicitly stated, we may assume that religious instruction is incorporated into the curriculum one day of the week.

Given Luther's critique of his own schooling and of that which he saw occurring in the schools, what is perhaps most remarkable about this basic, three-part, curriculum is what it does not include. There is no mention of history or geography or arithmetic, studies that Luther and Melanchthon elsewhere celebrated and encouraged. Instead, the stress falls above all on the learning of Latin grammar. There are certainly some changes—Donatus is not endlessly repeated for 20 and 30 years, as Luther had complained was done in the past. Carefully selected classical works and Scripture form the core of the curriculum, with singing a vital part of each stage of learning. We may perhaps find hints here that Luther and Melanchthon were already being confronted with the task of balancing their ideal curriculum with the realization that parents were willing to part with their children—when at all— for only a few hours a day, and that during that time only a limited amount could be learned and remembered. Under such conditions, the two reformers recognized that their goal must be

---

[91] W A 26, 238, 45–239, 1; L W 40, 318.

twofold. First, it must lay the foundation for further study, thus the stress upon the various components of grammar. Second, it should evoke in students a love of learning, gained through the reading of such accessible classical works as Aesop and Terence, and through such biblical texts as the Psalms, which also are a foundation for Christian living. As curricular reformers, Luther and Melanchthon began with what they had. They sought to improve it, to change it where necessary and possible, and, most of all, to widen the parameters of education. Equally crucial was the building within society of a new attitude toward education, on the part of secular rulers and parents.

To address parents directly, Luther took pen to paper during the weeks he spent on the sidelines at the Diet of Augsburg in 1530. Committed nobles and councilmen who built schools and supported them were essential, but the entire enterprise might yet flounder if parents were not convinced to send their children to school. *A Sermon on Keeping Children in School* was published in August and was dedicated to Lazarus Spengler, the secretary to the city council of Nuremberg. It was Spengler who had journeyed to Wittenberg in 1525 to consult with Luther and Melanchthon on the founding of a new humanistic school, the school that Melanchthon inaugurated in 1526.[92]

Luther portrayed education as a contest between God and the devil. Realizing that he can no longer control education as he once did, the devil now attempts to drive people from it, recognizing that if "Scriptures and learning disappear, what will remain in the German lands but a disorderly and wild crowd of Tartars or Turks, indeed a pigsty and mob of wild beasts."[93] In his efforts, the devil enlists parents, who neglect their duty. Luther's task then is to win over parents. His strategy is to appeal to their desire for profit: "I propose, therefore, to take up the question of what is at stake in this matter in the way of gains and losses, first those that are

---

[92] Harold J. Grimm, *Lazarus Spengler: A Lay Leader of the Reformation* (Columbus: Ohio State University Press, 1978), 86.

[93] *WA* 30 II, 523, 8–11; *L W* 46, 217.

spiritual or eternal, and then those that are temporal or worldly."[94]

Recognizing that parents were genuinely concerned for their children's welfare but misguided in their understanding of it, Luther proceeded very pragmatically, using the language of business and finance to persuade his readers of the benefits of the education. Fulfilling one's parental responsibilities in educating the young yields temporal and eternal rewards for both parent and offspring. Looking at the long term benefit, he questioned: "Is not the money and the labor you expend on such a son so highly honored, so gloriously blessed, so profitably invested that it counts in God's sight as better than any kingdom or empire?"[95]

Luther focused not only on the long term, spiritual benefits of parental investment. He also warned parents of the judgments that would befall themselves and society in general if they failed in their duties. Famine and pestilence were only two of the results that people might expect. But Luther sought mostly to motivate his readers through self-interest, spiritual and secular, rather than through threat. For example, becoming a pastor is a fine career: "To put it in a word, your son can easily get as good a living from the preaching office as from a trade—unless of course you are thinking of great wealth."[96] He reminded his readers that the reform movement had caused significant change within the church, with an accompanying need for new personnel to fill the posts that have now been deserted by the unqualified. Indeed, a job is just waiting for the well-educated young man! Luther held out to parents the promise of full employment for their sons, reminding them to "think ... how many parishes, pulpits, schools, and sacristanships there are. ... Vacancies are occurring every day. ... His living is ready for him before he needs it."[97]

Education also benefits the secular enterprise. The person who has been educated to help individual souls against "sin,

---

[94] WA 30 II, 526, 31–34; L W 46, 219.

[95] W A 30 II, 540, 9–12; L W 46, 228.

[96] WA 30 II, 553, 2–5; L W 46, 236.

[97] W A 30 II, 549, 6–10; LW 46, 234.

death, and the devil," also acts as teacher and guide to the temporal estates "on how they are to conduct themselves outwardly in their several offices and estates, so that they may do what is right in the sight of God. ... In a word, he gives direction to all the temporal estates and offices."[98] The result of this work is the preservation of peace within the community, the highest and most essential work, although it enjoys little respect and esteem from men. Only the pastor can sustain peace through the effects of his preaching. What human enterprise can thrive in the midst of tumult and war?[99] Education enables the secular administrator to know the law and rightly to administer it. Again, Luther admonishes parents to be grateful for the roles their sons might play:

> You would have to be a gross, ungrateful clod, worthy of being numbered among the beasts, if you should see that your son could become a man to help the emperor preserve his empire, sword, and crown; to help the prince rule his principality; to counsel and help cities and lands; to help protect so many men's bodies, wives, children, property, and honor—and yet would not risk enough on it to let him study and come to such a position.[100]

Indeed, for those who are born without great wealth and advantage, education offers the means to achieve extraordinary possibilities. Luther was certainly not above appealing to the ambitions of his readers, noting that in the courts of kings and princes, one "will find jurists, doctors, counselors, writers, preachers, who for the most part were poor and who have certainly all attended school, and who by means of the pen have risen to where they are lords ... helping to rule land and people like princes."[101] These people who have risen to their positions without benefit of high birth prove that it is God

---

[98] W A 30 II, 537, 5–7, 12–13; L W 46, 226.

[99] W A 30 II, 538, 4–6; L W 46, 226.

[100] W A 30 II, 561, 5–10; LW 46, 241.

[101] WA 30 II, 575, 17–576,4; LW 46, 250.

alone, not "nobility at birth," who raises men to positions of power. But education is the means.

Luther's arguments mix threat with admonition with promise, above all stressing that the parent who fails to give his son in service to God is aiding the devil and damaging both human society and God's kingdom. Thus,

> you are depriving God of an angel ... a king and prince in his kingdom; a savior and comforter of men in matters that pertain to body and soul, property and honor. ... Thus you are making a place for the devil and advancing his kingdom so that he brings more souls into sin, death, and hell every day ... the kingdom of God goes down to destruction, along with Christian faith. ... All of this need not have happened and could have been prevented, things could even have been improved, if your son had been trained for this work and entered it.[102]

Nor was Luther adverse to reminding parents that on their deathbeds they will be called to account for their actions. Those that failed to educate their children and thereby enable them to utilize the gifts they received from God for the benefit of God's kingdom will be judged as enemies. In the same vein Luther attacked the argument of parents who try to avoid their responsibility by placing it upon their neighbors. By such selfish reasoning they fail their duty and God's word is lost. Behind such arguments is a false conception of the relationship between parent and child, for such parents act as if their children belong to them. Children belong to God who has given them to the parents for safekeeping and to prepare them for their appropriate role in furthering His kingdom.

Luther did not argue that all children should receive the same amount and type of education. This decision should be governed by natural ability, as well as by the responsibilities associated with the position into which one is born. The sons of nobles should receive an education appropriate to their future roles (although Luther does not specify how that education should differ from that of prospective pastors and schoolteachers). The common people who do not need heirs should send their sons to school according to their ability.

---

[102] *WA* 30 II, 542, 10–543, 1; 543, 3–5; *L W* 46, 229.

However, even the boy who engages in a trade, business, or craft, should learn Latin. These young men thus form a ready reserve of pastors and teachers if the need arises, although that may not be their first calling. James Kittelson notes that in this treatise, in distinction from his 1524 tract *To the Councilmen*, Luther emphasized far more education as the tool for creating an educated clergy. Whereas in 1524, he had "given equal weight to the temporal and spiritual benefits of universal education," the visitations, as well as the events at Augsburg, had led him by 1530 to emphasize the role of education in preparing spiritual leaders.[103]

The influence of educated people extends to the whole world. Without educated people performing their spiritual and secular duties, all of society will crumble, for "when the theologians disappear, God's word also disappears, and nothing but heathen remain, indeed, nothing but devils. When the jurists disappear, then the law disappears, and peace with it, and nothing but robbery, murder, crime, and violence remain."[104] In the midst of such chaos, not even the most dedicated businessman, opposed to devoting time to education, will be able to maintain his position—"what earnings and profits the businessman will have when peace is gone, I shall let his ledger tell him."[105]

If people fail to realize and perform their duty of educating their young, the secular authorities must step in and compel them to do so. This is especially true in the case of the most gifted young people. If the civic authorities can compel people to military duty in defense of society, they can certainly compel people to send their children to school so that the inner defenses of society are maintained, in other words, so that there is an adequate number of "preachers, jurists, pastors, writers, physicians, schoolmasters, and the like, for we cannot do without them."[106] Society is at war. Indeed, the war is all the

---

[103] Kittelson, *Luther the Reformer,* 243, and James Kittelson, "Luther on Education for Ordination," *Lutheran Theological Seminary Bulletin,* vol. 65, no. 1 (Winter 1985), 33.

[104] *W A* 30 II, 578, 5-8; *LW* 46, 251–52.

[105] *W A* 30 II, 578, 8–10; *L W* 46, 252.

[106] *W A* 30 II, 586, 10–11; *L W* 46, 256.

more dangerous because the devil fights the war in secret, "sap[ping] the strength of the cities and principalities, emptying them of their able persons until he has bored out the pity and left only an empty shell of useless people whom he can manipulate and toy with as he will."[107] Within this war, education is the best and only defense.

Scattered throughout this tract are positive references to the many vocations that may be obtained with the benefit of education, from that of jurist to physician to preacher. Singled out for special praise, along with the vocation of pastor and preacher, is that of schoolteacher. Luther recognized the special challenges the teacher faces in educating the young. Indeed, he regarded the vocation of teaching so highly that he proclaimed: "If I could leave the preaching office and my other duties, or had to do so, there is no other office I would rather have than that of schoolmaster or teacher of boys."[108] Much the way that pastors and preachers shape and direct society through God's Word, so do teachers shape the future by preparing God's instruments, those who will teach and preach, judge and heal.

Luther's arguments throughout this writing were driven both by his love of learning and by his recognition of the danger in the present situation. It is impossible to overestimate the urgency that pulses through this tract or to fail to recognize the anger that ebbs below the surface. God's Word has been made known, the battle has been joined, and people have the opportunity to choose sides and battle on behalf of the Word. Indeed, now the victory is in sight. Instead, parents act as if their children exist only for their benefit. They fail to recognize that they are only the caretakers, preparing their children for their roles in secular and spiritual affairs. Luther's anger stemmed from his perception that God calls each individual to a particular task or vocation. By failing to allow children to realize and develop their gifts and thus to fulfill their vocations, parents impede God's will and give support to the devil's wiles. Luther's judgment on such parents is harsh indeed: "You are

---

[107] WA 30 II, 586, 16–587, 1; L W 46, 257.

[108] W A 30 II, 579, 16–580, 1; L W 46, 253.

making a place for the devil and advancing his kingdom so that he brings more souls into sin, death, and hell every day."[109]

The reformers had not fully halted the rejection of learning by "enthusiasts" and misguided parents alike. However, they had begun to wage an effective counter-assault during the decade of the 1520s. Facing innumerable challenges, which appeared to Luther to be the devil's own attacks, he nonetheless focused on what he regarded as his guiding purpose, "our chief purpose in life, namely, the care of the young."[110] Only where learning thrives will the gospel be carried from generation to generation. However, the schools by themselves could not meet all of society's educational needs. And education could not only be an opportunity for the young. Older people too must understand the changes that were occurring. Education in church and home became the next challenge.

---

[109] *W A* 30 II, 542, 31–33; *L W* 46, 229.

[110] *W A* 15, 33, 4–5; *LW* 45, 353.

6

Martin Luther: "A Child and Student of the Catechism"

In his *Large Catechism* of 1529, Luther voiced anew his commitment to the young and expressed his frustration with their elders. He complained:

> For it is clearly useless to try to change old people. We cannot perpetuate these and other teachings unless we train the people who come after us and succeed us in our office and work, so that they in turn may bring up their children successfully. Thus the Word of God and the Christian church will be preserved.[1]

The future of the reform movement lay with the new generation.

In the last chapter we traced Luther's dedicated effort to reform and revitalize education in school and university. While the future rested with the young, the present depended on the efforts of parents, pastors, and teachers. Therefore, the challenge to educate adults to become effective teachers of the young could not be ignored. Adult education, what we might call "continuing education," became a necessity. How did Luther and his colleagues go about this? What did they hope to achieve? And what were their pedagogical methods?

The visitations dramatically demonstrated the dismal conditions prevalent in many parishes where congregations were ignorant and confused, and pastors were sometimes only a small step ahead of their congregations in knowledge. Luther

---

[1] *W A* 30 I, 233, 7–11; Theodore G. Tappert, trans. and ed., *The Book of Concord: The Confessions of the Evangelical Lutheran Church* (Philadelphia: Fortress Press, 1959), 456.

recognized that many priests lived on the edge of poverty, forced to do other work to support themselves. This situation became even more critical as priests began to realize their freedom to marry. To attract knowledgeable and hard working pastors, they must be paid decently. This was a major concern of Luther's during the visitations. Other problems existed as well.

Some interpreted the reform movement as freedom from all ecclesiastical restraints. No longer obliged to observe saints' days, people used their new freedom not as Luther had hoped they would—to study the Scriptures and to become better Christians—but to indulge in drinking and debauchery. Such adults provided very poor models indeed for the young. Thus, while the long term success of the reform movement depended on educating the young, this goal was threatened if adults were left to their own devices. Luther sought the support of the secular authorities to assure that parents would be forced if necessary to send their youngsters to school. At the same time he realized how much children learn at home, from the behavior of their parents. If practices at home were different than those in school and church, children could become confused and uncertain. Thus, the need for adult education was urgent, for the sake of both adults and children. The preparation of catechisms, the revision of the liturgy, and the writing of new hymns, in the language of the people, became crucial tasks.

Parental responsibility took on even greater meaning for Luther as he came to experience the triumphs and trials of marriage and fatherhood. Much to the consternation of Melanchthon in particular, who thought the timing of his colleague's decision ill advised, Luther made the leap from single to married life in 1525. It was apparently a rather sudden decision. In a late November 1524 letter to his friend Georg Spalatin he reflected on the gossip circulating about his rumored plans to marry and declared: "Nevertheless, the way I feel now, and have felt thus far, I will not marry. It is not that I do not feel my flesh or sex, since I am neither wood nor stone, but my mind is far removed from marriage, since I daily expect death and the punishment due to a heretic."[2] A variety of factors appear to have contributed to his decision to marry. Not only would marriage spite his enemies and the devil, it would please

---

[2] *WA Br* 3, 394, 21–25; *L W* 49; 93.

his elderly father and provide a home for the former nun, Katherine von Bora. Arranging a marriage for her had proven difficult, not least because Katherine was not shy in stating her objections to any suitor she found unappealing. Initially a marriage had been arranged between Katherine and the son of a well-to-do Nuremberg family, but the young man's parents had opposed his marrying a former nun.[3] Efforts to arrange a marriage between Katherine and Caspar Glatz also proved unsuccessful. Glatz was a member of the theology faculty who had recently served as rector of the university and had replaced Andreas Carlstadt as pastor in Orlamünde. Katherine herself opposed this match, a judgment that was proven correct several years later when Glatz was accused of inappropriate financial dealings as rector and of negligence as pastor.[4] She made it known that there were only two men she would willingly marry, Nikolaus von Amsdorf, who remained a confirmed bachelor, and Luther himself. With Amsdorf vociferously refusing, the decision fell to Luther.

Marriage opened up a new world to Luther, one that yielded him much joy. Although he could speak of the trials and tribulations of married life, these negatives were more than matched by the benefits he discovered. From the pleasure of working with Katie in the garden to holding his newborn son in his arms, Luther found married life filled with unexpected blessings. In a letter of August 11, 1526 to Michael Stiefel, he declared,

> God in his great goodness has blessed me with a healthy and vigorous son, John, a little Luther. Katie, my rib, sends her greetings. ... She is well, by God's grace, compliant, and in every way is obedient and obliging to me, more than I had ever dared to hope (thank God), so that I would not want to exchange my poverty for the riches of Croseus.[5]

---

[3] Bornkamm, *Luther in Mid-Career*, 403.

[4] Bornkamm, *Luther in Mid-Career*, 403–404; Brecht, *Martin Luther: Shaping and Defining the Reformation*, 195–96.

[5] *WA Br* 4, 109, 7–12; *LW* 49, 154. See also Werner Reiningshaus, *Elternstand, Obrigkeit und Schule bei Luther* (Heidelberg: Quelle & Meyer, 1969.

The birth of his son was followed by that of his daughter Elisabeth a little over a year later, and ultimately, by the birth of four additional children. The seriousness with which Luther took his responsibilities as a father is demonstrated in his approach to the catechism and his stress on Christian education within the home. Luther professed that "every parent is a bishop in his house."[6] The home is the center and foundation of education.

Knowledge of Christian doctrine is essential for the laity, and especially for parents. For parents to function as teachers in the home, they must be able to understand and explain their beliefs as Christians. For the congregation to participate actively and knowledgeably in the worship service, they must be informed. The concepts of the priesthood of believers and Christian freedom demanded this understanding. The new services encouraged active participation and therefore necessitated dramatic changes in the services themselves. Both the revised Latin service and the new German service required the reeducation of clergy and congregations. Where the congregation did not understand Latin, the mass was to be offered in German. Luther himself turned to the task of composing a German mass in 1523. He had initially hoped that others might respond to the challenge of preparing a tool, a catechism, to educate pastors and laity. He had asked both Justus Jonas and Johann Agricola to complete such a work. However, neither they nor Melanchthon, to whom Luther also appealed, were able to do so. As a result, Luther turned to the task, completing the *German Catechism* or *Large Catechism*, as it later came to be known, in April 1529. It was designed primarily to educate the clergy.

In the Preface to the *German Mass and Order of Worship* Luther voiced his concerns about the pressing need to educate people in worship. He professed that "to train the young and to call and attract others to faith, I shall—besides preaching—help

---

[6] Harold J. Grimm, "Luther and Education," in George W. Forell, Harold J. Grimm, and Theodore Hoelty-Nickel, *Luther and Culture.* Martin Luther Lectures, vol. 4. (Decorah, Iowa: Luther College Press, 1960), 103, citing *Predigten D. Martin Luthers,* ed. Georg Buchwald, I, 72–73.

to further such public services for the people, until Christians, who earnestly love the Word find each other and join together."[7] Essential to those services was a "plain and simple, fair and square catechism."[8] Such a catechism would unite people, young and old, pastors and congregations, in understanding and celebrating their common faith.

The catechism was by no means an innovation. It had been widely used in the early church. By the fifteenth century, however, the catechism was most often associated with the sacrament of penance where people were called to reflect upon the Creed and the Ten Commandments as preparation for confession.[9] Thus, the catechism functioned as a "mirror" to perceive and confess sin.[10] Luther may have been drawn to the idea of the catechism not only by necessity but by a desire to reaffirm this connection with a practice of the early church. He envisioned the catechism as providing more than a "mirror" for sin. Similar to the role it had played in the early church, it was to function as a source that "taught and guided in what they should believe, know, do, and leave undone, according to the Christian faith."[11] The catechism, drawing from Scripture and the confessions of the early church, was to serve as a series of

---

[7] WA 19, 75, 23–27; *Luther's Works*, vol. 53: *Liturgy and Hymns*, ed. Ulrich S. Leupold (Philadelphia: Fortress Press, 1965), 64.

[8] WA 19, 76, 2; LW 53, 64.

[9] Denis Janz, *Three Reformation Catechisms: Catholic, Anabaptist, Lutheran*. Texts and Studies in Religion, vol. 13 (New York and Toronto: The Edwin Mellen Press, 1982), 6. For a discussion of preparation for confession and manuals of confession, see Thomas Tentler, *Sin and Confession on the Eve of the Reformation* (Princeton: Princeton University Press, 1977).

[10] Janz, *Three Reformation Catechisms*, 6. For information on medieval catechisms and the relation of Luther's catechism to them, see Lewis W. Spitz, "Further Lines of Inquiry for the Study of 'Reformation and Pedagogy'," in Charles Trinkaus and Heiko Oberman, eds., *The Pursuit of Holiness in Late Medieval and Renaissance Religion* (Leiden: E. J. Brill, 1974), 294–306.

[11] W A 19, 76, 4–5; L W 53, 64.

signposts leading people to Scripture. In Luther's hands, the catechism underscores both individual faith and relationship with God on the one hand, and the responsibilities of life as a member of a community of faith, on the other.

Our initial reaction to the word "catechism" may not be very positive. The idea of memorization rarely draws much enthusiasm! Luther regarded memorization as the essential first step in learning the catechism, but he was too innovative and perceptive a student of human nature in general and of children's nature in particular to believe that memorization is sufficient. Nonetheless, it provides the essential foundation for building understanding. Luther had enough experience of rote memorization in his own youth to know that memorization without interpretation is not true learning. Instead, he thought of the catechism in its original context of "sounding forth," as oral teaching and learning, in short, as dialogue. For him, the "good news" of the rediscovery of the gospel, of salvation by faith through grace, was energizing and joyful. He hoped to bring others to that same perception. The catechism was an essential tool in that process. Thus, the first stage of memorization was to be followed by conversation, by questions and responses, dialogue. Through dialogue a person demonstrates that he or she truly understands the meaning of what has been learned.

At the same time as Luther was composing the *Large Catechism* for the clergy, he was working on the *Small Catechism* for the laity, including children, and the more unlearned among the clergy. Theodore Tappert notes that it would be a mistake to regard the *Small Catechism* as a "condensation" of the *Large Catechism* or the *Large Catechism* as an "expansion" of the *Small Catechism*.[12] The fact that Luther worked on them simultaneously tells us that he viewed them as addressing two different sets of needs and directed toward two different groups. While the *Large Catechism* is sometimes polemical, the *Small Catechism* conveys the fundamentals of faith in as direct and straightforward a tone as possible.[13] Unlike the *Small Catechism*, the *Large Catechism* does not use a straightforward question and answer organization, since Luther intended it for

---

[12] Tappert, *The Book of Concord*, 337.

[13] Tappert, *The Book of Concord*, 337.

pastors and others who had progressed beyond a basic knowledge of Christian doctrine and practice and were now ready for more detailed knowledge. The *Large Catechism* is replete with examples on which the pastor was encouraged to draw in explaining Christian doctrine and practice to his congregation. For example, in discussing the fourth petition of the Lord's Prayer, "Give us this day our daily bread," Luther stressed God's providence and cited a current example of what happens when God withdraws his beneficence: "How much trouble there now is in the world simply on account of false coinage, yes, on account of daily exploitation and usury in public business, trading, and labor on the part of those who wantonly oppress the poor and deprive them of their daily bread!"[14] While affirming that Christians must bear this suffering, he also warned, "let exploiters and oppressors beware lest they lose the common intercession of the church, and let them take care lest this petition of the Lord's Prayer be turned against them."[15] Such concrete examples furnished pastors with ample sermon material!

The *Large Catechism* was rooted in Luther's own sermons. Already in March 1522 Luther sought to respond to the needs of struggling pastors. He published the first of his postils, collections of sermons that could be used as a source book for pastors writing their own sermons, or that could be read from the pulpit by those who were in especially dire straits.[16] Harold Grimm notes that Luther transformed the medieval sermon into a far more effective tool, changing it into a powerful mode of "adult education." Sermons now "became a means of public instruction in religious doctrine and ethics as the sermons of the Apostolic Church had been."[17] The first collection of sermons, the *Weihnachtspostille*, was followed the same year by his advent sermons, the *Adventspostille*. He soon published others, including the *Hauspostille*, which derived from the sermons that

---

[14] *W A* 30 I, 206, 3–6; Tappert, *The Book of Concord*, 431–32.

[15] *W A* 30 I, 206, 7–8; Tappert, *The Book of Concord*, 432.

[16] Grimm, "Luther and Education", 100.

[17] Grimm, "Luther and Education," 95–96.

Luther preached at home and which were recorded in much the way as his *Table Talk*.[18]

The catechisms aimed to provide both pastor and congregation with a firm and thorough understanding of the central aspects of the faith, beginning with the Ten Commandments, and proceeding through the Apostles' Creed, the Our Father, and the sacraments. As David Janz suggests, catechisms offer us an extraordinary opportunity to gain insight into what is most important to a theologian, the essential structure stripped of all accoutrements.[19] Both catechisms begin with the Ten Commandments rather than following the usual catechetical order of Apostles' Creed, Lord's Prayer, and Ten Commandments—creed, cult, and code.[20] Based upon his theological discovery, Luther changed this pattern, which assumed that "faith or belief (creed) makes possible the appropriation of grace (cult), the purpose of which is the way of life prescribed in the law (code)."[21] Luther reversed this pattern, beginning, rather than ending, with the Ten Commandments. Previously, as preparation for the sacrament of penance, this order made pedagogical sense, since it would leave most fresh in the mind of the person confessing the ways in which he or she had violated God's commands. Luther gave the catechism a much broader purpose, as ongoing preparation for daily life. In his Preface of 1530 he wrote that "anyone who knows the Ten Commandments perfectly knows the entire Scripture. ... What is the whole Psalter but meditations and exercises based on the First Commandment?"[22] Of course, he knew the impossibility of fulfilling the commandments and therefore the necessity of turning for salvation to Christ. Luther begins with the Ten Commandments as a way of bringing the

---

[18] Grimm, "Luther and Education," 100.

[19] Janz, *Three Reformation Catechisms*, 4.

[20] Janz, *Three Reformation Catechisms*, 17.

[21] Janz, *Three Reformation Catechisms*, 17.

[22] *W A* 30 I, 128, 22–23; 26–27; Tappert, *The Book of Concord*, 361. Luther's reordering also serves to emphasize the Law/Gospel dichotomy.

individual to an awareness of sin and to the acceptance of failure and recognition of need that comes with the struggle to attain salvation through works.[23] All the elements of Christian doctrine, including Creed, Lord's Prayer, and the sacraments, follow from that starting point, with the progression from "law to faith to prayer."[24] The commandments are also a rebuttal to the antinomianism then occurring.[25]

In his Preface to the *Small Catechism*, Luther urged that after instructing the people in this work, the pastor should proceed to the *Large Catechism*. His directive assumes that the pastor knows his congregation and its needs well so that he can devote more time to those commandments "which seem to require special attention among the people where you are."[26] Luther noted that in some congregations, composed largely of "laborers and shopkeepers," the seventh commandment which prohibits stealing may merit special attention.[27] When addressing children, the fourth commandment, which emphasizes obedience to one's parents, might be the one to receive special attention. Thus, the way the catechism is taught is conditioned by the special circumstances of each congregation. Luther demonstrates his commitment to a flexible pedagogy and to a creative use of the catechism.

The *Small Catechism* was initially published as posters that could be hung in church as a means of educating people visually. Soon thereafter, by mid-May 1529, Luther expanded it to include a Preface and Table of Duties and had it printed as a small book with illustrations.[28] Sections on "A Short Form for

---

[23] Strauss, *Luther's House of Learning*, 161–62. See also the helpful discussion of Luther's catechisms in relation to those of the Catholic Kolde and the Anabaptist Hubmaier, as well as a discussion of the significance of the order within the catechisms, in Janz, *Three Reformation Catechisms*, 17–21, especially 16.

[24] Strauss, *Luther's House of Learning*, 162.

[25] Strauss, *Luther's House of Learning*, 161.

[26] *W A* 30 I, 350, 13–15; Tappert, *The Book of Concord*, 340.

[27] *W A* 30 I, 350, 15–16; Tappert, *The Book of Concord*, 340.

[28] Tappert, *Formula of Concord*, 337.

Marriage, a Short Form for Baptism, and the Litany," were taken from other works by Luther and added by printers to subsequent editions.[29]

Luther gave the *Small Catechism (Der kleine Catechismus für die gemeine Pfarrher und Prediger)* another title as well, that of *Enchiridion*, a Greek word meaning "in the hand." This was a common title used by many authors, including Erasmus of Rotterdam who published his *Enchiridion* or *Handbook of the Militant Christian* in 1503.[30] As Roland Bainton discusses, *enchiridion* has a double meaning, that of either a small weapon one might hold in the hand or a manual or handbook.[31] While Erasmus saw his *Enchiridion* as a "dagger," which the Christian soldier might carry at his side, Luther envisioned his *Enchiridion* as the handbook that could guide the Christian to the Word and to faith.

The *Small Catechism* was designed for pastors, especially those in the rural areas, and congregations who were as yet beginners in faith and who were confused by the immense changes occurring. In his Preface to the work, Luther explained how the catechism is to be used by the pastor in teaching his congregation. In the midst of confusion, the goal is to establish a firm understanding of the basic precepts. Therefore, the text should not be changed lest confusion result: "Young and inexperienced people must be instructed on the basis of a uniform, fixed text and form. ... But when you are teaching the young, adhere to a fixed and unchanging form and method."[32] This admonition may seem to conflict with Luther's stress upon Christian freedom and the variety which he permits and even encourages in the liturgy of the mass itself. However, the catechism should be viewed within the context of the tumultuous events that were swirling around Luther and the reform movement.

---

[29] Tappert, *The Book of Concord,* 337.

[30] Roland Bainton, *Erasmus of Christendom* (New York: Charles Scribner's Sons, 1969), 66.

[31] Bainton, *Erasmus of Christendom,* 66.

[32] *W A* 30 I, 268, 11–13; 270, 4–5; Tappert, *The Book of Concord,* 339.

The Peasants' War and the revolutionary sermons of Thomas Muentzer, the differences with Ulrich Zwingli on the eucharist, and the appeals of the Anabaptists to cease infant baptism had yielded consternation and confusion. All too few pastors could adequately respond to the questions and concerns raised by their congregations. Thus, until the level of knowledge among both laity and clergy improved, Luther advocated a consistency of text as a baseline for interpretation and reflection. After the memorization of the text, pastors were encouraged to bring their congregations to the next level, that of genuine understanding: "After the people have become familiar with the text, teach them what it means. ... Take the explanations in this booklet, or choose any other brief and fixed explanations which you may prefer, and adhere to them without changing a single syllable."[33] Luther had no pride of authorship in insisting that his explanations be used, but he was adamant that the pastor be consistent in his teaching to avoid confusion. As a good teacher, he also admonished pastors and teachers not to seek to cover too much too fast, lest people be overwhelmed and forget what they had learned or become even more confused. Luther and Melanchthon advocated the same approach in their *Instructions to the Visitors* when they prohibited teachers from including too many books in the curriculum or teaching many languages to their young charges.[34]

The *Small Catechism* reaches out to the individual and stresses the personal relationship between the Christian and God. In the explanation to the first article of the Creed, "I believe in God, the Father almighty, maker of heaven and earth," Luther asked the most basic question: "What does this mean?"[35] He answered:

I believe that God has created me and all that exists; that he has given me and still sustains my body and soul, all my limbs and senses, my reason and all the faculties of

---

[33] *W A* 30 I, 272, 10–16; Tappert, *The Book of Concord*, 339–340.

[34] *W A* 26, 236, 37–42; 237, 1–2; *L W* 40, 315.

[35] *W A* 30 I, 247, 19; Tappert, *The Book of Concord*, 344.

> my mind, together with food and clothing, house and
> home, family [wife and child] and property.[36]

The answer is personal, direct, and unmistakable. All that the
Christian has and is; all that supports daily life—from food to
family—comes from God. God is the provider, the sustainer, the
nurturer, of goods, of relationships, of all that gives life and
supports life. No facet of life is lived apart from God's presence
and grace. This was the fundamental understanding Luther was
seeking to build among adults who would then teach their
children.

Creative images helped children and uneducated adults
learn from the catechism. A child was to think of all he or she is
learning as belonging in one of two pouches or purses, faith or
love. The one is for gold and the other for silver. Each purse in
turn has two pockets. Faith's pockets consist of the knowledge
of sin and condemnation through Adam, and of "the part [of
faith that trusts] that through Jesus Christ we are all redeemed
from this corruption, sin, and condemnation."[37] Love's purse
has one pocket for the knowledge "that we should serve and do
good to everyone, even as Christ has done for us," and a
second pocket that includes the knowledge "that we should
gladly endure and suffer all kinds of evil."[38] With these purses
and pockets in mind, the child is to be encouraged "to bring
home verses of Scripture from the sermon and to repeat them at
mealtime for the parents, even as they formerly used to recite
their Latin. And then these verses should be put into the
pouches and pockets, just as pennies, groschen, and gulden are
put into a purse."[39] Through this imaginative technique, the
child gains a framework or organizing principle for learning. A
child who delights in this learning is far ahead of an adult who
attends sermons "for three or four years and does not retain
enough to give a single answer concerning his faith—as I

---

[36] *W A* 30 I, 247, 20–21; 248, 1–5; Tappert, *The Book of Concord*, 345.

[37] *W A* 19, 77, 18–19; *LW* 53, 66.

[38] *W A* 19, 77, 20–22; *LW* 53, 66.

[39] *W A* 19, 77, 23–27; *L W* 53, 66.

experience daily."[40] The goal of catechetical learning is summed up in these words: "Enough has been written in books, yes; but it has not been driven home to the hearts."[41] Both works, the *Large Catechism* and the *Small Catechism,* were intended to make knowledge a matter of the heart, as well as the head.

The reformer realized that children must be approached on their own terms in language they could understand. This approach is exemplified in a letter of August 22, 1530. He penned this letter to his son John, then four years old. In imagery understandable and appealing to a little boy, Luther described to his son

> a lovely garden where many children in golden frocks gather rosy apples under the trees, as well as pears, cherries and plums. ... And they have fine ponies with golden bridles and silver saddles. I asked the gardener who were these children, and he said, "They are the children who like to pray and learn and be good." ... So, my darling son, study and pray hard and tell Lippus and Jost to do this too, so that you may all come together into the garden.[42]

No father who sought to introduce his son to the concept of heaven in such a loving and poetic manner would have been satisfied with turning catechetical learning into meaningless memorization.

Luther's explanation to the first line of the Lord's Prayer in the 1531 revised edition of the *Small Catechism* exemplifies the catechism's orientation to the individual and to the building of faith. To the words, "Our Father who art in heaven," follows the question, "What does this mean?" He replied: "Here God would encourage us to believe that he is truly our Father and we are truly his children in order that we may approach him boldly and confidently in prayer, even as beloved children approach their dear father."[43] This phrase might have been interpreted as

---

[40] *W A* 19, 78, 21–23; *LW* 53, 67.

[41] *WA* 19, 78, 23–24; *L W* 53, 67.

[42] Cited in Bainton, *Here I Stand,* 303.

[43] *W A* 30 I, 369, 6; 370, 1–2; Tappert, *The Book of Concord,* 346.

one stressing the difference between God and man; God is in heaven, we are on earth, but instead Luther chose to focus his interpretation upon the word "father." He stressed not distance but the love and trust implicit in the relationship between father and child. However, this was not to become an individualistic piety that excluded community. From the foundation of personal relationship the Christian is to move into the world. Luther's explanation to the very next line of the prayer, "Hallowed be thy name," offers guidance as to how the honoring of God is to be achieved. He asked,

> How is this done? Answer: When the Word of God is taught clearly and purely and we, as children of God, lead holy lives in accordance with it. ... But whoever teaches and lives otherwise than as the Word of God teaches, profanes the name of God among us.[44]

Honoring God occurs not only through worship but through ethical action, through following the Word of God. Intended to bring people to an understanding of the Christian as lord of all and servant of all, the catechism is shaped and governed by Scripture as the authority for belief and action.

The brief section on baptism likewise stresses the Word as that which gives meaning and purpose to the sacrament. To the initial question "What is Baptism?" there is the response: "Baptism is not merely water, but it is water used according to God's command and connected with God's Word."[45] The question which follows from that is "What gifts or benefits does Baptism bestow?" Luther answered: "It effects forgiveness of sins, delivers from death and the devil, and grants eternal salvation to all who believe, as the Word and promise of God declare."[46] To the question "How can water produce such great effects?" Luther proceeded from the visible sign to that which gives the sign meaning, the Word of God, answering "It is not the water that produces these effects, but the Word of God

---

[44] W A 30 I, 251, 7–9, 10–13; Tappert, *The Book of Concord,* **346.**

[45] W A 30 I, 255, 20–23; Tappert, *The Book of Concord,* 348.

[46] WA 30 I, 256, 8–11; Tappert, *The Book of Concord,* 349.

connected with the water, and our faith which relies on the Word of God connected with the water. For without the Word of God, the water is merely water and no Baptism."[47] And to the concluding question in the section on baptism, "What does such baptizing with water signify?" Luther replied that it signifies the death of the old Adam and the birth of the new person in Christ.[48] Although baptism itself is a one-time act, the battle against sin, against the old Adam, remains a lifelong struggle. Thus, baptism serves as a reminder that "sins and evil lusts should be drowned by daily sorrow and repentance and be put to death, and that the new man should come forth daily and rise up."[49] As Luther indicated in his famous hymn, *Ein feste Burg ist unser Gott*, while the victory through Christ is certain, the battle rages on throughout our lives.

The struggle against sin is also reflected in Luther's discussion of confession in the *Small Catechism*, which is composed of two parts, the act of confession and the reception of forgiveness. People are again addressed as individuals for whom one or another of the Ten Commandments may be especially important. Different vocations lead to different possibilities for sin and for breaking the commandments. Thus, in answer to the question "What are such sins?" he replied,

> Reflect on your condition in the light of the Ten Commandments: whether you are a father or a mother, a son or a daughter, a master or servant; whether you have been disobedient, unfaithful, lazy, ill-tempered, or quarrelsome; whether you have harmed anyone by word or deed; and whether you have stolen, neglected, or wasted anything, or done other evil.[50]

Thus, a servant might confess, "I am unfaithful to my master, for here and there I have not done what I was told. ... I have grumbled and sworn at my mistress" while a master might

---

[47] *WA* 30 I, 256, 22–26; 257, 1; Tappert, *The Book of Concord*, 349.

[48] *WA* 30 I, 257, 16–24; Tappert, *The Book of Concord*, 349.

[49] *WA* 30 I, 257, 19–22; Tappert, *The Book of Concord*, 349.

[50] *W A* 30 I, 384, 9–13; Tappert, *The Book of Concord*, 350.

confess: "I have not been faithful in training my children, servants, and wife to the glory of God. ... I have set a bad example by my immodest language and actions."[51] Urging each individual to reflect upon his or her sin, Luther simultaneously fostered concentration upon the connectedness among individuals. The sinful act of one affects others. People live not only as individuals but as members of a community connected by faith.

In his early years as a monk, Luther had approached confession with fear and anxiety. Indeed, he had driven both himself and his confessors nearly crazy with his efforts to confess each and every sin. This attitude was linked to Luther's concept of God as a judge whom one was expected to appease and from whom one sought to earn righteousness. As he experienced the insights that led him to reject this concept of God, Luther also rejected a "works righteousness" concept of confession. This attitude had transformed an act of comfort and reconciliation into one of terror. Luther advised others not to become self-absorbed in searching their consciences. Such actions lead one not to God, but to a concern for self at the expense of both God and neighbor. Thus, "if ... anyone does not feel that his conscience is burdened by such or by greater sins, he should not worry, nor should he search for and invent other sins, for this would turn confession into torture; he should simply mention one or two sins of which he is aware."[52]

In his 1531 Preface to the *Small Catechism,* Luther indicated that he found especially worrisome the laity's attitude toward the eucharist. Some find no need to receive the sacrament and others "treat it with contempt."[53] It is thus particularly incumbent upon the diligent pastor to educate his flock so that they might joyfully approach the sacrament. While stressing that reception is now a matter of Christian liberty and "no one is to be compelled to believe or to receive the sacrament, no law is to be made concerning it, and no time or place should be appointed for it," it is the pastor's duty to preach and teach his

---

[51] *W A* 30 I, 385, 8–10, 12–13; 386, 2–4; Tappert, *The Book of Concord,* 350.

[52] *W A* 30 I, 386, 7–10; Tappert, *The Book of Concord,* 350.

[53] *W A* 30 I, 351, 10–11; Tappert, *The Book of Concord,* 340.

congregation so that they recognize the importance of the sacrament, stressing that Christ said to his disciples "Do this."[54] While not turning the sacrament into a law, the pastor is to be frank about the "advantage and disadvantage, the benefit and loss, the blessing and danger connected with this sacrament." He should call attention to the fact that anyone who lacks the desire for the sacrament several times a year "is no Christian."[55] The sacrament is vitally important to both individual and community of faith. Christ's admonition was being neglected through a false understanding of Christian freedom.

When Luther turned to discussing the sacrament in the *Small Catechism*, his instructions radiate a concern with making the sacrament meaningful to the individual. While the first two questions "What is the Sacrament of the Altar?" and "Where is this written?" receive objective responses, the next questions "What is the benefit of such eating and drinking?" and "How can bodily eating and drinking produce such great effects?" are answered in terms of the individual's attitude and experience.[56] The answer to the first question stresses the words "for you" and "for the forgiveness of sins." At the same time "for you" is also for us, for all those who approach the sacrament in faith, the priesthood of all believers.[57] The answer to the next question stresses those same words, noting that it is not the bread or the wine or the acts of eating and drinking that produce any effects, but *the words* themselves, when linked to those acts. The best preparation for the sacrament is not mortification of the flesh, although Luther notes that "fasting and bodily preparation are a good external discipline." Most necessary is approaching the sacrament in faith and trust that the words truly apply to oneself: "He is truly worthy and well prepared who believes these words: 'for you' and 'for the

---

[54] *W A* 30 I, 351, 12–13; 352, 6; Tappert, *The Book of Concord*, 340–41.

[55] *WA* 30 I, 352, 18–20; 351, 15–352, 3; Tappert, *The Book of Concord*, 341.

[56] *WA* 30 I, 388–391; Tappert, *The Book of Concord*, 351–52.

[57] *W A* 30 I, 390, 5–7 (1529: 260, 27–31); Tappert, *The Book of Concord*, 352.

forgiveness of sins.' On the other hand, he who does not believe these words, or doubts them, is unworthy and unprepared, for the words 'for you' require truly believing hearts."[58] The catechism stresses the Word and faith in the Word as central to participation in the sacrament and to Christian life. Christian community, the priesthood of all believers, is in turn rooted in this unified conviction. Only when Christians understand the importance of the sacrament to their individual spiritual lives and to their collective life as a Christian community will they return to celebrate the sacrament joyfully and thankfully.

The final sections of the *Small Catechism* emphasize worship within the home, the role of prayer at the beginning and end of the day; and grace at meals, with a concluding discourse on the Christian's role within society. The section on morning and evening prayers was adapted by Luther from the breviary. It is noteworthy on two points, first, the admonition after the morning prayer to sing a hymn, perhaps one on the Ten Commandments, before going to work joyfully, and second, the directive after the evening prayer to "quickly lie down and sleep in peace."[59] Luther loved and appreciated music and looked with suspicion on anyone who could not or was not willing to sing. Lifting up one's voice to the Lord sets the tone for which to begin one's work, to fulfill those activities to which God has called one. At the end of the day, the Christian who has joyfully fulfilled his or her duties, who approaches God in faith for forgiveness, may indeed sleep in peace. As Luther had learned after many a restless night, the Christian is justified by faith not by works, thus there should be no sleepless nights of pondering what one has left unaccomplished or what sins one has committed. In confidence and trust, the Christian sleeps in peace and rises joyfully to face a new day.

Tappert notes that in formulating the Table of Duties Luther was probably influenced by Jean Gerson's *Tractatus de modo vivendi omnium fidelium*.[60] Composed of biblical passages, the

---

[58] WA 30 I, 391, 5–6; 392, 1–3 (1529: 261, 16–24); Tappert, *The Book of Concord*, 352.

[59] WA 30 I, 262, 9–10, 21; Tappert, *The Book of Concord*, 353.

[60] Tappert, *The Book of Concord*, 354, n. 8. For a discussion of Gerson and Luther on confession, see Tentler, *Sin and Confession on the Eve of the Reformation*, especially 349-62.

Table addresses the duties of bishops, pastors, and preachers on the one hand, and the duties that Christians owe to their spiritual leaders on the other, as well as the obligations of both governing authorities and their subjects. It outlines the appropriate roles of husbands and wives; parents and children, servants and masters, young persons in general, and widows. The text concludes with the duties of "Christians in General," which are summarized by the statement to love one's neighbor as oneself and to pray for all people. Thus, this final passage of the catechism ends with an emphasis on ethics and worship, the twin cornerstones of Christian life. In the 1531 edition Luther concluded with the words, "Let each his lesson learn with care And all the household well will fare," the counterpoint to the preface's admonition about the responsibilities of the "governing authorities and parents to rule wisely and educate their children."[61] Those who fail in their responsibility to teach the young and prepare them to become "pastors, preachers, notaries, etc. ... lay waste both the kingdom of God and the kingdom of the world and are the worst enemies of God and man."[62] They are, in short, furthering the work of the devil who "has a horrible purpose in mind."[63]

Luther's 1530 Preface to the *Large Catechism* addressed some of the abuses of Christian freedom resulting from the failure of pastors to fulfill their duties in instructing their parishioners. Free now from the obligation to pray the monastic Hours, pastors should "every morning, noon, and evening ... read, instead, at least a page or two from the Catechism, the Prayer Book, the New Testament, or something else from the Bible and ... pray the Lord's Prayer for themselves and their parishioners."[64] Instead, both pastors and congregations have been taken over by an "insidious plague of security and

---

[61] *W A* 30 I, 402, 3–4; 350, 21; 351, 1; Tappert, *The Book of Concord*, 356 and 340.

[62] *W A* 30 I, 351, 3–6; Tappert, *The Book of Concord*, 340.

[63] *W A* 30 I, 351, 8–9; Tappert, *The Book of Concord*, 340.

[64] *W A* 30 I, 125, 17–21; Tappert, *The Book of Concord*, 358.

boredom."[65] This plague has led people to feel superior to the "simple" catechism, which they believe they can quickly master and then "toss the book into a corner as if they are ashamed to read it again."[66] The situation had degenerated so much that the nobility, those most responsible for supporting and providing for the church, rejected the need for pastors, "because we have everything in books and can learn it all by ourselves." The result is that "parishes fall into decay" while "pastors and preachers suffer ... distress and hunger."[67]

To correct these abuses in the future, Luther underscored the importance of educating the young and setting a pattern of Christian habits for them to follow as adults. Children should be taught to recite the three principal parts of Christian instruction, the Ten Commandments, the Creed, and the Our Father, when they arise, at mealtimes, and at bedtime. Indeed, Luther even suggested that once children have learned these essentials of Christian belief, they should not receive food or drink until they have recited them, with the same penalty holding for recalcitrant servants. Lest such words seem harsh, there is ample evidence throughout the *Large Catechism* that Luther understood that children learn gradually and that they learn best when taught with examples to which they can relate. Thus, as he reflected upon the first and second commandments, Luther admonished pastors to make use of "childish and playful methods ... [so that] we may bring up our youth in the fear and honor of God ... for when we preach to children, we must also speak their language."[68] Elsewhere he remarked that young people are not to be trained "only with blows and compulsion, like cattle, but in the fear and reverence of God."[69]

In this context too, Luther forcefully reminded parents of their responsibility in educating their children and pastors of their responsibility in telling parents that children are a divine

---

[65] *WA* 30 I, 126, 4–5; Tappert, *The Book of Concord*, 359.

[66] *WA* 30 I, 126, 5–7; *Tappert, The Book of Concord*, 359.

[67] *WA* 30 I, 126, 8–12; Tappert, *The Book of Concord*, 359.

[68] *WA* 30 I, 142, 37–38; 143, 9–10; Tappert, *The Book of Concord*, 375.

[69] *WA* 30 I, 143, 7–8; Tappert, *The Book of Concord*, 410.

gift. The future of Christianity depends on their fulfilling their responsibilities:

> Nor is it recognized how very necessary it is to devote serious attention to the young. If we want qualified and capable men for both civil and spiritual leadership, we must spare no effort, time, and expense in teaching and educating our children to serve God and mankind. ... He has given and entrusted children to us with the command that we train and govern them according to his will. ... Therefore let everybody know that it is his chief duty, on pain of losing grace, to bring up his children in the fear and knowledge of God, and if they are gifted to give them opportunity to learn and study so that they may be of service wherever they are needed.[70]

Parents who neglect their duty bring upon themselves "sin and wrath, thus earning hell by the way you have reared your own children, no matter how devout and holy you may be in other respects."[71] While Luther was consistently concerned with parental responsibility and education of the young, his concern was heightened by his recognition of both the growing divisions within the reform movement and by the fact that many had used change to satisfy their own desires rather than to grow in faith.

Luther offered himself as a model of the learned doctor of theology who was never too wise to return daily to the catechism and to recite the Lord's Prayer, the Creed, and the Ten Commandments. Indeed, Luther asserted, even for those who are advanced in the study of the catechism, there is always the need to return to its truths as "the subject of meditation and conversation."[72] In this way, through the working of the Holy Spirit the catechism builds faith and community, and appreciation of the catechism grows.[73] The catechism contains

---

[70] W A 30 I, 156, 24–27, 30–35; Tappert, *The Book of Concord*, 388–89.

[71] W A 30 I, 157, 4–6; Tappert, *The Book of Concord*, 389.

[72] WA 30 I, 127, 1; Tappert, *The Book of Concord*, 359.

[73] W A 30 I, 127, 1–4; Tappert, *The Book of Concord*, 359.

the Word of God on which Christians are commanded to meditate. Thus, all Christians, and most particularly pastors, should "exercise themselves in the Catechism daily, and constantly put it into practice, guarding themselves with the greatest care and diligence against the poisonous infection of such security or vanity. Let them continue to read and teach, to learn and meditate and ponder."[74] Learning is lifelong, with a progression from reading to teaching to reflection, followed by learning and reading with new knowledge. Pastors should not be "know it alls" who think themselves doctors when they are but children in the faith. With irony Luther noted: "Let them never stop until they have proved by experience that they have taught the devil to death and have become wiser than God himself and all his saints."[75] Those who pursue such daily study and meditation will come to know that "the longer they work with the Catechism, the less they know of it and the more they have to learn. Only then, hungry and thirsty, will they truly relish what now they cannot bear to smell because they are so bloated and surfeited."[76]

These statements offer important insights into Luther's understanding of Christian education. For while a Christian may make progress in learning through study and meditation, just as Luther described himself as having seen another side of Scripture as a result of his meditation on Romans 1:17, one is called back again and again to the Word, whose profundity can never be exhausted. Thus, one remains—as Luther describes himself—child and student of the catechism. Study of the catechism was an especially vital part of what Luther termed "house worship." These were not situations in which the father professed to know all—even though Luther affirmed parents were bishops in their own homes—while everyone else merely listened. By virtue of age and his own daily study of Bible and catechism, the father would be expected to guide the study of the catechism, but he would also be open to the insights shared by the youngest child. The center of study and the true teacher is not the person delivering the text of the catechism, but the

---

[74] W A 30 I, 128, 33–35; 129, 1; Tappert, *The Book of Concord*, 361.

[75] WA 30 I, 129, 1–4; Tappert, *The Book of Concord*, 361.

[76] W A 30 I, 129, 7–10; Tappert, *The Book of Concord*, 361.

Word itself. The Word sets the tone of teaching and learning, of sharing and meditating that envelops all present, provided they do not assume that they are too wise to learn. The catechism is both an unceasing source of knowledge and the standard against which an individual's knowledge is to be measured. Just as a person may learn more and more about his (or her) craft although he (she) may already be a master, so too must he or she have reached a certain level of ability to gain that title. The same holds true for the Christian, Luther affirmed, "just as a craftsman who does not know the rules and practices of his craft is rejected and considered incompetent. For this reason young people should be thoroughly instructed in the various parts of the Catechism or children's sermons and diligently drilled in their practice."[77]

Christians should also recite Psalms and hymns to reinforce their knowledge of the catechism. As Luther wrote, these texts "supplement and confirm their knowledge."[78] The pastor's sermons and preachings on the catechism also enhance knowledge and understanding. In this way, when people are questioned they will be able to explain what they have learned. Mere memorizing or rote knowledge is not sufficient. It is only the essential first step toward growing into a much more profound and personal understanding of Christian truth.

This concern for building knowledge is borne out by Luther's insistence that adequate time be devoted throughout the week to teaching the Word and reinforcing the teachings of the catechism. Thus, in his commentary in the *Large Catechism* on the Third Commandment, "You shall sanctify the holy day," Luther noted that while daily worship is to be desired, this unfortunately imposes too heavy a burden on working people, so that one day alone should be set aside when we can "deal especially with the Ten Commandments, the Creed, and the Lord's Prayer."[79] For the young, however, several additional hours are to be set aside.

Like the *Small Catechism*, the *Large Catechism* also builds connections between the individual and community; and

---

[77] *WA* 30 I, 129, 16–20; Tappert, *The Book of Concord*, 362.

[78] *W A* 30 I, 132, 16–19; Tappert, *The Book of Concord*, 364.

[79] *WA* 30 I, 145, 6–10; Tappert, *The Book of Concord*, 377.

between belief and action. In teaching the second article of the Apostles' Creed, Luther questioned "What is it 'to become a Lord'? It means that he has redeemed *me* (italics mine) from sin, from the devil, from death, and from all evil." Then in the third article, he questioned:

> How does this sanctifying take place? Answer: Just as the Son obtains dominion by purchasing *us* (italics mine) through his birth, death, and resurrection, etc., so the Holy Spirit effects *our* (italics mine) sanctification through the following, the communion of saints or Christian church, the forgiveness of sins, the resurrection of the body, and the life everlasting. In other words, he first leads us into his holy community, placing us upon the bosom of the church, where he preaches to us and brings us to Christ.[80]

In *Luther's House of Learning: Indoctrination of the Young in the German Reformation*, Gerald Strauss argues that in response to the tumult and confusion, Luther, Melanchthon and their colleagues came to espouse a concept of education that was linked to governmental support and enforcement. Recognizing the failure of parents to fulfill their responsibilities, "Luther gave his support to this shift of educational authority from private to public jurisdiction, from voluntary to compulsory participation, and from associative to institutional organization."[81] While it is true that the reformers emphasized the role of public officials in supporting education, particularly in cases where parents failed to perform their proper responsibility, Luther continued to affirm the centrality of education in both home and church. Indeed, his pedagogical theory is fundamentally collaborative and reinforcing. Emphasis fell on the civic sector only when education was not being realized in home and church. Education begins in the home, and is reinforced in church through catechism classes, sermons on the catechism, and the learning of hymns that reinforce catechetical teachings. In school, these same teachings are

---

[80] *W A* 30 I, 186, 11–13; 187, 36–38; 188, 1–5 ; Tappert, *The Book of Concord*, 414; 415.

[81] Strauss, *Luther's House of Learning*, 7.

reinforced through the study of Scripture and music, with children subsequently assuming leadership in teaching adults the hymns that embody these teachings.

Among the most serious problems the reformers faced were two types of parishioners, those who attended sermons without paying attention and learning anything, and those who perceived Evangelical freedom as the option not to attend church. Luther and his colleagues were concerned about such people both for their own sakes and for their influence upon their children. To inculcate genuine understanding of the faith and a sense of commitment to Christian community required starting where people were and winning them to the Gospel.

This process necessitated changes in the manner in which worship was conducted. Already in 1523 Luther had discussed the general shape of such services in his *Concerning the Order of Public Worship*, written to help guide those who wished to institute change but were unsure how to proceed. Weekday services were to be held in the early morning and in the evening, the equivalent of the earlier matins and vespers services.[82] Central to both services is the preaching of the Word, with the Old Testament being read in the morning and the New Testament in the evening or the reverse. Neither service is to exceed an hour "for one must not overload souls or weary them."[83] By the daily reading of the Bible and by hearing sermons upon specific texts, Luther hoped that people would become "proficient, skilful, and thus well versed in the Bible."[84] The mass was no longer offered daily, although it might be held if people so desired and if there was sufficient time. The reason for this fundamental change is clear "for the Word is important and not the mass."[85]

Both weekday services and Sunday mass were governed by the centrality of the Word and by Luther's desire to promote an active understanding of the priesthood of all believers. Truly to be priests—and to appreciate all that they have received

---

[82] Bornkamm, *Luther in Mid-Career*, 134.

[83] *W A* 12, 36, 13–16; *LW* 53, 12.

[84] *W A* 12, 36, 7–8; *LW* 53, 12.

[85] *W A* 12, 37, 6–7; *L W* 53, 13.

through faith—Christians must understand what is at the core of Christian belief and life. Thus, while the services are above all occasions for praise, they also are enveloped in an "inclusive pedagogical context."[86] In his comments on *The German Mass and Order of Service*, Luther outlined a schedule for the texts that are to be taught: "On Monday and Tuesday mornings we have a German lesson on the Ten Commandments, the Creed, Lord's Prayer, baptism, and sacrament, so that these two days preserve and deepen the understanding of the catechism."[87] On Wednesday follows another German lesson with the Gospel of Matthew; Thursday and Friday mornings have the "epistles of the apostles and the rest of the New Testament assigned to them" while the gospel of John is the focus of the Saturday vespers service.[88]

The changes in the mass were designed to reassert the centrality of the Word and to awaken thanksgiving and further growth in faith. Thus, the 1523 *Order of Mass and Communion at Wittenberg* established that services are to be constructed so that the "spirit of the faithful" is not "quenched ... with tedium."[89] Individual congregations and their pastors were also given the freedom to follow practices that are meaningful to them "as long as the Word of God is diligently and faithfully preached in the church."[90] While Luther addressed himself on this occasion to the mass conducted in Latin, he also called for hymns to be written in the vernacular. In this way, the "people could sing during mass, immediately after the gradual and also after the Sanctus and Agnus Dei."[91] He lamented the paucity of such hymns and called upon those who were able to write works that encourage devotion. Through the Latin service, children might be offered additional practice in the language,

---

[86] Bornkamm, *Luther in Mid-Career*, 475.

[87] *W A* 12, 79, 17–20; *L W* 53, 68.

[88] *WA* 12, 79, 20–27; 80, 1–3; *L W* 53, 68; 69.

[89] *WA* 12, 210, 7–8; *LW* 53, 24.

[90] *W A* 12, 218, 33–35; *LW* 53, 37.

[91] *W A* 12, 218, 15–16; *L W* 53, 36.

which would in turn prepare them one day to be able to "participate in worship services in other lands."[92] Luther announced that he had no intention of "discontinu[ing] the service in the Latin language, because the young are my chief concern."[93] Indeed, Luther proclaimed that if he could, he would have the service conducted in alternate weeks not only in German and Latin, but also in Greek and Hebrew, for it is "reasonable that the young should be trained in many languages; for who knows how God may use them in times to come? For this purpose our schools were founded."[94]

Luther envisioned the young as playing a vital role in worship, and he emphasized the pedagogical significance of daily services. Every weekday they were to "chant a few Psalms in Latin before the lesson" so that they might become knowledgeable in the Latin Bible. Two or three boys were then called upon, after the reading of the Psalms, to "read a chapter from the Latin New Testament, depending on the length."[95] The service must also benefit those adults who do not understand Latin. Thus, he advised, "another boy then reads the same chapter in German to familiarize them with it and for the benefit of any layman who might be present and listening."[96] The same pattern holds for the vespers service "throughout the week in cities where there are schools."[97] Guidance for worship was most desperately needed in the rural areas where there were no Latin schools and where the pastors themselves were the most deficient. Preceding Luther, Thomas Muentzer had prepared a German translation of the Mass. Luther believed that he had failed, however, to bring the task to completion, for he had left in place the plainchant melodies, albeit now accompanied by German, not Latin, words. Luther's goal was

---

[92] Brecht, *Martin Luther: Shaping and Defining*, 255.

[93] *W A* 19, 74, 4–5; *LW* 53, 63.

[94] *WA* 19, 74, 19–21; *LW* 53, 63.

[95] *W A* 19, 80, 4–6, 7–9; *L W* 53, 69.

[96] *W A* 19, 80, 9–11; *L W* 53, 69.

[97] *W A* 19, 80, 23–24; *L W* 53, 69.

far more ambitious. As he wrote, "I hate to see the Latin notes set over the German words. I told the publisher what the German manner of singing is. This is what I want to introduce here."[98] Luther perceived text and music as constituting a whole, reinforcing one another. Thus, when the words were translated, the music must be changed to fit the new rhythm and cadence of the words.

Luther regarded the process of joining music to text as far more than another arduous task that must be accomplished as part of reform. He approached the task joyfully, convinced that music is a tremendous gift. In his 1538 Preface to George Rhau's collection of music entitled *Symphoniae iucundae,* Luther praised music as the "excellent gift of God" and mused over the mystery of how the human voice produces song. He proclaimed that "next to the Word of God, music deserves the highest praise" because of its profound ability to move people's emotions.[99] Luther voiced such thoughts many times over the years, in prefaces to collections of songs, in letters, and in the conversations recorded in the *Table Talk.* Music is a creature of God and is intended above all to praise God. However, like many others of God's good creations, music too may be misused, and Luther wrote bitterly against those who did so. He proclaimed:

> Take special care to shun perverted minds who prostitute this lovely gift of nature and of art with their erotic rantings; and be quite assured that none but the devil goads them on to defy their very nature which would and should praise God its Maker with this gift, so that these bastards purloin the gift of God and use it to worship the foe of God, the enemy of nature and of this lovely art.[100]

In 1524 in his preface to the *Geistliches Gesangbüchlein* or Wittenberg Hymnal, Luther had made known his understanding of the proper and improper use of the divine gift of music.

---

[98] *WA Br* 3, 462, 2–5; cited in *L W* 53, 54.

[99] *WA* 50, 368, 4; 370, 15; 371, 1–4; *L W* 53, 321, 323.

[100] *W A* 50, 373, 11; 374, 1–5; *LW* 53, 324.

Speaking of his own compositions and others included in the hymnal, Luther noted that they were composed in four parts "to give the young—who should at any rate be trained in music and other fine arts—something to wean them away from love ballads and carnal songs and to teach them something of value in their place, thus combining the good with the pleasing, as is proper for youth."[101] Luther recognized that the young could be drawn to the Gospel by music and therefore stressed musical training. He also affirmed that children could be the music teachers of their elders.

In the context of setting the agenda for church councils in the 1539 writing *On the Councils and the Church,* Luther asserted that the councils should occupy themselves with "matters of faith" and not consider questions of ceremony that should be handled within each parish and left to the judgment of pastor and schoolmaster.[102] Luther maintained that it is from the children, under the guidance of the pastor and schoolmaster, that the "common people will learn ... what, when, and how to sing or pray in church. ... When the pupils kneel and fold their hands as the schoolmaster beats time with his baton during the singing of 'And was made man,' the common people will imitate them."[103] Several points are worth noting. First, and perhaps most alarming, is the fact that in 1539, over twenty years after the initiation of the reform movement, there were still many who were at the very earliest stages of understanding Evangelical doctrines and practices. Second, his statement tells us much about both his pedagogy and its roots in the concept of the priesthood of all believers. Precisely because there is spiritual equality and because salvation is by faith, not by works, their elders may without embarrassment or hesitation learn from the young, and the young without arrogance may become the teachers of their elders. Music becomes the link between education and worship, although Carl Schalk rightly stresses that Luther understood music as first and foremost as

---

[101] WA 35, 474, 18–21; 475, 1–2; L W 53, 316.

[102] WA 50, 618, 36; 619, 5–7; *Luther's Works,* vol. 41: *Church and Ministry III,* ed. Eric W. Gritsch (Philadelphia: Fortress Press, 1966), 136–37.

[103] WA 50, 619, 9-13; L W 41, 137.

the *viva vox evangelii,* not as a teaching tool.[104] Music is both praise *and* mode for learning the Gospel. It both celebrates *and* teaches so that celebration may be rightly understood. Paul Nettl notes that congregational singing of hymns was a new experience for most members of the laity, and perhaps surprisingly, not one which was always greeted enthusiastically. Rather than sitting or standing passively, the service now required the congregation to pay attention and become actively involved—very much in keeping with the concept of the priesthood of all believers. This was quite a change, especially for older adults, who must have approached the new services with both awe and trepidation. None understood musical notes. Nettl reminds us that

> hymnbooks were designed for the pastor and cantor alone. ... The children, however, learned the hymns and sang them in church. They became the music teacher of the grownups, and boys not infrequently were scattered among the worshipers to carry the latter along during the hymnsinging.[105]

Many books and articles have been written about Luther's compositions and the role music played in church. Debate continues about the sources which influenced him and the originality of his work. Luther was adamant that there should be powerful hymns in the vernacular, but he was equally certain that people must keep silent until they learn the hymns. He retained the chant and worked with Johann Walther and Konrad Rupsch, professional musicians whom he considered much more gifted than he, to change the chants to conform to the Evangelical service. Some 40 years later, Walther described Luther's musical knowledge and the intensity with which he pondered questions of mode, changing modes to attain the unity of speaker, words, and music he desired. Thus, Walther recorded that Luther set the mode for Christ's words as the sixth—a sweet sound—while those of the apostle were in the

---

[104] Carl Schalk, *Luther on Music: Paradigms of Praise* (St. Louis: Concordia Publishing House, 1988), 47–50.

[105] Paul Nettl, *Luther and Music,* trans. Frida Best and Ralph Wood (New York: Russell & Russell, 1967 [1948]), 82.

more somber eighth.[106] Luther underscored the role of the choir and utilized the organ both in combination with the choir and alone to provide the congregation with time for reflection. Paul Nettl asserts that in Luther's time

> the hymn was never sung by the congregation alone. It was the custom to alternate between choir and congregation, and the singing was responsive. ... The choir sang the polyphonic arrangement of the hymn, alternating with the congregation; at times the choir and congregation remained silent and the organ played a stanza. ... The singing of the minister or the choir boys, alternating with the congregation or the choir, gave the service an uplifting, joyous, and jubilant tone. The hymn was interspersed with the playing of the organ alone, to give the worshiper time for silent reflection.[107]

Although Luther was cautious in allowing the unschooled congregation to sing without adequate training, he may not have reckoned with the power of music. Just as Luther himself adapted folk songs to his purposes and sought through engaging music to wean the young from music that furthered misbehavior, so the laity adopted the music of the church as their own. Schalk describes Luther's accomplishment as shifting "the emphasis from music as a science about which one might speculate to *musica practica*, music as a performed art."[108] In her study *Lay Culture, Learned Culture: Books and Social Change in Strasbourg 1480–1599*, Miriam Chrisman suggests that the view of the sixteenth century Evangelical family as one seated around the table with the father reading from the Bible is "an optimistic view of the sixteenth century," but what families of that time were more likely to own was a "psalm book, especially psalms set to music." It was through such books and

---

[106] *LW* 53, 59.

[107] Nettl, *Luther and Music*, 92–94.

[108] Schalk, *Luther on Music*, 19.

congregational "singing that they became familiar with the Word."[109]

Luther and his colleagues insisted that both pastor and schoolteacher be proficient in music. In a letter to the composer Ludwig Senfl, Luther wrote:

> It is necessary indeed that music be taught in the schools. A teacher must be able to sing; otherwise I will not as much as look at him. Also, we should not ordain young men into the ministry unless they have become well acquainted with music in the schools. Music is a beautiful and glorious gift of God and close to theology.[110]

Luther hoped that music might flourish not only in church and school, but within the life of the family, as it did in his own. Church furnished opportunities for people to practice their singing of hymns during the week. Luther recommended that the singing of hymns follow upon catechetical study "to supplement and confirm their knowledge."[111] We know that Luther himself began and ended his day with prayer and the catechism. He loved to gather together friends and family for music after dinner. Dating back to his youth, he loved to sing and to play the lute. He was especially fond of Christmas hymns such as *Ein Kindelein so löbelich*.[112] Luther wrote a touching letter to Thomas Zink whose young son had been a student at the University, had spent much time with Luther and his family, and had died unexpectedly on April 22, 1532. He told the grieving father: "We were all very fond of the boy (*"ein lieber Bube gewesen ist"*); he was especially dear to me—so that I

[109] Miriam Usher Chrisman, *Lay Culture, Learned Culture: Books and Social Change in Strasbourg 1480–1599* (New Haven and London: Yale University Press, 1982), 155 and 166.

[110] Cited in Walter E. Buszin, *Luther on Music* (Saint Paul: Lutheran Society for Worship, Music, and Arts, pamphlet series no. 3, printed at the North Central Publishing Company, 1958), 8.

[111] *W A* 30 I, 132, 16–19; Tappert, *The Book of Concord*, 364. Bainton, *Here I Stand*, 346.

[112] Buszin, *Luther on Music*, 12.

made use of him many an evening for singing in my house."[113] In the fall of 1542 Luther sent his son Hans, then sixteen years old, to Marcus Crodel, rector of the humanistically oriented school in Torgau, "to be drilled in grammar and music."[114] In that same letter he sent his greetings to his friend, the composer and Torgau cantor, Johann Walther, commending Hans to him for music instruction and adding, "For I, of course, produce theologians, but I would also like to produce grammarians and musicians."[115] Luther stressed the ethical effect of music, describing it as " 'a disciplinarian and moral trainer' which makes man 'more gentle and refined, more conscientious and sensible.' "[116]

The Wittenberg reformers' high esteem for musicians and their contribution to society is manifested in letters written by Luther and Melanchthon to Frederick the Wise's successor, John the Constant. These letters protested his decision to do away with the choir of the Castle Church and the court orchestra—a decision that ended the employment of the distinguished cantor and composer Johann Walther. Luther reminded the elector that "the art [of music] is worthy of being supported and maintained by princes and lords, much more so than many other endeavors and enterprises for which there is not nearly so much need."[117] Melanchthon questioned: "Why should the noble art of music not remain active for God's sake, since it is used for the service and glory of God?"[118]

Luther utilized music to glorify God. He was not concerned with composing strictly original works but with creating those that would be, in the words of Carl Schalk, "paradigms of

---

[113] WA Br 6, 301, 8–10; *Luther's Works*, vol. 50: *Letters III*, ed. and trans. Gottfried Krodel (Philadelphia: Fortress Press, 1975), 51.

[114] WA Br 10, 134, 3–5; LW 50, 231.

[115] WA Br 10, 134, 19–20; LW 50, 232–33.

[116] Nettl, *Luther and Music*, 34.

[117] Cited in Buszin, *Luther on Music*, 9.

[118] Cited in Buszin, *Luther on Music*, 9.

praise."[119] Nonetheless, his contribution to music was significant. His works grew from his experience of the love and mercy of God, and the joys and trials of life. *Ein feste Burg,* Luther's most famous hymn, was probably written at some point during the years 1527 and 1528. Luther wrote it not to portray his "own feelings, but to interpret and apply the 46th Psalm to the church of his own time and its struggles."[120] The hymn communicates trust in Christ who will conquer in spite of the devil's raging, and confidence in the Word, which will endure through all opposition. Luther composed hymns that embodied the Gospel but also hymns on the Law, most specifically the Ten Commandments. Leupold notes that these "hymns were sung in the weekday services during Lent when the sermons were on the Catechism. According to the Wittenberg church order of 1533, the choir boys were supposed to sing this hymn, ["These Are the Holy Ten Commandments"] before catechism sermons and the other hymn ["Man, Wouldst Thou Live All Blissfully"] afterward."[121] Music reinforced the teachings in the catechism and enabled the congregation's affirmation with their own voices. Music also served to rally and unite Evangelicals in the fight with those who opposed their teachings. As Brecht notes, "religious music was also reclaimed as a subject for learning" and songs became in fact " 'the Bible of the simple'."[122] Brecht reminds us that in spite of the best efforts of Luther and his colleagues, the lessons did not always take, and the people sometimes failed, for whatever reason, to be engaged. Such a response led Luther to redouble his efforts to educate the young, the best hope for the future.

If for some the hymns failed to engage, educate, and transform as Luther had hoped, for others, like the Meistersinger of Nuremberg Hans Sachs, Luther's works heralded a religious revolution. For Sachs, who began to collect

---

[119] Schalk, *Luther and Music,* 31; Victor Gebauer, "Luther: The Musician," in *Pastoral Music,* vol. 8, no. 5 (June–July 1984), 18.

[120] Leupold's introduction in *LW* 53, 283.

[121] Leupold in *LW* 53, 277.

[122] Brecht, *Martin Luther: Shaping and Defining the Reformation,* 133 and 257.

Luther's works in 1520, Luther was "the Wittenberg nightingale." Like his predecessor in Greek legend, he would "rather die than stop singing."[123] Through a vernacular liturgy with congregational singing, and through the clarity and consistency of the catechisms, Luther educated people to become active worshipers who could embody the meaning of the priesthood of all believers. All of Luther's efforts at education, involving both adults and children, were founded upon a vision of the Christian community as composed of those spiritually equal by faith before God. In such a community, parents, as bishops in their homes, were responsible for teaching their households the catechism, and, at least as importantly, for modeling its importance in their own lives by returning to it daily. In this same community, children, learning to sing in school and church, were the teachers of their elders. Luther and his colleagues confronted two challenges: to convince adults to approach learning with the openness and joy of children, and to train children to realize their vocations, to become the pastors, the teachers, the Christian mothers and fathers of tomorrow.[124] The catechisms, the reformed liturgy, and the congregational hymns were their creative responses to those challenges.

---

[123] Eli Sobel, "Martin Luther and Hans Sachs," in Gerhard Dünnhaupt, ed., *The Martin Luther Quincentennial* (Detroit: Wayne State University, 1985), 129–41, 133.

[124] As with other topics treated or referenced in this volume, the scope and limits of this study do not permit a listing much less a discussion of the extensive literature on Luther's catechisms. Nevertheless, mention should be made of the exhaustive analysis in Albrecht Peters, *Kommentar zu Luthers Katechismus*, ed. Gottfried Seebaß, 5 vols. (Göttingen: Vandenhoeck & Ruprecht, 1990-1994). Modern efforts to help pastors, teachers, and parents make lively use of the catechism are offered, for example, by the following: Timothy Wengert, " 'Fear and Love' in the Ten Commandments," *Concordia Journal* 21 (1995): 14-27; Charles P. Arand, "Does Catechesis in the LCMS Aim for the *Ars Vivendi Fide*?" *Concordia Journal* 22 (1996): 57-65; Arand, " 'He Walks with Me and Talks with me ...': Today's New 'Creeds,' " *Concordia Journal* 22 (1996): 370-77; Arand, "Catechismal Services: A Bridge Between Evangelism and Assimilation," *Concordia Journal* 23 (1997): 177-91.

Der kleine
Catechiſmus fur
die gemeine Pfar-
herr vnd Pre-
diger.
Mart. Luther.
Wittemberg.

*Title page of Luther's Small Catechism, printed by Conrad Treffer,
Erfurt, s. d.*

7

Martin Luther: "The World Is Still the World"

From university and school reform to the education of clergy and laity through postils, catechisms, orders of worship, and hymnals, Martin Luther sought to change the structure of education in sixteenth-century Germany. Centering his efforts on theology and the church, Luther was challenged simultaneously to accomplish widespread change in universities, schools, and among the general populace. Careful strategic planning and the implementation of gradual change proved impossible as events escalated at a far more rapid pace than Luther had ever anticipated. However, proposing ideas and plans for reform was not the same as making them a reality.

Visitation records tell us that the reformers, beginning with Luther and Melanchthon, and extending into the next generations, faced constant and continuing problems—lack of money to attract and pay competent schoolteachers; lack of willingness on the part of parents to further their children's education; lack of support on the part of secular authorities to mandate, finance, and carry through massive educational change; lack of understanding and participation in the new Evangelical practices among the general populace. Indeed, the situation appeared so dismal to Erasmus that he complained that wherever Luther's ideas had triumphed, learning had perished. This observation leads us to our central questions in this chapter. To what extent were Luther's educational goals achieved in the sixteenth century? And, if not in his own time, did he and his colleagues lay a strong foundation for the future? Or, are Erasmus and more recent critics correct in stating that the reformers' goals ended in failure? To answer these questions fully would require an exhaustive analysis of visitation protocols that goes far beyond this study. Indeed, the visitation protocols themselves must be balanced by other evidence since the visitors were primarily concerned with noting problems and concerns, not successes. Nonetheless, we can trace out some aspects of the changes that occurred over the decades of the 1520s through the 1580s, with the goal of reaching some general observations and conclusions.

In May 1518, at a time when the reform movement was still in its very earliest stage, Luther penned a heartfelt letter to Jodocus Trutfetter in Erfurt. In it he aimed to set the record straight with a former professor whom he admired. He also articulated his understanding of the process of reform, linking church and university. Thus, he wrote "it is impossible for the church to be reformed unless canon law, the decretals, scholastic theology, philosophy, and logic as they now exist are eradicated and other studies are instituted in their place."[1] In his 1520 *Address to the Christian Nobility* he referred to universities that fail in their duty of teaching the Holy Scriptures as "wide gates to hell," and he urged a thoroughgoing reform of their curricula.[2] Enduring ecclesiastical reform could only occur when the educational foundation of schools and universities was torn down and rebuilt. However, Luther did not have the luxury of implementing gradual reform, of slowly replacing the old with the new, along the lines advocated by Erasmus. He could not wait for reform to reach from the learned to the unlearned, from the universities to the parishes. While university reform remained a priority, it was not the only priority, as Luther was led to include within his horizon all aspects of society, including young and old, clergy and laity. At the same time, as Luther's horizon broadened, he never lost his focus on the university. He continued to turn to the universities as the source for educated and reliable pastors and teachers to preach and teach, men able to preach the Word and expound the catechism. And, no matter how many other tasks occupied his attention, Luther remained a university person, dedicated to teaching and to his students. Even more, he remained committed to *his* university, a commitment so strong that not even the plague could drive him from his post.

Not in 1518 nor even in 1520 did Luther fully grasp how far and wide reform would have to extend or how difficult it

---

[1] *WA Br* 1, 170, 33–36.

[2] *WA* 6, 462, 10; 457, 28–29; *LW* 44, 207; 200.

would be to bring people to a genuine understanding of why the gospel necessitated changes in both doctrine and practice. As we have seen, the catechisms, postils, and hymns were efforts to provide pastors and congregations with tools and guides that could lead them to an understanding of God's Word. Initially Luther may not have realized how extensively the clergy would need to be retrained. As his awareness grew, so too did his stress on education.

Several words of caution are necessary, however, with regard to what Luther expected from the universities and schools and from education in general. First, Luther understood reform to be a divine not a human activity, although people are called to serve as instruments of the Word. Any discussion of reform must center, as Gustav Wingren rightly notes, on individuals in relationship, both to God and to one another.[3] Second, within that context, Luther never lost sight of the centrality of the concept of the priesthood of believers. His growing recognition of the need for a learned pastorate was not a rejection of that fundamental belief. However, as he sought to respond to the tumult and disorder caused by the Peasants' Revolt and to find ways to address the ignorance and confusion which the visitations had brought to light, Luther and his colleagues found it imperative to establish procedures to ascertain that those who believed themselves called to preach the Word were truly prepared to do so. These procedures were not to replace divine *vocatio*, but to test that the call was genuine and to assure that the person called by God to preach and teach the Word was equipped with the necessary tools. Education could not replace *vocatio*, but without education, without knowledge of Scripture, *vocatio* lacked the means to become effective. In a time of confusion, setting standards and ascertaining who did and did not meet them became crucial, necessitating a centralized authority for ordination, for granting authority and credentials to those who were called to serve as pastors. Article XIV of the Augsburg Confession states "that nobody should publicly teach or preach or administer the sacraments in the church without a regular call."[4] While all

---

[3] Gustav Wingren, *Luther on Vocation,* trans. by Carl C. Rasmussen (Philadelphia: Muhlenberg Press, 1957), 163.

[4] Tappert, *The Book of Concord,* 36.

through baptism are priests, only some are called to the "function" of the ministry, and "after 1525 Luther emphasized an objective calling through an external sign from God or through a commission by the authorities."[5] Precisely who was to comprise this commission, whether theologians or pastors, was debated, but the Wittenberg University theologians assumed leadership through their examinations of candidates, thereby fulfilling Elector John Frederick's 1535 order that those wishing to serve as pastors be "sent to Wittenberg 'to our scholars of the Holy Scriptures, who have the command to ordain them and also to bestow the power and authority of their office of priest and deacon.'"[6] In 1535 the first ordination took place in Wittenberg, launching a practice that would draw men from throughout Germany and beyond.

The Wittenberg University theologians examined and certified those called to the ministry. Although this procedure might be viewed as one that set the pastor apart from his parishioners, Luther did not intend for that to be the case. His concern for the welfare of congregations mandated that those in authority be responsible for assuring that they were not guided by false teachers and preachers who would pervert the gospel and lead them astray. Education did not take the place of *vocatio*, and not all who passed the ordination examination had studied at the university, although increasingly that became the usual practice.[7] In 1564 the elector of Saxony stipulated that a

---

[5] Wolfgang Klausnitzer, "Ordination," in Hans Hillerbrand, ed., *The Oxford Encyclopedia of the Reformation*, vol. III (New York: Oxford University Press, 1996), 178. See also R. W. Scribner, "Practice and Principle in the German Towns: Preachers and People," in Peter Newman Brooks, ed., *Reformation Principle and Practice: Essays in Honour of Arthur Geoffrey Dickens* (London: Scolar Press, 1980), 99–100.

[6] Martin Brecht, *Martin Luther: The Preservation of the Church 1532–1546*, trans. James L. Schaaf (Minneapolis: Fortress Press, 1993), 124.

[7] For a discussion of clerical education in Germany before the Reformation and after, see James H. Overfield, "University Studies and the Clergy in Pre-Reformation Germany," in James M. Kittelson and Pamela J. Transue, eds., *Rebirth, Reform, and Resilience:*

university education was mandatory for anyone seeking ordination.[8] This demand assumed that the universities were themselves reformed and able to educate pastors and teachers in Evangelical principles. However, this too was no simple task.

Even the reform of Luther's own university faced obstacles. As we have seen, Luther initially faced opposition from his dean, the Thomist Andreas Bodenstein von Carlstadt, who was eventually won over to the biblical theology, as was the Scotist Nikolaus von Amsdorf.[9] While some, especially the students, welcomed these ideas enthusiastically, not all at the university were equally eager to support change. Even among those who were initially supportive, divisions occurred over time. For example, the distinguished jurist Hieronymous Schurf, who initially supported Luther in his confrontation with the ecclesiastical hierarchy, even accompanying him to the Diet of Worms, later broke with Luther over the teaching and authority of canon law.[10] In Carlstadt's case, study of Scripture, specifically Matthew 23:8–10, led him to conclude in 1523 that no academic degrees or titles should be granted and that he should resign his own titles. Ultimately, Carlstadt left the university for the pastorate. In short, while some could only travel with Luther part of the way, others diverged onto very different paths.

Nor were the faculty always focused upon the high topic of curricular reform. Then, as now, a university faced a multitude of daily problems. Sometimes the elector and the university leadership perceived these problems in the same way, sometimes not. Reform proceeded in spurts until Elector John Frederick's efforts in 1536. Reform was stymied by the lack of

---

Universities in Transition 1300–1700 (Columbus, Ohio: Ohio State University Press, 1984), 254–92.

[8] Olaf Pedersen, "Tradition and Innovation, " in Hilde de Ridder-Symoens, ed., *Universities in Early Modern Europe*, vol. II of *A History of the University in Europe* (Cambridge: Cambridge University Press, 1996), 476.

[9] Friedensburg, *Geschichte der Universität Wittenberg*, 100; Kolb, *Nikolaus von Amsdorf*, 27–30.

[10] Friedensburg, *Geschichte der Universität Wittenberg*, 200–201.

resources, by transitions in governance from Frederick the Wise to John the Constant to John Frederick, by the growing confrontation between Luther and his allies on the one hand and the papacy on the other, and by ensuing social turmoil, culminating in the Peasants' War. Under such circumstances, it is not surprising that even the best intentioned ruler often had to put the affairs of the university aside to cope with immediate problems and challenges. In this context Spalatin deserves another word of recognition, for it was he who kept the interests and needs of the university, from faculty salaries to building the library, constantly before the electors, and who served as a channel between the Wittenberg theologians and the court.

The statutes of the university from 1508 were revised in 1513, but remained fundamentally unchanged. As discussed earlier, in September 1517 the elector sent two emissaries to assess the state of the university. In our terms, we might consider this to have been a mini-accreditation visit prompted by the failure of the law professors to fulfill their obligation regularly to be present and to deliver their lectures, a problem that continued in spite of the elector's admonitions.[11] In part resulting from that visit, in 1518 curricular reform along humanist lines began in earnest. It was the decision to offer lectures in Greek, which brought Melanchthon to Wittenberg, the person who would give curricular reform new impetus and energy. While Luther provided the impetus for reform and focused his attention especially on the theological faculty, Melanchthon implemented the reforms and linked the reform in the upper faculty of theology to the reform of the liberal arts curriculum.[12] On the one hand, the study of the languages, learned within the arts faculty, became essential preparation for theological study. On the other hand, theological lectures were so in demand that they were even offered within the colleges

---

[11] Friedensburg, *Geschichte der Universität Wittenberg*, 109–10.

[12] Benrath, "Die deutsche evangelische Universität der Reformationszeit," in Rössler and Franz, ed., *Universität und Gelehrtenstand*, 69, and Gustav Adolf Benrath, "Die Universität der Reformationszeit," *Archiv für Reformationsgeschichte* 57, Heft 1/2 (1966), 39, 32–51,

serving primarily arts students.[13] In assessing their joint efforts, Benrath concludes that while the "reformation of the university" derives from Luther, the "university of the Reformation" should be traced back to Melanchthon.[14]

The thrust of the curricular reform was to push the old lectures delivered according to the two *viae* of Thomas and Scotus aside as Luther and his colleagues worked to establish a curriculum, in both the arts and theology, where students read the classical authors, the Bible, and the works of the church fathers. The 1518 reform also sought to address the problem of ill-prepared students, establishing a *paedagogium*, or preparatory program, with instruction in Latin, Greek, and Hebrew.[15] In 1536 the number of masters in the *paedagogium* was reduced from two to one, and the admissions criteria were changed, stipulating that, to be admitted, a candidate had to pass an examination in Latin and that he could not be younger than fourteen.

The new statutes of 1536 resulted in what is referred to as the second founding of the university under Elector John Frederick. The arts faculty and the higher faculties of theology, law, and medicine were reorganized. The theology faculty was now composed of three professors, including one who served as pastor of the Castle Church and therefore had reduced teaching responsibilities because of his duties as a preacher. The three were joined by the pastor of the City Church who was not required to hold a doctorate.[16] They were given differing responsibilities, with the first lecturing primarily on the New Testament; the second on important Old Testament texts, including Genesis, Isaiah, and the Psalms, while the third and fourth lectured on a variety of texts from both Old and New Testament, including the gospel of Matthew, Deuteronomy, the lesser prophets, and various letters of Paul, Peter, and John.[17]

---

[13] Friedensburg, *Geschichte der Universität Wittenberg*, 166.

[14] Benrath, "Die deutsche evangelische Universität der Reformationszeit," 69.

[15] Friedensburg, *Geschichte der Universität Wittenberg*, 114.

[16] Friedensburg, *Geschichte der Universität Wittenberg*, 180–81.

[17] Friedensburg, *Geschichte der Universität Wittenberg*, 181.

In a sequence that may seem surprising to us, students began their studies with the New Testament, with Paul's Letter to the Romans occupying a central position. Biblical study was not only textual in character but also dogmatic, as particular themes and precepts were highlighted and utilized as the central points in discussion of biblical texts.[18] Lombard's *Sentences* was no longer taught. Aristotle was excluded from the theological curriculum, but students would have encountered some of his ideas in Melanchthon's systematic theology, the *Loci communes*.[19] The revised theological curriculum responded to the demand of the times not only for more theologians but for capable pastors and preachers. The statutes for the theological faculty that Melanchthon had formulated in 1533 stressed exegesis as the core responsibility of the faculty and mandated that all who taught were to subscribe to the Augsburg Confession.[20] Subsequently members of the arts faculty were also required to affirm a confessional statement. Melanchthon regarded this affirmation as necessary, since the majority of the arts students went on to the higher faculties of law and theology.[21]

In law what is noteworthy is what remained unchanged by the 1536 statutes. One professor continued to be charged with lecturing on canon law, the decretals, suggesting that within the university there were still pockets of resistance to thoroughgoing reform.[22] The statutes also informed law and theology faculty of their additional obligations, in our terms, the "service" component of their contracts. Law faculty were to serve the elector's court in various capacities, both as judges and as advocates for the poor, while the theological faculty were to

---

[18] Hartfelder, *Philipp Melanchthon,* 474–76.

[19] Benrath, "Die deutsche evangelische Universität," 72.

[20] Friedensburg, *Geschichte der Universität Wittenberg,* 186.

[21] Hartfelder, *Philipp Melanchthon,* 447–48.

[22] Benrath, "Die deutsche evangelische Universität der Reformationszeit," 70. Friedensburg, *Geschichte der Universität Wittenberg,* 181; Hartfelder, *Philipp Melanchthon,* 441.

serve as consultants to the elector on spiritual questions and issues regarding marriage.

Both the 1536 statutes and the additions that were made after the visitation of the electoral commission in 1538 established curricular guidelines and outlined the faculty's responsibility for fulfilling them, as well as stipulating their duties as university citizens and indicating the rewards they were to receive for their labors. The pronouncements on such matters as residence and attendance suggest that then, as now, governing bodies and faculty were not always in agreement. Indeed, one could argue that by requiring faculty to serve as advisors and consultants to the electoral court John Frederick exacerbated a problem he had hoped to solve. While requiring professors to deliver their lectures at the stated times unless ill, he also frequently sought their advice and aid in resolving particular issues. Mediating crises and advising the elector often necessitated their absence from the lecture hall. On the one hand, these activities added to the esteem of the university, but on the other hand they often drew the most sought after professors away from their academic obligations. It comes as no surprise that this was especially the case for the two stars, Melanchthon and Luther, whose assistance was sought not only by their own ruler, but by many others. Indeed, Luther died away from home seeking to resolve a dispute among argumentative counts. Thus, although the new statutes clearly established the number of hours and days on which lectures in the various disciplines were to be held, these requirements were not always met. As Friedensburg notes, the involvement of the theologians in examining candidates for the ministry and in participating, along with the jurists, on the consistory with its multifaceted supervisory duties, constituted another series of extensive and time consuming demands. The benefit was that these same activities extended the influence and prestige of the University.[23]

Perhaps the most significant reforms of 1536 occurred in the liberal arts. The curriculum was revised and stabilized with a total of ten professorships, of which the classical languages, Greek and Hebrew, and mathematics, received nearly half. Both Cicero and Aristotle received their due—and Aristotle probably more than Luther might have wished, although he could rejoice

---

[23] Friedensburg, *Geschichte der Universität Wittenberg*, 189.

that he was no longer studied within the upper faculty of theology.[24] Melanchthon's focus on Aristotle has been termed "Ciceronian Aristotelianism, an Aristotelianism without a strict metaphysics and logical, occasionally rhetorical and Stoic."[25] Lewis Spitz has described this reform effort of 1533–36 as completing the "symbiosis of humanism and Reformation" in the Wittenberg curriculum.[26] No longer focused on breaking with the past, these new statutes solidified the changes of recent years and enforced "quality control." In the first phase of the reform, disputations, which had been such a central part of the medieval curriculum, had been dropped, but these were now reinstated, with disputations occurring at promotions for degrees and at regular times throughout the year in the upper faculties and every second Saturday in the arts faculty.[27] Students were expected to demonstrate both their knowledge and their ability to present it persuasively—eloquence—in required speeches or declamations for which Melanchthon had already pleaded in 1523.[28] Both professors and students were expected to participate regularly, with the professor of rhetoric overseeing the declamations of the students. Over the ten year period from 1535–45 when Luther served as dean of the theological faculty, he attended the disputations and speeches

---

[24] Lewis W. Spitz, "The Importance of the Reformation for the Universities: Culture and Confession in the Critical Years," in Kittelson and Transue, eds., *Rebirth, Reform, and Resilience*, 54; Benrath, "Die Universität der Reformationszeit," 42–43.

[25] Wilhelm Schmidt-Biggemann, "New Structures of Knowledge," in de Ridder-Symoens, ed., *Universities in Early Modern Europe*, 502. Benrath discusses Melanchthon's approach to Aristotle which maintained the distinction between theology and philosophy and which used Cicero to supplement Aristotle in "Die deutsche evangelische Universität der Reformationszeit," 71.

[26] Spitz, "The Importance of the Reformation for the Universities," 51.

[27] Hartfelder, *Philipp Melanchthon*, 451.

[28] Hartfelder, *Philipp Melanchthon*, 453.

as often as possible and enthusiastically affirmed their value.[29] No longer an occasion for meaningless argument and showmanship, under the guidance of Luther and Melanchthon, the declamations became occasions for students to debate the real issues of the day and to gain skill in presenting their arguments eloquently.[30] For pastors and teachers who would be caught in the increasing whirlwind of religious dissension such skill was absolutely essential. Luther valued the study of rhetoric, and both he and Melanchthon were at one with the humanists in admiring Cicero and his union of eloquence and wisdom.[31]

The initial impact of curricular reform on the University of Wittenberg had been positive, generating increased enrollments. There was, however, a negative side as the flood of new enrollments caused town and university to overflow. In just one semester, the summer of 1520, there were 332 new matriculations.[32] If expansion and new building projects seemed the right strategy at that time, events a few years later called those ideas into question. We can sympathize with those who were trying to plan the university's future in the midst of very unpredictable times. The Diet of Worms and Luther's subsequent absence from Wittenberg, as well as his condemnation by the pope as a heretic, led many to think twice about attending the university or about continuing their education at that institution. The university hit its nadir in 1525 during the tumultuous days of the Peasants' War when only 12 new students matriculated, but by 1528 enrollments were beginning to rebound.[33] Not only social turmoil but an outbreak

---

[29] Friedensburg, *Geschichte der Universität Wittenberg*, 192–93.

[30] Friedensburg, *Geschichte der Universität Wittenberg*, 193. James Kittelson, "Luther the Educational Reformer," in Harran, ed., *Luther and Learning*, 97–98.

[31] Walter Rüegg, "Themes," in de Ridder-Symoens, ed., *Universities in Early Modern Europe*, 28. Lewis W. Spitz, "Luther and Humanism," in Harran, ed., *Luther and Learning*, 86–87.

[32] Friedensburg, *Geschichte der Universität Wittenberg*, 147.

[33] Friedensburg, *Geschichte der Universität Wittenberg*, 177.

of the plague had deterred students from coming to Wittenberg. In summer 1527 most students and faculty had relocated to Jena until the wrath of the outbreak had passed.[34] As Lewis Spitz has observed, however, even this steep decline in enrollments must be seen in context.[35] Difficulties in both recruitment and retention were not new to German universities. Even before the tumult of the 1520s, only about one-third of the students who matriculated gained their degree at the University of Leipzig.[36] Nonetheless, for a time Wittenberg's problems were severe. Some rulers refused to allow their young men to study in an institution that had housed and supported a heretic and where his followers, even in his absence, took his ideas in more radical directions. Parents questioned whether a degree from the university associated with the heretic Luther would forward their sons' careers. Luther's reforms also ended the hope of a lucrative career in the church as a result of a university education. Carlstadt went even further, proclaiming the end of all academic titles, and thereby placing the value of higher education in question.

The problem that beset the reformers was whether the "liberty of the Gospel [was] to be reflected in academic liberty."[37] In short, if all Christians now had the freedom to interpret Scripture, should any one individual be regarded as having more theological authority than another? University

---

[34] Friedensburg, *Geschichte der Universität Wittenberg*, 177–78.

[35] Spitz, "The Importance of the Reformation for the Universities," in Kittelson and Transue, ed., *Rebirth, Reform, and Resilience*, 53. In the same volume, see the chapter by Overfield, "University Studies and the Clergy in Pre-Reformation Germany," 254–92. He notes that in the pre-Reformation period "most matriculants—70 percent or more at most institutions—received no degree whatsoever. In other words, most students remained at the university less than the one and a half or two years normally required for the Bachelor of Arts degree." 269.

[36] Spitz, "The Importance of the Reformation for the Universities," 53.

[37] Willem Frijhoff, "Graduations and Careers," in de Ridder-Symoens, ed., *Universities in Early Modern Europe*, 367.

records indicate that from 1526–1534 there were no candidates for degrees in theology.[38] This was a situation that threatened the very existence of the church. As we have seen, Luther prized his doctoral degree, seeing it as the emblem of his *vocatio* and as the foundation for his right to challenge, when necessary, the authority of church and state. The authority of the theological doctor itself had been hard won during the Middle Ages, emerging as one of the fruits of the conciliar movement and giving doctors of theology equal status in voting with the bishops.[39] The doctorate established one's right to debate ideas within the academy—academic freedom—a principle to which the Wittenberg faculty appealed in their defense of Luther and his right to speak as he had in the 95 Theses.[40] Oberman observes that "on the eve of the Reformation, the doctoral office had ... achieved a new height of respectability and authority."[41] Rather than being rejected as no longer necessary, through the Evangelical Reformation the doctorate came to assume new importance as the voice of educated authority. Willem Frijhoff suggests that

---

[38] Friedensburg, *Geschichte der Universität Wittenberg*, 172–73.

[39] Frijhoff, "Graduations and Careers," 366.

[40] On the faculty senate's defense of Luther's right as a doctor, see Heiko A. Oberman, "University and Society on the Threshold of Modern Times: The German Connection," in Kittelson and Transue, ed., *Rebirth, Reform, and Resilience,* 35. See also the discussion of the reformer's attitude toward the doctorate by Frijhoff, "Graduations and Careers," 366–67.

[41] Oberman, "University and Society on the Threshold of Modern Times," 29. Oberman discusses Luther's assertion of his right to challenge Albrecht's "indulgences policy on the basis of his, Luther's doctoral findings" and the parallel argument of Johann Eck, who would become Luther's antagonist, a few years earlier in a debate on interest in which he requested that the "University of Mainz confirm in an official *Gutachten* of 10 January 1515 that a sworn doctor has the right to announce and carry through a disputation irrespective of the approval of his bishop." 30.

the doctorate in theology was the very symbol of the renewal of the churches in that the renewal tended to replace the ritualistic role of the minister of religion with a more intellectual, cognitive, and educational conception ... [and] the abolition of the episcopate led to an extension of the theological role of the doctor in the Reformation churches.[42]

Emphasizing the authority of the doctor of theology was the reformers' response to the social and religious turmoil erupting around them. At the same time, Luther himself found deep personal meaning and value in the doctorate. For him, affirming the authority of the doctorate was tantamount to affirming the reality of God's *vocatio* and *ordo*.

During these years the university and the elector were faced not only with curricular problems, but with a variety of complex financial questions stemming from the secularization of church property. Elector John the Constant stipulated that the proceeds from the *Allerheiligenstift* were to go to the University.[43] At the same time as the *Allerheiligenstift* or All Saints' Foundation was reduced in size, the canons remaining there needed to be supported so a balance had to be struck between the commitments of the past and those of the present and future. Recognizing the value of Luther and Melanchthon to the university, John also acted to double their salaries, from 100 to 200 gulden a year, the highest of the faculty; subsequently their salaries were increased even more.[44] These raises recognized the enormous power of both men to attract students to the university and the fact that neither had charged fees for attending their lectures. Melanchthon in particular had in the early days of his Wittenberg career struggled financially, and we might imagine that his new salary was in part intended to reward him for his loyalty and years of hard work. The 1536 statutes continued to reward the theological faculty above all others, followed by the law faculty whose salaries ranged from 200 to 100 gulden, the medical faculty, and finally, at the

---

[42] Frijhoff, "Graduations and Careers," 367–68.

[43] Friedensburg, *Geschichte der Universität Wittenberg*, 176.

[44] Friedensburg, *Geschichte der Universität Wittenberg*, 175.

lowest rung of the salary ladder, the arts faculty, whose salaries generally averaged about 80 gulden.[45] The new theology also brought changes in the requirements for those elected and appointed to administer the University, with Melanchthon becoming the first married rector in the winter semester 1523.

The new situation likewise necessitated the formulation of a plan to support students during their university years. Luther himself was deeply concerned that promising students not be prevented from attending the University by a lack of financial support.[46] No longer living from prebends as the recipients of church income, students needed to be supported in other ways. Not surprisingly, given the ups and downs of the University and the enormous transitions that occurred over a relatively short span of time, addressing this challenge lagged behind others. The first plan came about in 1538, with additional clarification following in 1545, noting how many students from each social group were to be supported by funds from the church properties. Of the 150 scholarships awarded, 28 were to go to the sons of pastors, an implicit recognition that pastors lacked the funds to support their sons' higher education.[47] As a precursor to what we might regard as a "service component" to their education, these scholarship recipients were expected to serve either church or school in their home territory.[48] The elector set no time limit on the completion of studies, but he obviously recognized that some students might be inclined to enjoy the student life as long as it could be financially supported, and so he mandated that students had to pass exams assessing their progress and competency every six months.[49] In addition to this formal means of support, Luther

[45] Friedensburg, *Geschichte der Universität Wittenberg*, 183.

[46] Lewis W. Spitz, "Luther's Social Concern for Students," in Lawrence P. Buck and Jonathan W. Zophy, ed., *The Social History of the Reformation* (Columbus, Ohio: Ohio State University Press, 1972), 249–70.

[47] Friedensburg, *Geschichte der Universität Wittenberg*, 241.

[48] Friedensburg, *Geschichte der Universität Wittenberg*, 242.

[49] Friedensburg, *Geschichte der Universität Wittenberg*, 241.

sought private donations to keep students in school. Indeed, as Lewis Spitz reports, "approximately half the letters that Luther wrote on behalf of students over the course of thirty years sought financial aid for them."[50]

Wittenberg not only served as the center of the reform movement but became the touchstone and reference point for all that followed. By requiring that all men seeking ordination were to pass an examination at Wittenberg, the University and its faculty were granted enormous power to select those who were to become the next generation of pastors and to shape what their message would be. Thus, the University served as a centralizing force within the reform movement.

From Wittenberg reform proceeded to other universities, to schools, and to other territories. Melanchthon was the decisive voice behind the founding of the first evangelical university, Marburg, which opened its doors in 1527 and whose statutes date from 1529. Free of the problems of vested interests intrinsic to the older universities, Melanchthon shaped the curriculum according to his pedagogical priorities. Not surprisingly, the arts faculty emerged as by far the largest. It was composed of ten chairs, including the classical languages, Greek and Hebrew; Latin grammar; poetry; physics; mathematics; dialectics; two chairs in rhetoric; and one—for the first time—in the discipline of history.[51] The mathematics professor also taught astronomy, a topic dear to Melanchthon's heart, as, unfortunately, was astrology.[52] Those chosen to teach were to be both learned, *docti*, and pious, *pii*, but interestingly,

---

[50] Spitz, "Luther's Social Concern for Students, 251.

[51] Pedersen, "Tradition and Innovation," in de Ridder-Symoens, ed., *Universities in Early Modern Europe*, 462. See also Lewis W. Spitz, "The Impact of the Reformation on the Universities," in Leif Grane, ed., *University and Reformation: Lectures from the University of Copenhagen Symposium* (Leiden: E. J. Brill, 1981), 9–31. On Marburg, see especially 18–19.

[52] Pedersen, "Tradition and Innovation," in de Ridder-Symoens, ed., *Universities in Early Modern Europe*, 463. Spitz, "The Importance of the Reformation for the Universities," in Kittelson and Transue, ed., *Rebirth, Reform, and Resilience*, 53–54. Paulsen, *Geschichte des gelehrten Unterrichts*, 234.

perhaps because the orientation and goals of the university were clear to all from the start, they were not obliged to sign a confessional statement.[53]

The theological faculty consisted only of two professors, divided between Old and New Testament, while medicine was even smaller, with only one faculty member responsible for lecturing on texts by Galen, Avicenna, Hippocrates, and Aristotle's *Physics*. Law was the largest of the higher faculties, with three members, all lecturing on Roman law.[54] Ever concerned with the well-being of the young, Melanchthon provided for two professors in the *paedagogium* to provide training for entering students in Greek and Hebrew, as well as music, rhetoric, and dialectic, both utilizing Melanchthon's own texts.[55] Every arts student was assigned a praeceptor to guide his academic progress and supervise his work, as well as to assure his regular attendance at the required declamations and disputations.[56] The influence of Melanchthon and Wittenberg was reinforced by the fact that virtually all the Marburg professors had been trained at Wittenberg, and the first two rectors were both former students of Melanchthon.[57]

From its beginnings, Philip of Hesse directed the university toward the goal of providing his territory with young men to

---

[53] Benrath, "Die deutsche evangelische Universität," 70; Benrath "Die Universität der Reformationszeit," 41.

[54] Benrath, "Die deutsche evangelische Universität, 70; Benrath, "Die Universität der Reformationszeit," 40.

[55] Benrath, "Die deutsche evangelische Universität, 70. Lewis Spitz suggests that the "pedagogical department" may be viewed as constituting "an embryonic school of education." Spitz, "The Importance of the Reformation for the Universities," in Kittelson and Transue, ed., *Rebirth, Reform, and Resilience*, 54. Insofar as there may have been a more self-conscious attitude on the part of teachers toward the methods of preparing their students for university study, it seems possible to look upon the *paedagogium* in this light, although one might also understand it as a "prep school."

[56] Paulsen, *Geschichte des gelehrten Unterrichts*, 234.

[57] Paulsen, *Geschichte des gelehrten Unterrichts*, 234.

serve church and state. To that end, he mandated that towns and cities were to provide scholarship funds or stipends to support students from their areas. In return, upon graduation, students were obliged to perform public service. As Paulsen describes, well-intentioned as the program was, it suffered from a variety of problems, ranging from the failure of towns to provide the agreed upon sums in a timely manner, to students failing to fulfill their obligations upon graduation.[58] In other words, the difficulties the U.S. government encounters in collecting student loan repayment is by no means a new problem.

Largely under Melanchthon's influence, older universities also enacted reforms. Both Tübingen and Heidelberg revised their curricula and both sought to attract Melanchthon to their institutions. Rostock and Königsberg also followed Melanchthon's lead, with Rostock breaking new ground by implementing a college model combining study with housing—and thereby establishing a stricter student life—along the lines long envisioned by Melanchthon.[59]

Vexing as university reform could be, these difficulties could not compare to the immense challenges presented by the grassroots reform of schools.[60] Scholars differ widely in their assessments of the reformers' influence and their degree of success, especially in the country side. They agree that in the towns the reformers' educational efforts fared better, although here too there were problems in implementing reform. In

---

[58] Paulsen, *Geschichte des gelehrten Unterrichts*, 236.

[59] Hartfelder, *Philipp Melanchthon*, 523–24.

[60] While recognizing that primary education was very limited even at the time of the Reformation, there was a long history of schools in Saxony. Johannes Müller cites records of schools in nineteen locations from the end of the twelfth to the end of the fourteenth century in Saxony with the first school foundation occurring in Meissen where the boys were taught in three groups. The first foundation of a city school occurred in Dresden, with the second following in Zittau. "Die Anfänge des sächsischen Schulwesens," *Neues Archiv für Sächsische Geschichte und Alterthumskunde*, vol. 8 (1887), 2, 7, 19, 244, 251; 1–40; 243–71.

particular, pastors and city councils struggled over who had the right to appoint the schoolmaster.[61]

In his 1978 book *Luther's House of Learning* Gerald Strauss drew on visitation records from throughout Evangelical lands to conclude that the reformers failed in their educational goal of imbuing all Christians "with a Christian mindset, motivational drive, and way of life."[62] This statement asserts that Luther had a far more optimistic view of what education could accomplish than was in fact the case. More recently, C. Scott Dixon has examined the development of the Evangelical movement in the parishes of Brandenburg-Ansbach-Kulmbach over the period 1528 to 1603 and concluded that education made little progress, especially in the rural areas.[63]

Leaving aside the question of Strauss' interpretation of Luther's goals, there is no doubt that the reformers faced their greatest difficulties in the rural areas where reforms of church services, school curricula, and lay morality often encountered obstinate indifference or rejection, as well as a lack of resources. However, branding the reformers' efforts a failure does not take into account the often grim situations they faced, resulting from years of neglect. If the visitation records frequently offer evidence of only the most modest of improvements even over decades, they also establish how bad the situation was when the reformers began. For example, the 1529 visitation to Wercho in the Kurkreis Saxony established that the peasants knew neither the Ten Commandments nor the articles of faith and

---

[61] C. Scott Dixon, *The Reformation and Rural Society: The Parishes of Brandenburg-Ansbach-Kulmbach 1528–1603* (Cambridge: Cambridge University Press, 1996), 153–54. Similar problems existed in other parishes and towns, such as Zwickau, where such difficulties emerged as early as 1527 in concert with "the emerging Lutheran view ... that in Zwickau, as everywhere, teachers were lower level clergy and as such subject to the pastor in whatever parish they worked." Susan C. Karant-Nunn, *Zwickau in Transition, 1500–1547: The Reformation as an Agent of Change* (Columbus: Ohio State University Press, 1987), 157.

[62] Strauss, *Luther's House of Learning*, 307.

[63] Dixon, *The Reformation and Rural Society*, 207.

could not even pray.[64] In Zinna the peasants refused to pray the Lord's Prayer because *"es zu lang sei,"* it was too long![65] It would be naive to think that such longstanding ignorance could be altered by only a few years of reform or be completely transformed even in a few decades.

Transitions in pastors, such as that in Düben where six pastors served within a few years, yielded the result reported in the 1529 visitation of only three people attending Sunday services out of a village of 110 families.[66] This rapid turnover in spiritual leadership resulted in little continuity or support for gradual improvement. Such transitions in spiritual leadership in turn resulted from the difficulty in creating a strong infrastructure to support pastors. Endowments from monasteries, convents, and churches were intended to support pastors and teachers, but only slowly could the various problems in the utilization of these funds be addressed—from determining how much money should be used to support those who remained monks, nuns, or canons to establishing into whose coffers the remainder should flow. In their efforts to remedy the critical situation of the pastor and to address the most pressing spiritual needs of the parish, the school sometimes was a distant second in the visitors' priorities.

Visitation records from the diocese of Grimma gathered over several months in 1529 offer ample evidence of the visitors' main focus and concern. For example, after visiting Deuben, the visitors noted that the pastor Gregorius Sartoris was unlearned and unskilled in preaching, and that his parishioners complained that he was drunk and lazy—not preaching once in three Sundays![67] Given the central role of the pastor in

---

[64] C. A. H. Burckhardt, *Geschichte der sächsischen Kirchen- und Schulvisitation von 1524 bis 1545* (Leipzig: Verlag von Fr. Wilh. Grunow, 1879), 38.

[65] Burckhardt, *Geschichte der sächsischen Kirchen- und Schulvisitation*, 39.

[66] Burckhardt, *Geschichte der sächsischen Kirchen- und Schulvisitation*, 39.

[67] Karl Grossmann, ed., *Die Visitations-Acten der Diöces Grimma aus dem ersten Jahrhundert seit der Reformation* (Leipzig: J.C. Hinrichs'sche Buchhandlung, 1873), 115.

preaching and teaching both adults and children, it is not surprising that the visitors were above all concerned with finding a new pastor for the congregation.

The rapidly emerging divisions within the reform movement beginning in the 1520s also yielded new problems since the visitors increasingly had to ascertain not only the pastor's level of ability and devotion to duty, but his confessional commitment. Increasingly it was necessary to ascertain not only that he had parted from Catholic practices but that he had not adopted others judged by the visitors to be "schismatic." In their 1529 visitation of Polentz, also in the diocese of Grimma, the visitors noted that the pastor Johannes Kress had been accused by both laity and neighboring pastors of affirming the teachings of Zwingli and Oecolampadius.[68] The visitors carefully questioned not only the pastor but several in his congregation and established the accuracy of the accusations, necessitating the replacement of the pastor.

The visitation reports indicate that often the most skilled and devoted pastor had his hands full trying to preach and teach the Gospel to his congregation. The April 1540 report of the visitors to Chemnitz prohibits anyone from standing around in the churchyard or elsewhere engaging in idle conversation while the pastor is preaching. People are likewise admonished not to buy beer during this time! And, the visitors added, it was also forbidden to swear about the visitation![69]

In spite of their concentration upon these basic problems, the visitors sought, whenever they could, to improve the schools since they knew how essential they were for long-term progress in reform. As Julius Richter describes in his *Geschichte der sächsischen Volksschule*, the progress of the Evangelical reform altered and increased in responsibility the role of the sexton, the

---

[68]Grossmann, ed., *Die Visitations-Acten der Diöces Grimma*, 133–34.

[69] Emil Sehling, ed., *Die evangelische Kirchenordnung des XVI. Jahrhunderts. Erste Abteilung. Sachsen und Thüringen, nebst angrenzenden Gebiete. Erste Hälfte: Die Ordnungen Luthers. Die Ernestinischen und Albertinischen Gebiete* (Leipzig: O. R. Riesland, 1902), 541.

Küster or *Custos*.[70] This person performed manifold duties within the church, from locking and unlocking the door and cleaning the building, to increasingly assuming a more active role in assisting the pastor. His role expanded especially in those areas where the pastor was responsible not only for the main church but for those in neighboring areas affiliated with it, which required him frequently to travel. The duties of the sexton came to include teaching and quizzing the children on the catechism and sometimes teaching them "singing, reading, writing, and arithmetic."[71] Mention of a sexton in the visitation records, however, does not necessarily mean that he taught or even that he had the most rudimentary skills to teach. Richter points to the mention of a *Custodia* or sexton's house in the visitation protocols as an indication school may have been held.[72] This one room hut, usually quite small, in which the sexton lived, along with his family, and in which he taught his pupils during the day, was often in very poor shape. Both the mention of a dwelling and records indicating the payment of *Schulgeld* or a quarterly payment by pupils to the sexton are

---

[70] Julius Richter, *Geschichte der sächsischen Volksschule*, vol. LIX in Monumenta Germaniae Paedagogica (Berlin: Weidmannsche Buch-handlung, 1930), 35. On the duties of the sexton, see Hans Georg Kirchhoff, "Kirchspiels- und Küsterschulen in der Reformationszeit: Die niedere Schulwesen im Spiegel von Visitationsberichten des 16. Jahrhundert," in Klaus Goebel, ed., *Luther in der Schule*, Dortmunder Arbeiten zur Schulgeschichte und zur historischen Didaktik, vol. 6 (Bochum: Studienverlag Dr. N. Brockmeyer, 1985), 127–47, and the foundational article by K. Pallas, "Der Küster der evangelischen Kirche, sein Amt, seine Besoldung, seine Beschäftigung als Lehrer. Ein geschichtliche Betrachtung," *Zeitschrift des Vereins für Kirchengeschichte der Provinz Sachsen*, Jahrgang 19, Heft 1 & 2 (1922), 3–20.

[71] Richter, *Geschichte der sächsischen Volksschule*, 35. Pallas cites evidence that long before the Reformation in rural areas the sexton was expected to teach the children, especially the hymns. "Der Küster der evangelischen Kirche," 6.

[72] Richter, *Geschichte der sächsischen Volksschule*, 3, 6. He notes that this sexton's house or school house could also be the *Schreiberei*, literally "writing place." 5.

evidence that school was being held.[73] Of course, it is quite another matter to glean from these records both how competent the sexton was and how engaged the children were in learning.

Records from visitations to the diocese of Grimma in 1529 indicate a very low set of educational expectations from the sexton. In Trebissen he was instructed to gather the children together and teach them the Lord's Prayer and the Ten Commandments. In addition, he was to help the pastor during the services and teach the people the German hymns.[74] There is no indication that he was to instruct the children in reading and writing. It is therefore possible that all teaching was oral. This may also have been the nature of the teaching that occurred in at least some of the German schools in Braunschweig. In the school order he prepared for that city, Johannes Bugenhagen proposed that, in addition to the two Latin schools, there should be German schools where children are taught "the Word of God, the Ten Commandments, the Creed, the Lord's Prayer," as well as the meaning of the sacraments of baptism and communion and various hymns.[75] Bugenhagen makes no reference to reading or writing, suggesting that this teaching too was entirely oral in character. In such cases, there is a good chance that the sexton was illiterate.

Especially in the rural areas, many teachers were lacking in the skills to be effective pedagogues. In the 1529 visitation to Dubro in the Kurkreis, the visitors noted that the community praised their sexton, but he was unable to read or write.[76] Expectations were usually low, with many villagers content if

---

[73] Richter, *Geschichte der sächsischen Volksschule*, 36.

[74] Grossmann, *Die Visitations-Acten der Diöces Grimma*, 102.

[75] Kirchhoff, "Kirchspiels- und Küsterschulen in der Reformationszeit," 135–36.

[76] Burckhardt, *Geschichte der sächsischen Kirchen- und Schulvisitation*, 41. It should be noted that the records do not indicate that Dubro has a school. The fact that the sexton could not read or write would, of course, mean that even if a Custodia were present he would not have been able to teach the children anything beyond his own oral knowledge.

the sexton instructed the children once a week.[77] In many cases, not even that proved possible, as there were simply not enough sextons to go around. The third visitation of 1533 in Thuringia listed some 738 locations, but a total of only 250 sextons.[78] A more sweeping and inclusive approach toward education would have required the constitution of a "job corps," and the princes and city councils were unwilling to dip into their coffers to initiate such a massive project. Even in a community where a sexton was present and somewhat skilled, it was unimaginable to think of a teacher instructing the children in Latin as the reformers wished. Although Luther and his colleagues sought to instill Latin as the essential educational foundation, especially in rural areas, the reality was that although the reformers "may have disdained German-language schools as inadequate to the attainment of their goals, ... German-language schools is what they got."[79]

There were, however, cases in which higher goals were set even for the rural sexton, suggesting that some progress was occurring and that the sexton was a capable teacher. The sexton in Nawenhof was addressed in 1529 as schoolmaster and was instructed to teach the children "writing, reading, hymns, and as much as possible of the subjects indicated in the *Instructions to the Visitors.*"[80] In Mutschen the expectations were even higher, indicating that an educational foundation was already in place. The teacher was instructed to work with the pastor, Dietterichen von Starschedel, to hold school, during which time the boys were to be taught their prayers, along with reading and writing in Latin, grammar, and as much as feasible from the *Instructions.*[81] This entry offers a signpost for the future, since it

---

[77] Burckhardt, *Geschichte der sächsischen Kirchen- und Schulvisitation,* 41.

[78] Burckhardt, *Geschichte der sächsischen Kirchen- und Schulvisitation,* 140.

[79] Karant-Nunn, "The Reality of Early Lutheran Education: The Electoral District of Saxony—A Case Study," *Lutherjahrbuch* 57 (1990), 135; Davis, *The Reformation and Rural Society,* 151.

[80] Grossmann, ed., *Die Visitations-Acten der Diöces Grimma,* 131–32.

[81] Grossmann, ed., *Die Visitations-Acten der Diöces Grimma,* 141–42.

reverses the normal order of referring to the sexton as also the schoolmaster and states instead "the schoolmaster who is provided with the sexton's position," perhaps an indication of the growing stress upon the function of the teacher in the parish. Frequently repeated as well was the sexton's obligation to teach the children the catechism and to assign them a passage from Holy Scripture to be memorized and repeated at home.[82] Following Luther, this instruction from the visitors demonstrates both the value of repetition and the significance of the home as the place where learning is reinforced. As with children teaching adults hymns at church, this admonition may reflect the visitors' awareness that also with Scripture children might act as the teachers of their parents in the home.

Depending in part on the payments they were to receive from each child, the rural sexton or school teacher often lived on the brink of poverty. The Kulmbach visitation of 1572 noted, "With the sextons, or schoolmasters, the situation is such. ... Their upkeep is mean and wretched; [they] must earn more than just that of their church office from trade and labour."[83] The church order issued under the name of August of Saxony in 1580 recognized the poverty of the sexton and permitted him to pursue a trade at home, although he was not to compete with workers in other areas.[84] It was not enough that the schoolmaster had to perform the myriad tasks of the sexton in addition to teaching. He often had to take on additional employment to support himself and his family. Reports suggest that many sextons used the "free day" from school on Saturday to sell their handwork or crafts at market, sales that were essential for their economic survival.[85] It does not take much imagination to recognize that such a person could hardly afford—even if he so wished—to be a dedicated teacher who

---

[82] Grossmann, ed., *Die Visitations-Acten der Diöces Grimma*, 149–50.

[83] Dixon, *The Reformation and Rural Society*, 152.

[84] Sehling, ed., *Die evangelische Kirchenordnungen des XVI. Jahrhunderts. Ersten Abteiling ... Erste Hälfte*, 454.

[85] Richter, *Geschichte der sächsischen Volksschule*, 52. Kirchhoff, "Kirchspiels- und Küsterschulen in der Reformationszeit," 137–38.

exceeded the expectations of his job. In addition to the teachers' poor pay, they experienced "poverty in housing, poverty of security, poverty of status."[86] This poverty continued in spite of Luther's laudatory words about the role of teachers and the esteem in which they should be held, and the efforts by church superintendents such as Friedrich Mecum in Gotha to have John Frederick mandate that Wittenberg students should serve as teachers before receiving a parish.[87] Given their poverty and low status, rural teachers must only rarely have been role models who inspired their pupils to pursue learning and become teachers themselves. Of course, most of these children and their families were as poor, if not poorer, than the teacher, and few could therefore dedicate themselves to long years of schooling. This was the case even in a town such as Zwickau where Burckhardt reports that scarcely one child in twenty would think of becoming a teacher.[88] Dependent as such teachers were on other means to augment their salaries, it is not surprising that those who served as town scribes may have been reticent to encourage the learning of writing among their pupils.[89]

Not even in the case of the more "practical" German schools did all parents, especially in rural areas, readily embrace education.[90] Village schools were often established just before a

---

[86] Dixon, *The Reformation and Rural Society*, 152.

[87] Pallas cites this letter of October 23, 1537 as an example of the efforts that church authorities made to address the problem of unlearned teachers/sextons. "Der Küster der evangelischen Kirche," 7.

[88] Burckhardt, *Geschichte der sächsischen Kirchen- und Schulvisitation*, 190. Müller discusses the history of the first school in Zwickau, dating back to the end of the thirteenth century, and eventually coming under the control of the city council. "Die Anfänge des sächsischen Schulwesens," 32–33.

[89] Susan C. Karant-Nunn, "The Reality of Early Lutheran Education," 135.

[90] Günther Wartenberg notes the slow progress of education outside the towns in Albertine Saxony, noting that before 1580 there was little development, in part due to the lack of interest on the part of

visitation and quickly lost their pupils and support after the visitors had departed.[91] The concerns that Luther had noted in 1530 continued to be the case through the end of the century. Parents often saw little value to education, and, even when they did, they often lacked the funds to pay the requisite *Schulgeld*, small as that amount was.[92] Especially for peasants, their children's contribution to the family's income was essential and they could not be spared for schooling, except during those times when there was less work. Thus, many children learned little more than the basics.

If this dismal outline of Evangelical education represented the whole picture, then we would have little choice but to regard Luther's educational program as a failure. Educating children, especially those in the countryside, proved to be a long term struggle. Yet there were promising signs of improvement. Records cited by Richter indicate that in 1574 there were Latin schools in many of the cities of Saxony, including Dresden, Leipzig, and such locales as Borna and Grimma.[93] Already in 1524, under Luther's influence "Magdeburg, Nordhausen, Halberstadt, and Gotha" were inspired to establish schools.[94] Smaller Latin schools existed in a variety of other towns, including several such as Bischofswerda and Zschopau with three teachers, and German schools existed in a considerable number of others, including Dohna, Dahlen (with three teachers), and some 38 others.[95]

---

the populace. Wartenberg asserts that the goal of learning to read the Bible in German was not sufficient to draw sustained interest from the village people. "Visitationen des Schulwesens im albertinischen Sachsen zwischen 1540 und 1580," in Goebel, ed., *Luther in der Schule*, 55–78; 66, 67.

[91] Karant-Nunn, "The Reality of Early Lutheran Education," 134.

[92] Karant-Nunn, "The Reality of Early Lutheran Education," 135.

[93] Richter, *Geschichte der sächsischen Volksschule*, 36.

[94] Klaus Goebel, "Luther als Reformer der Schule," in Goebel, ed., *Luther in der Schule*, 17.

[95] Richter, *Geschichte der sächsischen Volksschule*, 37.

In 1617, a century after Luther had posted his *95 Theses*, and in contrast even with the situation in 1574, records indicate that the term *Custos* or sexton had been replaced with *Schulmeister* or schoolmaster in most villages in Saxony.[96] These records cited by Richter do not of course tell us at what level education was being conducted, how regular attendance was, nor how much the children were learning. Nonetheless, if Richter's reporting is accurate, it is an indication both of the spread of schools into the rural areas, and of a significant transformation in the job description and expectations of the sexton, now seen primarily as teacher.

The education of girls, a goal to which Luther was very much committed, also made progress. The school in Grimma, for example, was founded at the time of the 1529 visitation and was directed by the former nun, Magdalena von Staupitz, sister of Luther's mentor and superior in the Augustinian Order, Johann von Staupitz.[97] The visitation report mandates that girls in the school are to be "brought to the fear of God," learning the Ten Commandments, other appropriate passages from the Scriptures, as well as reading and writing.[98] The instructions do not indicate if the girls are to learn Latin or German, but we may be certain that, as a former nun and abbess, Magdalena Staupitz was proficient in Latin.[99]

The *Schulordnungen* or regulations for the Latin schools generally hold to the initial plan outlined by Melanchthon and Luther in the *Instructions to the Visitors*. Children are to be divided into three groups, proceeding on the basis of their

---

[96] Richter, *Geschichte der sächsischen Volksschule*, 47–48.

[97] Richter, *Geschichte der sächsischen Volksschule*, 38. Grossmann, ed., *Die Visitations-Acten der Diöces Grimma*, 96–97.

[98] Grossmann, ed., *Die Visitations-Acten der Diöces Grimma*, 97.

[99] The *Schulordnung* stemming from the visitation to Meissen in 1533 states that those in the girls' school should learn the Lord's Prayer, the Creed, the Ten Commandments, various psalms, and should also learn to read and write. In this case, the reading is clearly in German—"Und dises lesen mag man uben in tetutzchen kinder buechlein, vater unser etc. item in dem neuen testament." Sehling, ed., *Die evangelische Kirchenordnungen des XVI. Jahrhunderts*, 194.

progress from learning the basics, Cato, and Donatus in the beginning group to Vergil, rhetoric, and dialectic in the most advanced. There is concern both to establish a consistent curriculum and to offer enough variation throughout the day and week to avoid boredom.[100]

Those orders formulated for the German schools establish a much simpler curriculum. Children are divided into three groups, with the first learning the alphabet, the second syllables, and the third to read and write.[101] Above all, the teacher is instructed to teach the children the "fear of God," and therefore no books that are "sectarian" or "damaging" are to be brought into the school, but instead the children are to be taught from the Psalms, the New Testament, and above all, the catechism of Luther.[102] The children are to learn the catechism by heart, but the schoolmaster is also instructed to teach the children so that they "understand and grasp" (*damit sie denselbigen auswendig lernen, und recht verstehen und begreifen mögen*).[103] The teacher is thus to set aside certain hours both for the children to practice reciting, but also to "teach and explain" it (*also mit ihnen üben und exerciren, auch einfältig dieselben unterrichten, und ihnen verständlich erklären*).[104] Once groups of children have achieved the same basic knowledge of

---

[100] The 1580 *Schulordnung aus der Kursächsischen Schulordnung* explicitly denounces teachers who on the basis of their own preference omit authors, thereby damaging their pupils' education. Reinhold Vormbaum, ed., *Die evangelische Schulordnung des sechszehnten Jahrhunderts*, vol. 1 (Gütersloh: Druck und Verlag von C. Bertelsmann, 1860), 232. In the section on *Particular-Schulen* (Latin schools) the problem of variation of curriculum from city to town to village is explicitly addressed, with authorities instructed whenever possible to divide pupils into five classes, while recognizing that village schools do not have adequate resources for so many classes, 234.

[101] Vormbaum, ed., *Die evangelische Schulordnungen*, 293.

[102] Vormbaum, ed., *Die evangelische Schulordnungen*, 294.

[103] Vormbaum, ed., *Die evangelische Schulordnungen*, 294.

[104] Vormbaum, ed., *Die evangelische Schulordnungen*, 294.

the catechism, they are to be divided into groups, with one posing questions and the other responses so that the learning is reinforced and the children gain practice in reciting the catechism publicly.

If the German schools represent the low end of the reformers' educational expectations as indicated in the *Schulordnungen* from the latter part of the sixteenth century, the Latin schools in towns and cities represent the high end. Beginning with the Magdeburg school founded in 1524 to the Eisleben one of the following year to the *Fürstenschulen* founded by Moritz of Saxony in the 1540s, education did make strides. Curricular plans were developed; funds from church properties were secured; committed and proficient teachers were hired and were paid decent salaries; support was gained from princes and city councils. In these locations the teacher enjoyed respect and served as a role model.

The three *Fürstenschulen* of Moritz and the Academy directed by Johann Sturm were especially significant achievements. In January 1543 Moritz of Saxony proclaimed his desire to establish three schools, one at Meissen for 70 boys, one at Merseburg for 60, and one at Pforta for 100.[105] Of the 230 boys, one-third were to be selected from the nobility. While the school in Meissen was founded in 1543 and that in Pforta in 1550, the school in Merseburg was never established. Both an outbreak of the plague that killed many in the town and Moritz's dispute over endowments with the resident bishop deterred him from establishing the school there.[106] Instead, the

---

[105] Wartenberg, "Visitationen des Schulwesens in albertinischen Sachsen," 56–57. Karl Julius Roessler, *Geschichte der Königlich Sächsischen Fürsten- und Landesschule Grimma* (Leipzig: Druck und Verlag von B. G. Teubner, 1891), 4; Ulrich Michael Kremer, "Zur Geschichte der sächsischen Fürstenschulen," in Hans Assa v. Polenz and Gabrielle v. Seydewitz, eds., *900-Jahr-Feier des Hauses Wettin 1089–1989. Festschrift des Vereins zur Vorbereitung der 900-Jahr Feier des Hauses Wettin e.v.* (Bamberg: St. Otto Verlag, 1989), 81–92.

[106] Roessler, *Geschichte der Königlich Sächsischen Fürsten- und Landesschule Grimma*, 9–13. On Moritz of Saxony's policies for church and state, see Günther Wartenberg, *Landesherrschaft und Reformation: Moritz von Sachsen und die albertinische Kirchenpolitik bis 1546* (Weimar: Hermann Böhlaus Nachfolger,

third school was established in Grimma, probably in 1550. To attend any of these three schools, boys were not to be younger than eleven or older than fifteen when admitted.[107] According to the 1580 *Schulordnung*, to be admitted a boy must already have completed the first three levels of a Latin school and be knowledgeable in Latin grammar. The course of study was extremely rigorous, with the boys arising at 5 in the morning and going to bed at 8 in the evening. In the three classes or levels of these schools, the boys proceeded through a more intensive study of Latin grammar to the study of Greek, as well as poetry, dialectic, rhetoric, astronomy, and, if a teacher was so able, even to the teaching of Hebrew on Saturdays.[108] The teachers were instructed to correct their pupils' errors gently but firmly, especially in dialectic, where correction must not be too harsh if it is not to intimidate a boy from developing further skill in argument.[109] To assure that the boys were making adequate progress, there were two exams a year.[110] Moritz's goal through such an intensive classical education was to prepare leaders for church and state.

In Strasbourg, Johann Sturm sought to endow boys with a classical education as preparation for worthwhile lives. Sturm, however, saw the matter rather differently than did Moritz. While Moritz supported the schools in order that young men might be prepared to serve the state, Sturm "wrote that the only justification for government was the promotion of education,

---

1988). Moritz's first order with regard to religion was to repeat a command of his father that every parish was to have on hand certain books essential to the building and maintaining of Christian community and order, 121–22.

[107] Roessler, *Geschichte der Königlich Sächsischen Fürsten- und Landesschule Grimma*, 5.

[108] Vormbaum, ed., *Die evangelische Schulordnungen*, 282.

[109] Vormbaum, ed., *Die evangelische Schulordnungen*, 285–86.

[110] Roessler, *Geschichte der Königlich Sächsischen Fürsten- und Landesschule Grimma*, 38.

for only then would society flourish."[111] Divided into nine classes, Sturm's gymnasium sought to endow its graduates with *pietas litterata*, "learned piety," a love of learning conjoined with faith. Such men would continue as scholars even while serving as leaders in the spheres of church and state.[112]

State support proved essential to the furthering of education, as Luther had recognized by 1524. Yet the authorities' support of education and of the reformers' goals has often been viewed in a negative light. As Dixon writes, "Lutheran theology was soon manipulated by the territorial princes to sanction an increased encroachment of the state into the moral and religious lives of its subjects."[113] According to this interpretation, in the specific case of education, the state used the schools as a means to indoctrinate the young into obedience. When the state supported young people through school and university, it came with a price, that of service either to the territory or to the territorial church.[114] Strauss' assessment is even harsher, suggesting that the efforts to indoctrinate the young by rod and catechism failed to engage both minds and hearts. By his findings, the result, at the end of the sixteenth century, was largely indifference and apathy, if not downright hostility. Especially in the rural areas, folk

---

[111] Lewis W. Spitz and Barbara Sher Tinsley, *Johann Sturm on Education: The Reformation and Humanist Learning* (St. Louis: Concordia Publishing House, 1995), 49.

[112] Spitz and Tinsley, *Johann Sturm on Education*, 57. On Strasbourg, see also Lorna Jane Abray, *The People's Reformation: Magistrates, Clergy, and Commons in Strasbourg, 1500-1598* (Ithaca: Cornell University Press, 1985). Abray notes that in Strasbourg too it was sometimes a struggle to win the minds and hearts of the laity: "By the mid-1530s Strasbourg had become a Protestant city. ... From the beginning, the lay response to the reformation varied. ... There were parents in Strasbourg who preferred to send their children to unlicensed schoolmasters or schoolmistresses to learn to read and write and count, because the legal parish schools spent too much time on religious instruction." 163.

[113] Dixon, *The Reformation and Rural Society*, 207.

[114] Paulsen, *Geschichte des gelehrten Unterrichts*, 298.

culture persisted, with people continuing to place their trust more in ancient remedies and magic than in the gospel.[115] Education of young and old, in schools and churches, had largely failed to uproot old beliefs and foster a new understanding of the Christian life.

Thus, historians critique Evangelical education of the sixteenth century on two fronts—in the rural areas because it failed to engage the people, and in the urban areas because it succeeded to some extent, but only through state support and at times compulsion. Luther had recognized early on that parents could not always be relied upon to educate their children or even to take their best interests to heart. For this reason, he stressed the importance of the authorities' role in mandating education, which he regarded as essential to the welfare of both church and state. Yet, Strauss and Dixon, for example, argue that even over the course of a hundred years, the educational plan did not achieve widespread success. Many schools remained as they had been, following almost the same curriculum, and often achieving little real learning. Memorization continued, as did a respect for the authorities that were to be learned and obeyed before being questioned.

The repetition of earlier goals in the *Schulordnungen* of 1580 may suggest that the reformers continued to pursue without success the same aims they had since the first visitation in 1529. However, another reading is also plausible, one that posits that while the reformers' goals, both the modest ones connected to the German schools and the much more idealistic ones connected to the Latin schools, did not fully succeed, the goals were deemed worthy enough and successful enough to be reiterated in the anticipation of greater accomplishments. If there had been no success, it seems hard to believe that there would have been a continuing commitment to these goals. Certainly the reformers did not succeed everywhere, most especially in the rural areas, where pastor and teacher encountered superstition, hostility, and most often, apathy and a desire simply to be left alone to follow familiar customs. To know that compulsory schooling was first instituted in Germany only in the nineteenth century, beginning with Prussia in 1825, is to know that the reformers did not win fully the minds and hearts of either the rulers or the people in the

---

[115] Dixon, *The Reformation and Rural Society*, 168–93.

sixteenth century.[116] Yet, as we have seen, there were successes that became the foundation for the future. It was a small beginning, and as Luther well recognized, "the world was still the world."[117] But every time a child learned the catechism and prayerfully pondered its meaning, every time a verse of Scripture was shared around the table in the evening or a hymn was sung, every time a scholarship or private donation allowed a gifted child to continue his studies, a beginning was made to overcome the darkness of ignorance with the light of learning.

---

[116] Kirchhoff, "Kirchspiels- und Küsterschulen in der Reformationszeit," 127. For a still valuable discussion of Luther's goals with regard to schools and the relationship between the schools of the reformers and older humanistic schools, see Otto Scheel, "Luther und die Schule seiner Zeit," *Lutherjahrbuch* (1925), 141–75. Scheel characterizes Luther's goal as articulated in his 1524 writing *To the Councilmen* as that of establishing "protestantische Bürgerschule", Protestant civic schools, rather than either humanistic gymnasia or German schools (Volksschule), 175.

[117]*WA* 30 II, 552, 13; *LW* 46, 236.

Conclusion

Martin Luther
Learning for Life

Martin Luther was shaped both by the education he received and by what he wished he had been taught. As teacher and theologian, he put to good use the skill in memorization, in Latin grammar, and in music, that he learned as a schoolboy and student. His university education developed his skills in analysis and argument, even though Luther rejected a scholasticism that stressed Aristotle at the expense of the classical and biblical sources. His encounters with humanism yielded a commitment to the study of the classical languages as a valuable tool in the service of knowledge. He admired those, like Philipp Melanchthon, whose linguistic expertise in Greek and possibly in Latin, though not in Hebrew, exceeded his own. Luther's energetic engagement with the biblical text, his struggle to interpret Romans 1:17 and Romans 3:23–5, profoundly changed not only his life but the history of the church. As theologian and exegete he collaborated with his colleagues in translating the Bible into German so that others might share his discovery of God's Word. Utilizing the technology of his time, the printing press, Luther shared his learning and his ideas more widely than had anyone before him.

At the same time, as an educator, Luther often took an independent path. He never joined those humanists who pursued learning for its own sake. Nor did he conceive of education as a realm belonging only to the intellectually elite, although he did believe that only those who were genuinely gifted and called to appropriate vocations should attend the university, especially its higher faculties of law, theology, and medicine. He had no patience with those who considered learning a status symbol and who simply wished to claim a doctor or lawyer as a family member. At the same time, he expanded the possibilities of education as never before. By his concept of the priesthood of all believers, Luther widened the boundaries of the spiritual estate beyond the monastic and clerical orders to include all Christians. This concept transformed the status of the laity and gave new importance to education, especially to gaining literacy, for it was through reading, as well as hearing the Word that one could make truly one's own the crucial tenet of justification by faith.

An advocate of education, Luther never ascribed a spiritually transformational role to it. For Luther, the individual remains *simul iustus et peccator*, both justified and a sinner. Thus, those scholars who argue that Luther and his colleagues believed that education could fundamentally alter human behavior ignore the fact that Luther and the magisterial reformers never lost sight of humankind's sinful condition. But Luther also affirmed the possibilities now open through the proclamation of the Word. Education could be celebrated both for its illumination of vocation and its building of expertise in one's calling, as well as for its intrinsic beauty and joy. In his treatise *The Freedom of a Christian* Luther described the Christian as both lord of all and through love the servant of all. Education becomes a crucial instrument in orienting the Christian toward service in the world. Thus, Luther protested against a narrow view of education as preparation for career, a problem with which contemporary educators must also struggle. He sought to defend a broad curriculum against those who would undermine it either in the name of religion or a narrow-minded materialism. He reminded parents that they could not offer their children a better preparation for the future than a sound education in the liberal arts: "House and home burn down and disappear, but an education is easy to carry off."[1] He was not above enticing skeptical parents with the promise of plentiful job openings for their sons as teachers and pastors if they succeeded in school and university.

Luther espoused a view of education that was anchored in the home, but he was realistic enough to recognize that not all parents are able, either through ability or desire, to rise to the pedagogical challenge before them. Thus, Luther reached out to the civic sphere to establish schools, to appoint well-prepared and caring teachers, and to require attendance. He firmly

---

1 Plass, ed., *What Luther Says*, vol. I, 447, citing WA TR 4, 217, 2–3.

believed that government has no higher responsibility than to care for its young. Only through education can both church and state gain knowledgeable and ethical people to serve as leaders. Luther's plea to the authorities of his time to remember that the best defense for any society lies not in its weapons but in its well-prepared and skilled people stands as a warning to us and our elected leaders as well.

Today educators debate both the most appropriate curriculum for schools and the principles on which it should be based. Scholars, such as developmental psychologist Lawrence Kohlberg and professor of education Richard Hersh, have recognized that schools themselves often lack a firm foundation in values. In an article entitled "Moral Development: A Review of the Theory," they write:

At present, the schools themselves are not especially moral institutions. Institutional relationships tend to be based more on authority than on ideas of justice. Adults are often less interested in discovering how children are thinking than in telling them *what* to think.[2]

Luther, of course, had very definite ideas about *what* should be included in a curriculum, and his ideas on discipline still are in many respects more medieval than modern. However, he also perceived education as a liberating enterprise. While at the same time maintaining much from the medieval curriculum, he advocated teaching that leads children to discover and appreciate the world, through science and experimentation, as well as languages, literature, and history. Indeed, he especially stressed history, noting that it offers a "mirror" to see the whole of human endeavor and thereby prepares young people "to take their own place in the stream of human events".[3]

Luther recognized, as do many contemporary critics of American education, that education cannot be left to the schools, but it must occur also, and perhaps even more

---

[2] Lawrence Kohlberg and Richard H. Hersh, "Moral Development: A Review of the Theory," in John Martin Rich, ed., *Innovations in Education: Reformers and Their Critics* (Boston: Allyn and Bacon, Inc., 1975), 264.

[3] *WA* 15, 45, 12–20; *L W* 45, 369.

importantly, in the home. Luther advocated that each school child be given a passage from the catechism or the Bible to bring home and practice as daily homework, as a way of learning Latin, increasing skill in remembering, and establishing learning as a family activity. He advocated the study of the catechism for all Christians, young and old. For him the catechism was not a dead document to be memorized without understanding, but a vibrant source of ongoing reflection and discussion, and a link among the generations. It was to be learned and taught in dialogue as a means of building a community of faith. Luther's concept of education was fundamentally collaborative, involving the entire community. That too is a fact of which contemporary educators are all too aware as they realize that without the active participation and support of parents and community schools can not meet the challenge of educating the young.

Like Luther, we too stand in the midst of a powerful stream of events at a turning point in history. We are the beneficiaries of a flood of knowledge generated by the new technology of the internet, but anyone who has "surfed the net" knows that one must bring to it a foundation of knowledge and analysis to separate fact from fiction, truth from lie. The resources of the new technology will allow education to overcome boundaries of time and space, but it will make even more crucial the gaining of both skill in critical thinking and a strong foundation in the liberal arts and in ethics.

On February 19, 1546 Melanchthon announced to his students the passing of Martin Luther. It seems only appropriate that these students were in a class on Romans, the text that was so central to Luther's theology and that played such a role in his conversion. Melanchthon told the students that their beloved professor had "been 'called to the heavenly university'."[4] For a man who loved learning, who expanded the realm of education to include all of society, and who described himself even as a mature theologian as a child of the catechism, no pronouncement could have been more fitting. From a small university on the edges of civilization, Luther launched ideas that would change the world and that would leave church and

---

[4] Brecht, *Martin Luther: Preservation of the Church*, 378. Melanchthon's funeral oration for Martin Luther may be found in Lewis W. Spitz, ed., *The Protestant Reformation: Major Documents* (St. Louis: Concordia Publishing House, 1997), 68–76.

society profoundly altered. He had transformed education into learning for life.

The *Lutherbild* from Neukirch, near Liegnitz, Cranach school 1540, 1570, or 1580, since 1903 in the diocesan museum of Breslau, today's Wroclaw. It shows how the Word of the Lord created a new culture. In a Renaissance architectural setting, Luther points to the Redeemer and his resurrection against the background of a ruined medieval castle. Melanchthon hears confession. Melchior Hoffmann, in 1518 Luther's first emissary from Wittenberg to Silesia, or Johannes Hauptmann, his successor in Neukirch, continue to celebrate mass. Above all, the *Verbum Dei* illuminates the landscape. Behind the *pastor loci* stand his patrons, the barons von Zedlitz, students of Trozendorf and Flacius Illyricus, who commissioned the painting. Members of the Zedlitz family fill eight pages in the *Allgemeine Deutsche Biographie* as *milites Christiani*, statesmen and poets, to say nothing of the progeny of the pastors from Neukirch.

Suggestions for Further Reading

There is a huge literature available on Martin Luther. The following is a list of books in English that relate to various aspects of the topic Luther and education and that are widely available in libraries. The interested reader, and those able to read German, are referred to the notes for additional sources.

Bainton, Roland. *Here I Stand: A Life of Martin Luther*. New York and Nashville: Abingdon Press, 1960.

Bornkamm, Heinrich. *Luther in Mid-Career (1521–1530)*. Translated by E. Theodore Bachmann. Philadelphia: Fortress Press, 1983.

Brecht, Martin. *Martin Luther: His Road to Reformation 1483–1521*. Translated by James L. Schaaf. Philadelphia: Fortress Press, 1985.

_____. *Martin Luther: The Preservation of the Church 1532–1546*. Translated by James L. Schaaf. Minneapolis: Fortress Press, 1993.

_____. *Martin Luther: Shaping and Defining the Reformation 1521–1532*. Translated by James L. Schaaf. Minneapolis: Fortress Press, 1990.

Buszin, Walter E. *Luther on Music*. Pamphlet series no. 3. Saint Paul: Lutheran Society for Worship, Music, and Arts, 1958.

De Ridder-Symoens, Hilde, ed. *Universities in Early Modern Europe (1500–1800)*. Vol. II of *A History of the University in Europe*. General editor, Walter Rüegg. Cambridge: Cambridge University Press, 1996.

Dixon, C. Scott. *The Reformation and Rural Society: The Parishes of Brandenburg-Ansbach-Kulmbach 1528–1603*. Cambridge: Cambridge University Press, 1996.

Erikson, Erik H. *Young Man Luther: A Study in Psychoanalysis and History*. New York: W.W. Norton & Company, 1962.

Fleischer, Manfred P., ed. *The Harvest of Humanism in Central Europe*. St. Louis: Concordia Publishing House, 1992.

Forell, George W., Harold J. Grimm, and Theodore Hoelty-Nickel. *Luther and Culture*. Martin Luther Lectures, vol. 4. Decorah, Iowa: Luther College Press, 1960.

Grane, Leif. *Martinus Noster: Luther in the German Reform Movement 1518–1521*. Veröffentlichungen des Instituts für Europäische Geschichte Mainz, Abteilung Religionsgeschichte, vol. 155. Mainz: Verlag Philipp von Zabern, 1994.

Grimm, Harold J. *Lazarus Spengler: A Lay Leader of the Reformation*. Columbus: Ohio State University Press, 1978.

Gritsch, Eric. *Martin—God's Court Jester: Luther in Retrospect*. Philadelphia: Fortress Press, 1983.

Grossmann, Maria. *Humanism in Wittenberg 1485—517*. Nieuwkoop: B. de Graaf, 1975.

Harran, Marilyn. *Luther on Conversion: The Early Years*. Ithaca and London: Cornell University Press, 1983.

_____,ed. *Luther and Learning: The Wittenberg University Luther Symposium*. Selinsgrove: Susquehanna University Press, 1985.

Janz, Denis. *Three Reformation Catechisms: Catholic, Anabaptist, Lutheran*. Texts and Studies in Religion, vol. 13. New York and Toronto: The Edwin Mellen Press, 1982.

Johnson, Roger A. *Psychohistory and Religion: The Case of Young Man Luther*. Philadelphia: Fortress Press, 1977.

Karant-Nunn, Susan C. "The Reality of Early Lutheran Education: The Electoral District of Saxony—A Case Study." *Lutherjahrbuch* 57 (1990), 128–146.

Kittelson, James. *Luther the Reformer*. Minneapolis: Augsburg Publishing House, 1986.

_____ and Pamela J. Transue, eds. *Rebirth, Reform, and Resilience: Universities in Transition 1300–1700*. Columbus: Ohio State University Press, 1984.

Lohse, Bernhard. *Martin Luther: An Introduction to His Life and Work*. Trans. by Robert C. Schultz. Philadelphia: Fortress Press, 1986.

Manschreck, Clyde Leonard. *Melanchthon: The Quiet Reformer*. New York and Nashville: Abingdon Press, 1958.

Oberman, Heiko. *Luther: Man Between God and the Devil*. Translated by Eileen Walliser-Schwarzbart. New Haven and London: Yale University Press, 1987.

_____. *The Reformation: Roots and Ramifications.* Translated by Andrew Colin Gow. Grand Rapids, Michigan: William B. Eerdmans Publishing Company, 1994.

Ozment, Steven. *When Fathers Ruled: Family Life in Reformation Europe.* Cambridge, MA: Harvard University Press, 1983.

Rosin, Robert. "The Reformation, Humanism, and Education: The Wittenberg Model for Reform." *Concordia Journal,* vol. 16, no. 4 (October 1990), 301–318.

Schalk, Carl. *Luther on Music: Paradigms of Praise.* St. Louis: Concordia Publishing House, 1988.

Schwiebert, Ernest G. *The Reformation.* Vol. I: *The Setting of the Reformation.* Volume II: *The Reformation as a University Movement.* Minneapolis: Augsburg Fortress, 1996.

Siggins, Ian. *Luther and His Mother.* Philadelphia: Fortress Press, 1981.

Spitz, Lewis W. *Luther and German Humanism.* Aldershot, Hampshire, England: Ashgate Publishing Ltd., 1996.

_____. *The Reformation: Education and History.* Aldershot, Hampshire, England: Ashgate Publishing Ltd., 1997.

_____. *The Protestant Reformation: Major Documents.* St. Louis: Concordia Publishing House, 1997.

_____. *The Religious Renaissance of the German Humanists.* Cambridge, MA.: Harvard University Press, 1963.

_____. *The Renaissance and Reformation Movements,* 2 vols. St. Louis: Concordia Publishing House, 1987.

_____ and Barbara Sher Tinsley. *Johann Sturm and Education: The Reformation and Humanist Learning.* St. Louis: Concordia Publishing House, 1995.

Strauss, Gerald. *Luther's House of Learning: Indoctrination of the Young in the German Reformation.* Baltimore and London: The Johns Hopkins University Press, 1978.

Stupperich, Robert. *Melanchthon.* Translated by Robert Fischer. Philadelphia: The Westminster Press, 1965.

Tentler, Thomas. *Sin and Confession on the Eve of the Reformation.* Princeton: Princeton University Press, 1977.

Todd, John M. *Luther: A Life.* New York: Crossroad Publishing Company, 1982.

Wingren, Gustav. *Luther on Vocation.* Translated by Carl C. Rasmussen. Philadelphia: Muhlenberg Press, 1957.

Der Buchdrucker.

Der Teppichmacher.

Der Papyrer.

Der Organist.

Der Schrifftgiesser.

Der Uhrmacher.

Der Apotecker.

Der Buchbinder.

Index

Concordia Scholarship Today

12-3256—Raj, A. R. Victor. *The Hindu Connection: Roots of the New Age.* 240 pp.

12-3257—Oden, Thomas C. *Corrective Love: The Power of Communion Discipline.* 224 pp.

12-3272—Schalk, Carl F. *God's Song in a New Land: Lutheran Hymnals in America.* 240 pp.

12-3276—Arand, Charles P. *Testing the Boundaries: Windows to Lutheran Identity.* 270 pp.

12-3205—Miller, Roland E. *Muslim Friends: Their Faith and Feeling. An Introduction to Islam.* 432 pp.

99-1620—Schalk, Carl F. *Source Documents in American Lutheran Hymnody.* 174 pp.

Order from Concordia Publishing House
3558 S. Jefferson Ave.
St. Louis, MO 63118
or call 1–800–325–3040

Marilyn J. Harran is currently Professor of Religion and History at Chapman University, Orange, California. Before joining the Chapman faculty in 1985, she was Assistant Professor of Religion at Barnard College, Columbia University. At Chapman University she has served as chair of the faculty and of the Department of Religion, director of the honors program, and director of the university's nationally recognized freshman seminar program.

A graduate of Scripps College, she studied at the University of Tuebingen and Stanford University, where she received the M.A. and Ph.D. degrees. She has been a guest lecturer at various universities and seminaries, including Lutheran Theological Seminary in Gettysburg, Emory University, and Wittenberg University.

Professor Harran has been the recipient of fellowships and grants from the National Endowment for the Humanities and the International Research and Exchanges Board and has been a Mellon Fellow at the Aspen Institute for Humanistic Studies.

Her previous publications include *Luther on Conversion: The Early Years* (Cornell University Press, 1983) and *Luther and Learning: The Wittenberg University Luther Symposium* (Associated University Presses, 1985). She has published in the *Concordia Journal* and the *Archiv fuer Reformationsgeschichte* and has contributed articles to *The Encyclopedia of Religion*, and the *Oxford Encyclopedia of the Reformation*.

The impetus for this volume, *Martin Luther—Learning for Life*, stems in part from the author's experiences in Leipzig, Germany, during the fall of 1989 when she witnessed firsthand the dramatic events that unfolded during that time, including the central role played by pastors and members of the Evangelical Church in leading the way to a peaceful revolution. Recognizing the vast implications that this political revolution would have for education and for society as a whole gave her a new perspective on the transitions that occurred within sixteenth century German society, including dramatic changes for education as a result of Luther's stress on the priesthood of all believers and the need for each Christian personally to read and understand the Word of God.